THE
SIGN OF
THE DOUBLE 'T'

THE
SIGN OF
THE DOUBLE 'T'

(The 50th Northumbrian Division – July 1943 to December 1944)

BY
B. S. BARNES

British Library Cataloguing-in-Publication Data.
A catalogue record for this book is available
from the British Library.

Copyright © 1999 B. S. Barnes

Published by

Sentinel Press,

3 Mansfield Court, Newland Park,
Kingston upon Hull, HU5 2DF, East Yorkshire

Printed by

Pardy and Son (Printers) Ltd., Ringwood, Hampshire

ISBN 0-9534262-0-3

First edition 1999

Maps by B S Barnes

DEDICATION

For my children Nicholas, David and Rachel.

May the pleasant lands of France and Sicily mean for them only holidays and fun.

Many thanks to the following for their invaluable assistance.

Miss Elizabeth Talbot-Rice for her painstaking research.

Steve Hamilton for advice on armoured units.

Lynne Dooley for her meticulous work on this manuscript.

The Commonwealth War Graves Commission
for the loan of cemetery registers.

The Imperial War Museum
for the supply of original photographs.

All the old soldiers who appear in this study.

Mr T.M.D. Ball: London Irish Rifles' Museum.

Mr C. Webb, London Scottish H.Q.

J. N. Rhodes, curator of the Royal Engineers Museum.

R. A. Moore MM and G. E. Tidey, the Sharpshooters
Yeomanry Association.

The Royal Marines Museum, Portsmouth.

A special mention must be given to Ewart W. Clay MBE,
who wrote the original regimental history:
The Path of the 50th. 1950.
His work has provided me with a detailed account
of the whole of the 50th Divisions activities from 1939 to 1944,
in whose ranks he served.

CONTENTS

N. W. EUROPE: 1944

FOOTNOTES

BIBLIOGRAPHY

APPENDIX 'A'

HONOURS AND AWARDS: 6TH TO 12TH JUNE 1944

APPENDIX 'B'

THE FALLEN: 6TH, 7TH AND 8TH JUNE 1944

APPENDIX 'C'

ORDER OF BATTLE. 50TH NORTHUMBRIAN DIVISION: MAY 1944

APPENDIX 'D'

GERMAN ORDER OF BATTLE. GOLD BEACH, 6TH JUNE 1944

APPENDIX 'E'

BRITISH FORCES ASSAULTING 'GOLD BEACH',
0725 HRS, 6TH JUNE 1944

APPENDIX 'F'

COMPANY SERGEANT MAJOR STANLEY ELTON HOLLIS VC
BRIEF BIOGRAPHICAL OUTLINE

APPENDIX 'G'

50 DIV: CASUALTIES, REINFORCEMENTS AND POW'S:
6TH JUNE TO 1ST DECEMBER 1944

APPENDIX 'H'

MESSAGE FROM DIVISIONAL COMMANDER: 6TH JUNE 1944

APPENDIX 'I'

MESSAGE FROM CO 8TH ARMOURED DIVISION: 12TH JUNE 1944

APPENDIX 'J'

MESSAGE FROM ARMY COMMANDER: 14TH JUNE 1944

FOREWORD
by
Major I. R. English. MC and Three Bars. TD.

Some regiments win fame by virtue of their achievements which become known to a wider circle than purely the Army. More rarely Divisions can do the same; for example the 7 Armoured Division - the 'Desert Rats' and the 2nd New Zealand Division.

50 (Northumbrian) Division can be included in that small select group. This springs from the distinguished part it played in many battles. These included the Counter Attack at Arras May 1940, Gazala June 1942, El Alamein and Mareth. Also of course the two campaigns so ably described in this book - Sicily and North West Europe. General Horrocks the Commander of 30 Corps had good reason to describe the 50th Division as the "most experienced battle-fighting division in the British Army".

Major Ian English. MC and Three Bars. 8th Bn DLI.

The previous history of the division in the Second World War - "The Path of the 50th" by Ewart Clay published in 1950 has long been out of print, and is now virtually unobtainable. So it is very timely that Barrie Barnes has written this book.

He describes the general situations, the divisional plan to carry out the given task, and gives a vivid picture of the detailed actions of brigades, battalions and regiments in the various battles. These are augmented by a large number of personal accounts told by other ranks equally with officers. They are immensely valuable and give a sharper focus on what life is like for the front line soldier than any general history can do. Some of these accounts are poignant and moving.

Before the war the 50th Division was recruited from Durham and north and east Yorkshire. Later units received drafts from other parts of the country - the Scottish borders, Lancashire and Shropshire. As the war went on and after so much hard fighting, it was inevitable that reinforcements were collected from wherever they cound be found. For example my company received a draft of

MEN OF THE 50TH NORTHUMBRIAN DIVISION LEAVE YORK MINSTER AFTER A
SERVICE OF THANKSGIVING. 16 MAY 1945. (*AUTHOR'S COLLECTION*)

about thirty five Welshmen who did not want to join the DLI. But after a few weeks the new comers and the veterans got to know each other, and the Welsh lads were soon proud to call themselves Durhams. In this way the division always kept its north country character. Tough, hardy and resolute men, whether they were Durham miners or Yorkshire country stock. Most did not want to be soldiers, but they realised their country needed them and they had a job to do. They just wanted to do it to the best of their ability and get home again. Sadly many never came home.

As one who served in '50 Div' from the beginning of the war, apart from nine months as a prisoner of war in 1943, to the very end - so fittingly marked by the magnificent Service of Thanksgiving and Remembrance in York Minster on 16 May 1945 - I warmly welcome this book and commend it equally to young and old soldiers, and indeed to the general public. Let us never forget the part played by the men of '50 Div' with many others, in the defeat of the armies of one of the greatest tyrannies known to man.

Ian English

CHAPTER ONE

THE LANDINGS
10th July 1943, Sicily

The Allied re-entry into Europe via Sicily was to be a hazardous leap hedged with uncertainties. The capitulation of eight divisions in Tunisia left Italy and its islands almost bereft of defensive cover. With these forces the axis powers could have provided a very strong defence for the Italian gate-ways into Europe and the chances of an allied invasion succeeding would have been very slim. The eventual success of the Sicilian landings owed much to factors that were not at once obvious. Firstly, Hitler and Mussolini had poured in men and resources into the latter part of the Tunisian Campaign in an attempt to save face. Both leaders would not listen to any argument in favour of evacuating the German and Italian Forces while there was still time and opportunity to get them away. Secondly, Italy had no strong mechanical forces left and the Italian Generals asked the Germans to provide a powerful reinforcement of Panzer style units. Hitler at once offered five divisions but Mussolini, fearful of so many German troops on Italian soil, sent a reply asking for only three, expressing the view that no more after these should be dispatched. Mussolini's pride did not want the world to know he was dependant upon German aid and although he was anxious to keep out the allies, he was equally as anxious to keep out the Germans.

Mussolini's chief of the Army Staff eventually persuaded him more German troops were necessary if a successful defence of Italy and its islands was to be made, but by the time he accepted the need to have more German help, Hitler was becoming more dubious about providing it. He suspected the Italian people may overthrow Mussolini and sue for peace, thus isolating badly needed German Forces that had been pushed in so deeply they could be cut off if their allies changed sides. Hitler also thought that the Italian command and Kesselring were mistaken in their view that the allies next assault would come on the shores of Sicily, he expected landings in Sardinia and Greece.

These ideas were encouraged further by documents found on the dead body of a British officer washed up on the shores of Spain; German spies acquired them and handed them on to their superiors. Both the corpse and the documents had been planted by British Intelligence but the plan worked so well that the Germans were totally convinced of its genuineness; and although it did not alter the view of the Italian High Command and Kesselring that the next blow would fall in Sicily, on Hitler's orders, troops and tanks were sent to Sardinia and Greece.

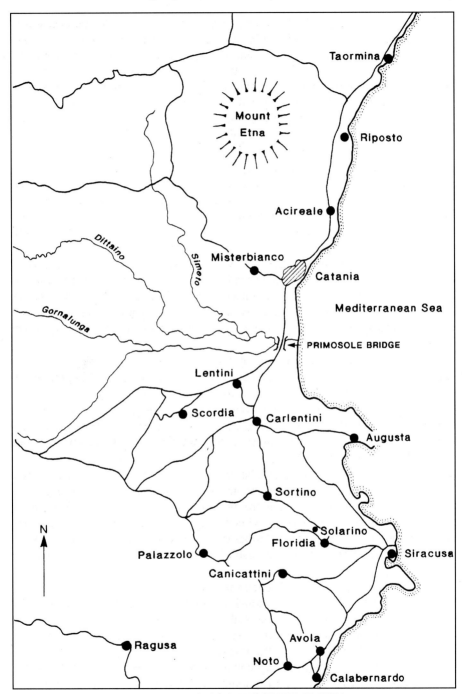

THE COASTAL ROADS FROM MOUNT ETNA TO AVOLA

On the 19th January 1943, the allied combined chiefs came to the decision to move against Sicily, with the intention of relieving the pressure on the Russian Front, securing the Mediterranean line of communications and increasing the pressure on the Italian main land. On the 20th January, the British put forward an outline plan code-named 'Operation Husky'. Eisenhower became Supreme Commander with Alexander as his deputy, this emphasised the role of the United States as senior partner in the alliance, even though Alexander was senior in rank and experience and the British were to provide the bulk of the forces.

A swift landing in Sicily immediately after the fall of the Axis Forces in Africa would have found the island almost defenceless. The pause that followed enabled the enemy to reinforce the defences of the island and would have been longer but for Churchill's insistence that the landing should be made in June. As it turned out the Army Commanders were not able to launch the invasion until July 10th.

In the new plan, Patton's Army (THE WESTERN TASK FORCE) would now land in the south east near Monty's army, instead of at the western end of Sicily, and the British forces would now be more concentrated with their landing points closer together. This tight massing of the invading forces was good preparation in the event of a heavy counter attack by the enemy. Though with hind sight we know it was unnecessary.

In scale, this simultaneous landing by eight divisions was to be bigger than the landings in Normandy eleven months later and it was to be the first big sea borne assault, in the second world war, on a coast held by the enemy.

In the afternoon of 9th July, the convoys began their journey west of Malta, wind speed increased dramatically and churned the sea up to such an extent that it threatened to dislocate the landings. Later that night conditions improved but left a troublesome swell.

The airborne forces of the British 1st and American 82nd Divisions were worst affected by the winds, the American parachute troops were scattered over an area of fifty miles and the British glider troops, also widely scattered, lost forty seven of their one hundred and thirty four gliders in the sea. However, the unintentionally scattered distribution of these troops caused alarm and confusion over a wide area behind the enemy's front and enabled key bridges and road junctions to be seized.

The sudden storm that had plagued the attackers served to lull the defenders into a state of false security, even though during the afternoon convoys had been sighted advancing from Malta. The Italian troops had been on alert for many nights and were worn-out physically. However, their weariness was more than just physical, many were tired of the war itself. The troops defending the coast were Sicilian men. The reasoning behind this was that they would fight all the harder for their own homes and reputation as fighting men. This did not take into account the long-standing dislike of the German's by the Sicilians nor the realisation that the harder they resisted the invasion the less there would be left of their homes.

On the morning of 10th July 1943, the coastal defenders looked out to see a vast array of ships that filled the sea to the horizon, Private Norman (Gee) Hardy was with 69th Brigade preparing for the landing:

> "I was on one of the big ships in the mess-deck when one of the lads said 'come and take a look at the island'. It was beautiful. You could see shells bursting and smoke coming up, but otherwise it was perfect. The landing was quite easy, we had 2lb bombs with fuses ready to be lit to blow a gap in the barbed wire, but we just walked up the beach." [1]

As the landing craft, loaded with men and equipment, made their way to the coast, many became scattered and lost touch with their neighbours. 'A' and 'B' Companies of the 6th Durham Light Infantry should have landed at 0245 hours, 'C' Company at 0300 hours and 'D' Company at 0315 hours. The first Durham's ashore were the men of 'B' Company who landed, less one platoon, one and a half hours late and some three thousand yards from their planned landing position. The remaining companies landed at 0430 hours, some four thousand, five hundred yards south of their planned landing positions. The 9th Battalion was a little more fortunate, but not much. Two companies landed within five hundred yards of their allotted beach, but the remainder landed in scattered parties between three and four thousand yards too far south. However, despite these set backs, the main beach was cleared of the enemy relatively easily, though enemy shell fire continued for quite some time. Once ashore the troops quickly re-organised themselves and, as it was now daylight, a number of clearly discernible landmarks enabled companies to redeploy, mopping up any enemy resistance as they went.

At dawn the 8th D.L.I. landed in broad daylight, some three thousand yards north of their allocated beach. They came under heavy shell fire and aircraft attacked them. Private Ralph Hymer was with 'C' Company and can clearly recall the difficult passage:

> "The sea was very rough and the landing craft was blown all over the place, so when we landed we wasn't in our own battalions. We joined anything to go forward and the Germans was there. We had a struggle on the beaches, there was that many craft together, the German aircraft couldn't miss 'em. There was a lot of casualties lying about and lots of shells dropping round us." [2]

Private J H Clarke was in a neighbouring craft:

> "We were tossed about quite a bit. As we were approaching we picked up quite a few parachutists, who missed the land and dropped into the sea. There was a good bit of opposition. Our landing craft stuck fast on a sand bank. The officer in charge told people to get off, about half a dozen stepped off into twenty feet of water and was drowned. The landing craft

8TH ARMY TROOPS LANDING IN SICILY.
10TH JULY 1943

along side got a direct hit and was set on fire, there was quite a few casualties." [3]

As soon as 151st Brigade had begun to move inland to their concentration area, 69th Brigade was ordered ashore and, expecting the worst, got a pleasant surprise, recalls Private Harry Forth:

"We clambered down the ropes into the landing craft. On the approach the matelot dropped us in twelve feet of water. The front goes down and yer off, the boat was still moving as the front lads stepped off and carried on over them - they was drowned. Myself and some of the lads got wise and jumped off the side. I had me bren gun, my Mae West, three or four bandoliers of ammunition, grenades and all my other equipment. You floated thanks to yer Mae West but when a boat went over the top of you - you had no chance. The landing was simple, the Italians was with their suit cases waiting to come off. We had very little opposition until we got further inland, we knew then we was meeting the Germans again." [4]

Lance Sergeant Ken Rutherford felt uneasy about the lack of resistance on the beach:

"We expected everything to be shot at us, we got practically nothing. It was like being on a picnic until the night. We thought we was walking into a trap, it felt uncanny. There was dog fighting above, we were under a tree when an Italian pilot came down on a parachute, he was OK but he'd lost the bag from his testicles - all he could say was 'no bambino' - 'no bambino'." [5]

Private Tommy Atkinson expected the worst when his unit landed but found the landing easy:

"We'd had a few days rest on our journey from Port Said along the Medi, apart from daily P.T. and lectures on the attack on Avola Lido, Sicily. We had seen models of the coastline and photographs of the beaches. We'd been told that it would be a piece of cake because the Italian homeguard were defending our beaches. We'd heard that tale before!

So we assembled on the boat deck, loaded like pack mules and boarded our allocated assault craft which we then swung out in the davits as this armada closed in on the shoreline, still unseen in the darkness. We heard the engines of aircraft passing over as they took paratroops for the first assault - so we were told. Later, we heard that some had been dropped short in the sea. Then as the skies lightened and we could see other landing craft scattered around us as we were lowered into the sea for our journey ashore. As dawn broke so did air attacks and shellfire from the land.

The naval escort put up a good show in knocking out enemy guns so it was only the occasional shell that dropped on the beach as we laid mesh tracking for the half-tracks and bren-carriers. We had no trouble with mines or small-arms fire so in effect it was a piece of cake.

We had landed and formed a beach-head. The rest of the company advanced with the Green Howards along the coast eastwards. This campaign introduced us to compo rations which were a great improvement on what we were used to. They consisted of rations for eight men for 24 hours: Tinned bacon or sausage; dried porridge; tea powder and dried milk, which used to leave thick scum on the top of liquid; dried mince; tinned potatoes; tinned rice; hard oatmeal biscuits; tinned margarine; tinned cigarettes and even toilet paper. Included was boiled sweets and plain chocolate - all this was packed in a box 12in. x 12in. x 18in.

Having handed over the beach track maintenance to support troops, we rejoined our company heading towards Augusta. So far resistance had been slight and our advance had been steady."

All beach defences were quickly over-run and the discomfort of sea sickness, suffered by many of the attacking troops, was more than offset by the low casualties from enemy fire when getting ashore. The coastal divisions disintegrated without firing a shot and the field divisions were soon driven back, mass surrenders were not uncommon. The first day had been singularly successful in spite of the early mishaps and Montgomery was jubilant as his 8th Army seized all of its objectives.

Once assured of the success of the 8th Army assault, Montgomery exhorted both corps commanders to push inland with great haste. Leese was ordered to advance on Noto and Avola, while Dempsey was told to head for Syracuse and then Augusta. Montgomery landed early on 11th July to find Syracuse had fallen to 13th Corps and that it's important port had been seized undamaged.

During the critical period before the invading troops were firmly established on shore, there came a dangerous counter attack by the Herman Göering Division, equipped with the new 56-ton Tiger tanks. This unit had been stationed at Caltagirone overlooking the Gela Plain - where the American 1st Infantry Division had landed. On 11th February only a few American tanks were ashore owing to the congested state of the beaches and unloading problems caused by the heaving surf. There was also a shortage of anti tank guns and artillery ashore. As the attacking Panzers advanced, the American outposts were overrun. It was not long before the Germans had reached the sand dunes bordering the beaches prepared to drive the invaders back into the sea. Accurate naval gun fire, however, saved the day and broke up the attack. Another German thrust on the left flank of the 45th Division was broken up in the same way.

In three days, the 8th Army had captured all of South Eastern Sicily, but despite their early successes, the British and American soldiers soon learnt it was going to be an infantryman's war. The troops had spent many months fighting in the deserts of North Africa, now they saw green fields, vegetables growing and olive groves lined along the dry stone walls that criss-crossed the land in every direction. The easy landing gave the promise of a short painless campaign, but things were soon to change. After visiting the front, Montgomery decided to make a break-through into the Plain of Catania from the Lentini area, he wrote:

"I was confirmed in my view that the 'Battle of Sicily' would be primarily a matter of securing the main centres of road communication. Movement off the roads and tracks in the hilly country was very difficult and often impossible, so that if the nodal points were gained it was clear that the enemy would be unable to operate.

On the 13th Corps flank, I decided that we should make a great effort to break-through into the 'Plain of Catania' from the Lentini area and ordered a major attack for the night of 13th/14th July. A Parachute Brigade and a Commando Brigade were made available for the operation, in which the main problems were to force the bottle-neck through the difficult country between Carlertini and Lentini and secure two bridges, one north of the Lentini Ridge and the other, the Primosole, over the River Simeto.

The plan was to land the Parachute Brigade during the night near Primosole with orders to capture it and establish a small bridge-head on the north bank. Contact was then to be made with the commando whose task, having landed west of Agnore, was to secure the other bridge. The main thrust, directed on Catania, was to be delivered by the 50th Division with an armoured brigade leading." [6]

The 50th Division prepared itself to push north through the foot hills of Lentini, at the southern edge of the Plain of Catania. The 151st Brigade moved into the area around Floridia-Solarino, positions vacated by 13th Brigade. This brigade was in contact with the enemy who were very active with artillery, mortars and machine-guns. The 69th Brigade concentrated south east of Floridia in preparation for an advance on Lentini and prepared a mobile column consisting of one squadron of tanks, carriers and self propelled guns to advance through Canicattini Bagni with the intention of cutting the Solarino-Palazzolo Road, then attacking the enemy at Solarino in the rear. This mobile column was late in assembling and was hindered in its progress by the difficult terrain it had to advance over. Contact with the enemy was made west of Solarino and after a brief fight and the taking of several prisoners the column withdrew the way it had come. The Italian troops west of Solarino made two abortive attempts to break-through the British lines, once with an infantry attack and again with infantry and tanks - French R35's. Five tanks came down the road from Palazzolo heading for Solarino, four were quickly knocked out but the fifth carried on through Solarino and onto Floridia - shooting up anything in sight. As a 15 cwt truck loaded with ammunition exploded the advancing troops of the 5th Bn East Yorkshire Regiment and the 6th Bn Durham Light Infantry scattered into the roadside ditches and behind stone walls. The Commanding Officer of the 5th Bn East Yorkshire Regiment, Lt Colonel R. B. James, was driving a motor-bike from Floridia to Sortino accompanied by his intelligence officer in a carrier when this rogue tank came into view, both the bike and the carrier spun round and beat a hasty retreat. The carrier had a track blown off and ended in a ditch, but the tank pursued Colonel James on his motor-bike for another half mile, firing bursts with its machine gun until knocked out by a 105 mm self propelled gun near Floridia. The attacking Italian infantry formations were met by heavy concentrations of artillery fire and were soon broken up; the attack petered out.

Late in the evening 69th Brigade Headquarters received orders from Divisional Headquarters to continue the advance through Sortino and Lentini. The 151st Brigade were to occupy Sortino once it had fallen to 69th Brigade and to concentrate in that area and make contact with 30 Corps. The Durhams were also to patrol the area to the east of the Sortino road with the intention of clearing up any isolated pockets of Italians still present.

The transport situation was still acute and the nature of the country often made matters worse, a brief description of the land at this point will give some idea of the problems to be over come. A coastal plain seven miles in width runs between

Cassibile and Syracuse. North of the road that links Syracuse, Floridia and Solarino lies a great mass of broken hilly country which runs all the way to the 'Plain of Catania'. Of the two roads running northwards one was a good coastal road used by the 5th Division for their advance, the other inland road runs through the hills from Floridia to Sortino. Both converge on Lentini on the edge of the 'Catania Plain', from there, one main road crosses the Leonardo River, running along a low commanding ridge until it drops again to the 'Primosole Bridge' over the Simeto River. Past this point the road runs over very flat terrain, over looked by Mount Etna in the distance, to Catania itself.

The 50th Division was about to advance along the inland road, which runs for much of its length along valleys dominated on both sides by steep hills rising some two to three hundred feet above it. As it draws nearer to Sortino the hills are closer to the road until they form a gorge with sides covered with trees and shrubs. About a mile and a half from Sortino the road climbs in a series of sharp bends to the town on top of the ridge.

Beyond Sortino which is half way between Floridia and Lentini, the nature of the land is more open as the road drops to Carlentini and Lentini. Every inch of the way it is winding, dust covered and narrow, not at all made to accommodate two way traffic of the military kind. Stone walls and olive trees border the road sides. The bends in the road are often of the hair pin variety.

The 5th Battalion East Yorkshire Regiment led by their advanced guard, 'C' Company, headed for Sortino. Little opposition was expected and the troops pressed on along the road. Just south east of Sortino, in well concealed positions, German and Italian troops waited on both sides of a gorge. Sortino was within sight when the enemy opened fire on 'C' Company. An anti tank transport had moved too quickly up the column and as it reached the head of 'D' Company, turning a bend in the road, it was met by a hail of Spandau fire. Both companies deployed and a heavy fire fight took place as the troops moved up the steep slopes. Major K C Harrison was a platoon commander at that time and describes the action as seen from the rear of the battalion column:

> "Sudden and exciting, I heard from my position in 'B' Company the unmistakeable purr of Spandau's. Bren guns replied from our leading companies, then the heavy thumps of German mortar bombs echoed down the valley. We halted for a while, hoping that 'D' and 'C' Companies might soon overrun the enemy. But the noises of battle continued spasmodically, and without knowing much about the situation 'B' Company was told to advance further down the narrow valley. Further ahead at a road junction we were ordered to establish ourselves on a hill to our right.
>
> The enemy could not see to fire it's spandaus at us, as we were still climbing the slopes and hidden by stone walls and trees, but a regular procession of mortar bombs hit the valley below, near the road junction we had just left. Dusk was rapidly approaching and, in my platoon area, I found the CO with my Company Commander. The CO's plan was that 'B'

SOLDIERS OF THE DURHAM BRIGADE TAKE GENERAL PORGINI, COMMANDER OF THE NAPOLI DIVISION, AND HIS STAFF INTO CAPTIVITY. 14TH JULY 1943. (*IMPERIAL WAR MUSEUM*)

Company should occupy one of the enemy hills during the darkness, while 'D' and 'C' Companies were given similar assignments.

Although the men were tired, hungry and thirsty after the long march in the almost tropical sun, they welcomed the move and set off with a good heart. The CO led us in the darkness, the Company Commander with him. I was immediately behind with my platoon, but the exceedingly rough ground and the many stone walls made it hard going for my men with their rifles, Brens and other platoon weapons." [7]

'B' Company arrived at the foot of a hill criss-crossed with stone walls at 0230 hours, everything was quiet now and the moon made a welcome appearance. The troops clambered up the sides of the steep hill only to find the enemy had withdrawn, sentries were posted and a couple of hours precious sleep was had. All objectives had been taken by the East Yorkshiremen and during the early hours of the new day enemy stragglers were rounded up.

By dawn on 13th of July, 69th Brigade was firmly established on the high ground beyond Sortino having lost contact with the retreating Axis forces. The troops were by now hungry and exhausted yet still the 50th pressed on in the heat and dust fighting actions as they went. It now became imperative that the high ground, overlooking the Catania Plain, should be taken before the enemy could re group and co-ordinate any serious opposition in this difficult terrain. The 6th

D.L.I. of 151st Brigade had been attacked by the troops and tanks of the Napoli Division. By 5.30 am on 13th July, the Durham's had taken the Italian positions and found the enemy very demoralised. This action resulted in the destruction of the Napoli Division, the capture of several hundred troops and the taking of the enemy Divisional Commander, General Porgini.

By dawn on the 13th July, 168th Brigade, now part of the 50th Division, having landed at Syracuse, had moved to a concentration area east of Floridia and from there to north of Melilli. Montgomery was by now very keen to push his troops forward into the heart of Sicily. He issued a personal message, to be read out to all of his divisions, with the intention of spurring them on in their quest for victory:

"The beginning had been very good, thanks to your splendid fighting qualities and to the hard work and devotion to duty of all those who work in the ports, on the roads and in rear areas. We must not forget to give thanks to 'The Lord Mighty in battle' for giving us such a good beginning towards the attainment of our objective, and now let us get on with the job. Together with our American Allies we have knocked Mussolini off his perch. We will now drive the Germans out of Sicily. Into battle with stout hearts, good luck to you all." [8]

The troops of the 69th and 151st Brigades continued to press remorselessly on to the Catania Plain against determined opposition. The going was hard over this harsh terrain, the sun merciless and the fighting bitter. By midnight on 13th July, the 6th Green Howards had captured part of the approach to Mount Pancali, but could advance no further because of heavy fire coming from this feature. At 0500 hrs on 14th July, the 7th Green Howards made an attack on the Mount, supported by artillery and the machine guns of the 2nd Cheshires. Here is an account of this action written by Captain K A Nash who took part in the assault.

"We are to attack Mount Pancali, a high hill on our left - alive with machine guns. 'A' Company goes left and we make the frontal assault. I can see the objective rising suddenly about two thousand yards away, with a flat plain between us. This waiting before an attack is bloody, the men don't like it and neither do I. The guns open up and we move forward, at the foot of the hill at last, looks bloody steep from here. There are big boulders as we climb, the men are splendid, climbing up grimly, not knowing what to expect at the top. We reach a ledge just before the summit and pause for breath and then I hear a shout, 'follow me eleven platoon', and I find myself on the top. Now machine guns open up all around, a miserable Bosche crawls from behind a boulder with the inevitable shout of 'Kamerad'. He could have killed me twenty times over as I stood there, but he is too shaken to press the trigger. I ran past him, bullets are whining everywhere, but our blood is up - we are shouting, swearing, cheering - it's easy, they're giving themselves up - they've had it. Except, that on the right there's no sign of

Nigel and a lot of fire is coming from behind that wall. The rest of the company has swept forward, I can hear the C.S.M. yelling encouragement to them. Geoff is quiet and looks bad, he was hit in the thigh but staggered on to the top and collapsed in a hail of bullets.

I am as excited as hell now and get a bren to open up towards the copse and Jerry quietens down. I must be excited now as I do a darned silly thing - I zig-zag forward under cover of the bren. Two blokes say 'good luck sir' and one voice says 'I'm coming with you sir' - grand troops - it's Corporal Kendrick. We dash forward among the spandau lead, our bren silences one machine gun. Another twenty yards then more spandau and a dash for cover behind a big boulder - I turn round to see Kendrick shot clean through the throat. I grab his tommy gun and loose off the magazine. Poor Kendrick - courage evaporates - I hug the ground and pray. Then Jerry starts shelling us, I shout back for a smoke screen on the copse only to find the mortar crews have been knocked out, I lay there nearly half an hour sweating. Presently the Bosche gets browned off and come out with their hands up. What a morning !"

The objective was captured by 1000 hrs, the German troops left the area littered with their dead and wounded. Some twenty nine enemy machine guns were found on top of the mountain.

The great fatigue of the troops and the stubborn enemy rear guards delayed the advance, the landscape to the south of Carlentini and Lentini bore witness to the grim struggle that had taken place there. Burning vehicles obstructed roads and during the morning of the 14th July, enemy air attacks had harassed the slow moving columns. By the early afternoon, Carlentini and Lentini had been secured by the 69th Brigade. The 5th East Yorkshires joined up with No 3 Commando north of Lentini, and the bridge over the Lentini was intact. The 4th Armoured Brigade passed through Lentini with the object of pressing on to Primosole Bridge and relieving the hard pressed airborne troops. By dusk on the 14th July, the 4th Armoured Brigade and the 9th Battalion Durham Light Infantry were only a mile from Primosole Bridge, many of these north country-men, who looked down upon that ugly structure, would have good cause to remember the sight, others would not live to tell the tale.

Pte Kerans of the 9th D.L.I. recalls the hazardous march to Primosole, as he and his comrades pressed on in the oppressive heat, and the dangers that they faced along the way:

"We marched each side of the road, on constant look out for the two Me. 109s or any other action. At the first sign of the two planes everybody shouted at once and vanished, as if by magic, into fields that edged the road and into any cover there was. From it they sent a shower of bullets at the aircraft. The bren carriers and ammunition trucks were not always so lucky. An ammo truck was hit and was a danger to everybody in the area. I suppose the driver could have jumped off and run like hell but, instead, he drove it up the hillside as far as he could before it exploded, killing him, Poor blighter.

Two of the carriers were hit and left blazing on the road. As I resumed my march a charred lump of smoking flesh, for all the world looking like an over cooked turkey, fell at my feet, and that smell, that only a front line soldier knows, filled my nostrils and made me feel sick. I often came across that smell and still do in my worst nightmares. I don't know who buried our dead, I rarely did. We marched on, and on, and on, mile after mile over dusty, rough Sicilian roads, nursing the precious contents of our water bottles." [9]

During the first three days of the advance the 8th Army had met only minimal opposition, but Montgomery's bold plan now focussed the success of the Sicilian campaign upon an ugly structure of steel girders, 400 feet long, called the Primosole Bridge. Highway 114 passes over it to the city of Catania, 7 miles distant to the north. To the south, some 10 miles away lies Lentini. At this point, the River Simeto winds its muddy way, in a series of loops; through a marshland devoid of cover; its banks overgrown with tall reeds.

At each end of the bridge stood a concrete block house. Close to the northern end was a series of farm buildings. To the east and west of Highway 114, to a width of over 1,000 yards in each direction, were lines of vineyards and olive trees that extended to 500 yards in depth. Along the northern edge of the vineyards ran a sunken track, while further north the plain opened out devoid of cover and treacherous with gullies and other such natural obstacles. Nearly three miles north of the bridge Highway 114 passed over a dry irrigation canal called Fosso Bottaceto, which outlined the southern defences of the Catania airfield.

During the planning of the campaign Montgomery had seen that the Primosole Bridge was the key to securing the Catania Plain and the city, though in the event of a successful British advance it could turn out to be a dangerous bottle neck. This steel structure was now to become a focus of attention for the British and German forces in a deadly game that would alter the course of the campaign.

The ease of 8th Army's advance led Montgomery to believe he could successfully attack on two fronts, the main assault along the coast was to cut through the Plain of Catania and take the city. The second assault by Harpoon Force, was to track inland to capture Vizzini, Caltagirone, Enna and Leonforte. Patton's force would hold off the Gela counter-attacks while Harpoon Force would sweep around the rear of the Herman Goering Division, trapping the German forces between II Corps and 30 Corps.

At Vizzini, Harpoon Force ran into stiff resistance from the Herman Goering Division, which held the city until the 15th July, stopping the inland thrust in its tracks. At this point Montgomery turned his attention to the coastal thrust. The 1st Airborne was alerted and was to take Primosole Bridge on the night of 13th/ 14th July.

Montgomery's plan was simple and audacious, the 1st Parachute Brigade was to drop around the bridge, followed by a small glider force carrying ten light artillery pieces. Simultaneously, No 3 Commando would land by sea and take the bridge at Malati, which crosses the River Lentini three miles to the north of the City of Lentini. While these bridges were being held, the 50th Division, reinforced by the 4th Armoured Brigade, would drive north, take Carlentini and Lentini, relieve the Commandos, press on to Primosole Bridge to relieve the Airborne, and establish a bridge head north of the river by nightfall on 14th July. On the 15th, the then combined force would seize the City of Catania.

The 1st Parachute Brigade, led by Brigadier Lathbury, prepared itself for the trial ahead. The Battalion was to drop north and south of the bridge taking it from two sides. The 3rd Battalion was to land 1,000 yards north where the river ran to the sea, establish a bridge head and counter any enemy moves from the direction of Catania. To the south, the 2nd Battalion was to capture the high ground, these were three small hills of vital importance, code named Johnny I, II and III. From these, all access to the bridge from the south was controlled.

As the airborne troops made ready the Germans responded at last to relieve their beleaguered troops holding the line. Reinforcements were sent in the form of Lieutenant Colonel Ludwig Heilmann's 3rd Parachute Regiment, as the advanced guard, followed by a Machine Gun Battalion and Signal Company. These forces were to be joined shortly by anti tank units, Engineers and finally by the 4th Parachute Regiment. These men were mostly veterans and had seen action in Poland, the Netherlands, Crete and Russia. They were young and tough, believing themselves to be the cream of the Wehrmacht, and would prove this by their actions throughout the war.

Heilmann and his paratroops were transported to an area north of Lentini where they came under the command of Group Schmalz, his 2nd Battalion being sent to Francoforte where they would help plug the gap between Schmalz and the Herman Goering Division defending Vizzini. On the 13th July, the 1st Parachute Machine gun Battalion arrived and was ordered to move south to Primosole Bridge, when they arrived they at once dug in on the edge of an orange grove, west of Highway 114. Schmalz now had some extra muscle and made good use of its fresh paratroops to slow down 13 Corps' drive for Lentini and the Plain of Catania.

On 13th July, the 5th Division, thrusting for Lentini, collided with 115 Panzer Regiment and two fresh battalions of Paratroops. The 15th Brigade was stalled all that day. Montgomery's audacious plan was running into trouble, so he turned the heat on Kirkman, who drove up to his leading troops of the 50th Division to urge them on. He found them brewing up after a hard battle the night before. Kirkman told Brigadier Cooke-Collis:

"You're not going to sit down and rest, you go on now until you drop if necessary, occupying the ground you'll have to fight for tomorrow. Get em all on the move, now's the time to go on."

On the evening of 13th July, No 3 Commando was put ashore behind enemy lines, in bright moonlight, in the Bay of Agnone. Once on the land they were to force march five miles to the Malati Bridge and take it intact. This crucially important bridge spanned the Lentini River four kilometres north of the town and it was an important lynch-pin in Montgomery's strategy. This highway bridge carried about 300 yards of Highway 114 and was the main route joining Lentini and Catania - the only direct road to Primosole Bridge.

The first commandos landed at 2200 hours and instead of finding the expected Italian defenders, they ran into Heilmann's paratroopers who stood their ground. All of the high ground between the landing point and the objective was held by the 3rd Battalion of the Herman Goering Regiment. For the next five hours the commandos fought their way over rugged country until they took the bridge at 0300 hours. The Italian defenders there were soon routed and demolition charges removed. As dawn broke the commandos were shooting up anything that came into range - causing great confusion in the enemy ranks.

The main problem was now to hold the bridge until the 50th arrived, for Highway 114 was as important to the Germans as it was to the British. It was their main supply route to all units fighting to the south of Lentini and their route of escape to the north. The Germans poured mortar, rifle, and machine gun fire upon the commandos. A Tiger tank pounded the bridge with its 88 mm gun and casualties mounted at an alarming rate.

The 50th Division, which was to have relieved the commandos at dawn on the 14th, were still battling their way forward against Group Schmalz and Heilmann's Paratroopers. After holding out for the best part of the day, in the face of constant attacks, the commandos that survived were forced to fight their way out of the position to avoid capture or certain death and make for friendly lines. On 14th July, at 1700 hours, the lead elements of the 50th, the 5th East Yorkshires, reach the bridge at Malati and took it intact. In their haste to retreat, the Germans had not had time to destroy it. Montgomery was so moved by the commando operation that he renamed the bridge 'No 3 Commando Bridge' and had a stone mason carve the name which was placed nearby. Casualties within the ranks of the commando's were as follows:

28 Killed
66 Wounded
59 Missing

At this point, 151 Brigade took the place of the exhausted 69th Brigade as the 50th Divisions lead troops.

On the night of the 13th July, the 1st Parachute Brigade was flying through a black sky towards the Primosole Bridge and the Plain of Catania. 145 aircraft packed with paratroops, 126 towing Horsas, gliders carrying anti-tank guns and artillery. The drop was to commence at 2200 hours with the gliders landing at 0100 hours on the 14th July.

As this aerial convoy moved en masse five miles from the coast line they were fired on by their own ships lying off Malta and the Sicilian coast. Heavy enemy flak added to its problems, the convoy now being dispersed in great confusion. Eleven planes were shot down by flak, three others lost in the sea, twenty six never dropped their load but returned to their North African base. Only thirty craft dropped their troops in the correct DZ (Dropping Zone), nine dropped them just outside the DZ and forty eight others were wide of the mark by anything up to twenty miles. Out of the 1,856 men who set out on 'Operation Fustian', only 295 of them landed close to or at Primosole Bridge.

As the paratroops fell to earth, the sight that greeted their eyes was akin to Dante's Inferno, Medic Robert Smith recalls how he hung in the air and viewed the scene:

> "Fires were burning to the four points of the compass and I could see the bridge shining in the light of the moon, the machine gun and small arms fire intensified as I approached mother earth, then I was on the ground, hugging it grimly in a depression that was not nearly deep enough. As I lay on the ground, a plane was hit in the under belly and I saw a pin point of flame then almost simultaneously she exploded." [10]

Fires lit up the area as the paratroopers tried to gather their senses and bearings. Artillery and flak fire was constant, as small groups gathered together and made for their respective areas and, in the early hours of 14th July, Primosole Bridge was captured. The Italian force defending this feature fled in panic when a glider collided with one end of the bridge. As dawn broke other men arrived and engineers dismantled the explosive charges strapped to the steel girders. Lt Colonel Pearson organised the defence of the now secured objective with 120 men from his own battalion (The 1st), two platoons of the 3rd Battalion and three anti tank guns. Other weapons, those of the Germans and Italians, were collected from the area and employed by the paratroopers to make up for their own losses.

Pte Priestley jumped from his aircraft and made a landing some distance away from his objective - the hill named Johnny I - and found himself in close proximity to his German counterparts:

> "We flew in at almost sea level until the approach then went up to about five hundred feet. Equipped with all our gear, we thought 'this is a pantomime'. It was. All hell broke loose, ships and artillery opened up, we all stepped out of the planes. One hell of a drop! What a job sorting things out. One shouted for comrades and was answered in German. This went on for some time. Eventually we got more or less organised and set off for our objective Johnny I, named after our Col. John Frost." [11]

The confusion of the night evaporated with the clear Sicilian dawn of the 14th July, and the struggle for this iron bridge would soon begin in earnest. In the

A VIEW OF PRIMOSOLE BRIDGE

lull before the storm, both sides prepared for the coming battle, whose outcome would determine Montgomery's failure or success in trying to seize Catania and bring the campaign to a swift end.

The morning of the 14th July began with still no sign of the 50th Division whose lead elements still battled their way to the Plain of Catania. The troops of that unit were exhausted, racked with diarrhoea and short of water. The men moved forward in a haze of white dust mile after mile, with strained, grey faces sweating under steel helmets and looking like unearthly apparitions. The heat rose to 35° in the shade and in this, the advancing 50th pushed back the stubborn German forces who made a stand at every opportunity. The road leading to the 'Primosole Bridge' was littered with dead and wounded north countrymen whose corpses were identified by the sign of the double 'T' on their shoulders.

CHAPTER TWO

THE BATTLE OF PRIMOSOLE BRIDGE

(14th-17th July 1943)

In the early hours of the 14th July, Frost's 2nd Parachute Battalion took the full weight of the German counter attacks. The enemy 1st Parachute Machine-gun Battalion was in position between Johnny I and Johnny III in order to prevent any British attempt to take the bridge via route 114. The British Paratroops holding Johnny I came under intense mortar and machine gun fire resulting in many casualties. The British were astonished at the presence of crack German troops attacking from the west just south of the Simeto. The Green Devils (German Paras) and Red Devils fought it out around Johnny III, which finally fell to the attacking Germans. From this position they delivered a withering fire upon the British. The war diary of the 2nd Parachute Battalion stated as follows:

> "0800 hrs - Forward troops are withdrawing inside the perimeter. At this time it was apparent that we were under MG fire from three sides and the enemy were closing in on us, not in very great strength but with heavy fire power and considerable skill. A great deal of sniping had taken place on both sides."

Casualties began to mount as blazing grasses to the south forced the British into an ever shrinking perimeter, ammunition was now running low and it became obvious that any co-ordinated enemy counter attack could not be held. The situation was saved by the six inch guns of the cruiser H.M.S. Newfoundland. Once radio contact was made, her high velocity shells began to arrive with great precision among the Germans and the danger receded.

As this battle raged, the defenders on the bridge were left relatively in peace. At mid morning the fun started, as a Focke-Wulf machine-gunned the area around the bridge. At noon, German 88s plastered the bridge for an hour. The bulk of the British Paras were north of the river facing Catania and it was here that the counter attacks came in, just after 1300 hours. The first was easily repulsed, to be followed by another from the right flank, which forced the British to shorten their defensive perimeter.

But now the defenders came under fire from more anti tank guns that rained down a tempest of steel on the paratroops. Captain Gammon was in a pill box at the end of the bridge and recalls the devastating effects of the 88s as they fired solid shot rounds into them:

"To this day I swear as each round of solid shot struck the pill-box, it keeled over and bounced up again. Perhaps it was the heat haze of the dust or my fevered imagination - it was made of reinforced concrete - but I swear it did. Suddenly there was a crash, fumes and dust and something hit me in the chest. I could hardly see. Where's the door? Had it collapsed? A shaft of light and I groped my way out into the blinding sunshine." [12]

Ammunition was now running low and casualties began to mount from the heavy artillery fire. At the southern end of the bridge a surgical unit of the 16th Parachute Field Ambulance Company set up shop and managed to perform numerous operations in difficult circumstances. The wounded were evacuated on a mule drawn cart with Sgt Stevens, RAMC, running alongside braving the flying steel, he was awarded the Military Medal for his courage.

The Green Devils now began to take their first prisoners, Major Rudolf Bohmler commented later on the captured Red Devils:

"There was considerable mutual respect between the two opponents. They were splendid fellows, each single one an athletic type. Now it was clear the British had air landed and we were involved with 'colleagues'! Really a pity that one had to fight against such spirited types so similar to our German Paratroopers, and who did not seem to be annoyed that they had been captured by their German brothers in arms." [13]

The only contact the Red Devils made with the outside world was at 0930 hours. This was with the 4th Armoured Brigade which informed them they were having great difficulty getting through to relieve the force holding the bridge. By 1000 hours all radio contact had been lost, never to be regained. British radio sets were notoriously unreliable and all too often gave out at critical moments in many actions.

The battle being fought along the Simeto and around Johnny I was fierce and a basic fight for survival. No quarter was asked for, or given, as the Green and Red Devils continued to blood each other. The British looked in vain for the relieving force throughout the day. Radio contact had gone so no help could be obtained from the cruiser Newfoundland. Colonel Pearson was forced to the conclusion that the dire circumstances they found themselves in, meant the position could not withstand the growing German pressure for long.

Under cover of the fire of their 88s the Green Devils crept forward using the stunted trees growing near the river as a shield and set fire to reeds on the river bank, these burned furiously and gave off clouds of acrid smoke. The British troops on the Northern bank withdrew as their comrades on the bridge gave them covering fire. At 1730 hours the situation was so bad the order was given to abandon the bridge and those troops that were able fell back to the Johnny positions, under heavy fire, leaving behind them many badly wounded comrades. The bridge had been in British hands for just 16 hours.

A DEAD GERMAN PARATROOPER IN THE DRY GRASS NEAR THE BRIDGE. HIS BOOTS HAVE BEEN TAKEN
BUT HIS IRON CROSS IS STILL ON HIS UNIFORM. (*IMPERIAL WAR MUSEUM*)

Pte Priestley and his comrades were caught in a hail of mortar bombs, but their position was now untenable and they were forced to withdraw:

"A lot of men died there. Almost all my friends died there. To name a few: George Weir, Bob Whittle, Harry Coppard and lots of others. Ken Stuart and myself were blown up by a mortar. We escaped to the quarry, as it was called, on the way we encountered a barbed wire fence, I don't remember very much having been wounded in the ankle, but it would appear I pushed poor Ken into the barbed wire and ran over him, all I wanted was a drink. Ken threatened an Italian prisoner he would shoot him if he did not hand over his water bottle, which he eventually did. I had a good drink and nearly choked, it was full of vino. I was then taken to the First Aid post. After a short time I was returned to duty. Doc Gordon had little mercy and quite right.

On my return I was walking back to Johnny I when I saw a dog-cart coming down the hill pulled by Ken, I almost threw a fit, we had been together for what seems a life time. Someone gave the order that it was every man for himself." [14]

That night, the Germans did not press on any further, but the British forces did, at 7.30 pm Sherman tanks arrived near Johnny III, followed by a company of the 9th Battalion Durham Light Infantry. The worn-out troops had covered some twenty miles in the blazing heat of the day and were in no fit state to commence offensive operations immediately, the acute shortages in transport had, not for the first time, affected the outcome of a major campaign.

Lt. Fenner of the 6th D.L.I. let his weary troops get some rest after their hard slog to Primosole. He recalls the bitterness of the British paratroops he met after they had fought so well and then been forced to withdraw:

> "During the night two tired and bitter paratroopers came up the road to the battalion. They had captured the bridge but could not hold it any longer. Most of their mates were dead or captured. So deep was their sorrow they tried to talk the I.O. and the C.O. into waking the lads and making an attack right away. There were tears in their eyes and anger in their voices as they talked. To the best of their knowledge they were the only ones left from the battle and it was definite that the bridge was in German hands. They swore they were coming in with us and taking no prisoners." [15]

A column of Italian troops that had been cut off by the advancing Durham's of the 9th Battalion tried to pass through their lines in an attempt to rejoin their own forces. Pte Kerans lay in wait with his comrades:

> "Things were more or less ready when the enemy's first vehicle started to come through us. The anti tank gun had been pulled just clear of the road and those men awakened were crouched down behind the low wall that verged it, with their weapons in their hands. The enemy consisted of six large, life boat shaped vehicles, packed, jammed full of heavily armed Italian commandos. For all the world like so many life boats and they could be driven either end. Open boats, just asking for grenades to be tossed into them. Nobby had not managed to caution men all the way through the battalion and a guard at the far end 'Let fly at them'. Then all hell broke loose.
>
> At the beginning the commandos were brave, just out of Italy, they were going to make a name for themselves. They could not see who was attacking them or from where so they put up a solid wall of fire from all sides of their armoured boats. Our lads, behind the wall, without even looking, tossed grenades into the boats, like so many balls into a bucket at the fair ground. Those further up the hill side fired at the flashes of their guns. The Italians realised they had run into a 'Hornets nest' and decided to withdraw. The rear car started to beat a hasty withdrawal. As it passed the anti-tank gun the latter 'let fly' and it burst into flames. The second managed to squeeze passed, but not before at least one grenade had exploded into it. As the third tried to get passed it was hit by a shell and the road was well and truly blocked. The three remaining still poured a withering fire into our hillside but this subsided as grenade after grenade exploded in them. The air was filled by flying steel and bits of Italians. Those able to do so threw themselves out of their machines and took cover

on the opposite side of the road. A lot of them were dead or dying and their screams and cries almost drowned what was left of the battle." [16]

Pte Kerans heard his officer calling him for a full five minutes, but he could not get there because of the heavy machine gun fire that had him pinned down:

"I found him, only to get the usual derogatory remarks, he ordered me to take a couple of Itie prisoners back. Just my luck, I'm going to miss my breakfast as I did my yesterday's meals. As we went back along the road the war hadn't finished, there were still the odd bullets whistling around. The prisoners were glad to come with me, I don't think they liked Mr Visher's company either. By now it was quite light. We passed the first two armoured cars both still burning merrily. I had to keep my eyes on my prisoners and on the many mutilated and dying lying around. One of the latter might decide to take an enemy with him when he left this life. First one then another would give himself up. I had eleven at the finish. As we passed the dead, dying and mutilated bodies of their comrades they wept and crossed themselves. One poor blighter had had both legs blown off and was still conscious. We propped him against a tree and put a cigarette in his mouth, but by the amount of blood around him it was obvious he was doomed. There were many wounded and my charges were reluctant to leave them. There was nothing we could do for them. As we walked towards the rear of the column a tearful and angry voice, from the hill side screamed, 'Kill them, kill the bastards, kill the hump-backed 'Gets'. They have got Jimmy Hall. It was Arthur Thompson. Through his tears, (he was crying like a baby) his hate could be felt. A bullet had killed Jimmy outright. I felt it too, he and I had been in the same training battalion in Blighty. We had fought together all the way up the Desert. But after seeing what we had done to the other Ities I could feel no hate for those who were left. I told Arthur so and he said, "Then turn your back for two minutes and I will." With Arthur in his present state I thought it sensible to add a little haste as we carried on up the road. My prisoners gave me no trouble, stunned by what they had been through, pale and dazed they walked quietly in front of me, talking in whispers amongst themselves. I thought it's a lovely morning, the birds are singing, there are flowers in the hedgerow. Maybe that's how it was, that's how I remembered it, or was it that I was just glad to be alive?" [17]

Lt David Cole, of the 2nd Inniskillings, remembers the view that met his eyes as he looked down upon the scene from the crest of a ridge:

"The panorama before us was magnificent, thirty miles to the north dominating the horizon was the huge, misty snow capped conical mass, ten thousand feet high, of Mount Etna. On the plain itself we could see through our binoculars, the Simeto River curling irregularly from the west down to the sea. Along the coast the City of Catania was dimly visible, shimmering in the heat. All this would have constituted a picture of great beauty and tranquillity, had it not been for the thud of shells, with their tell tale puffs of black smoke, exploding near the river. The reality was that down in front of us, concealed in slit trenches and ditches and sheltered behind buildings and whatever cover they could find, two armies were facing each other in mortal combat." [18]

One look at the Sherman's of the 44th Royal Tank Regiment and the Germans pulled back to the north bank and prepared themselves for the expected all out attack by the British ground forces. No attack was made that night as the leading unit, the 9th D.L.I., did not close until 2130 hours. The rest of the 151st Brigade was strung back along the Lentini Road and the last of them did not arrive until midnight. Both sides spent a quiet night, the worn-out Durham's rested in preparation of their coming battle.

The first phase of the 'Battle for Primosole Bridge' was over, for the British Airborne it had been a bitter disappointment, of the 1,856 troops that had flown from North Africa only 16% ever came into action on the objective and one third were never dropped. Many that did were captured and an unknown number were missing. During the battle Brigade casualty figures were 117, with 27 killed. With their work done the airborne troops left the battle to the men of the D.L.I. For the German paratroopers there was to be no relief and during the night they took up new positions in preparation for the ordeal to come.

The plan for the morning attack was for a conventional frontal assault. The CO of the D.L.I. did not like the hastily put together plan, but his Divisional Commander Kirkman had Montgomery breathing down his neck to achieve even greater speed in breaking through to the Plain of Catania and so, imperfect as it was, it had to be put into operation.

The area around the bridge in the dawn of the 15th July was quiet as the grave as both sides moved into position. The dim light showed the approach to the bridge to be littered with wrecked vehicles and the dead bodies of paratroopers in their camouflaged smocks. At 0730 hours the stillness was broken as the British artillery opened fire on suspected enemy positions. The 24th and 98th Field Regiments of the Royal Artillery rained down shells on the Germans. From behind the Johnny II position emerged Lt Colonel Clarke's 9th D.L.I. supported by the Sherman's of the 44th RTR, who began their move up Highway 114.

The Durhams spread out into attack formation, the tanks being interspersed among their number. Lt Colonel Frost and Pearson of the Parachute Brigade had a grand stand view of the drama now being played out before them as the German paratroopers cut the Durham's to pieces. Frost wrote of that morning:

"We had never taken part in such an operation and having seen this were determined never to do so. It all went according to plan. There was a massive expenditure of ammunition. Medium machine guns kept up continuous pressure and tanks were interspersed with the infantry. There was a smoke screen to cover the last and most dangerous stretch. The infantry plodded on remorselessly with bayonets fixed for the final assault across the river. The Germans held their fire until the Durham's were within some fifty yards, more or less point-blank range, then mowed the leading platoons down. Then they engaged the follow-up platoons. They fired burst after burst of machine gun fire at the tanks, which had the effect of forcing them to remain closed down and therefore unable to identify enemy targets. The enemy anti-tank fire appeared nevertheless to be ineffective, but without protection, the infantry attack just faded away and both Durham's and tanks came back" [19]

Pte Pope attacked with the 9th D.L.I. that morning and recalls only too well the stout defence that met them:

"The Germans defended the bridge very well. My mate from down the road was killed in the fighting which was very rough. There was snipers everywhere picking men off, when we finally crossed the bridge and got into the vineyards the enemy was so close we was engaged in hand to hand fighting." [20]

Those platoons that did manage to get across to the north bank were soon forced back over the Simeto leaving their dead and most of their wounded in enemy hands. The remnants of the battalion lined the south bank, while the Germans prepared to meet the next attack. Any movement on the Southern bank brought down a ferocious barrage from 88s, but the troops of the 9th D.L.I. prevented any attempt by enemy engineers to place explosive charges on the bridge.

By the time 9th D.L.I. made their attack, Pte Kerans had delivered his prisoners and returned to his company in time to watch the assault:

"They started to cross the river then all hell broke loose. On the other side of the river suddenly a row of heads, machine-guns and rifles popped up. Soon the river ran red, literally, with the blood of the Durham's. Some did reach the other side, scamper up the bank and engage the enemy in hand-to-hand fighting, but there was not enough to hang on to what they had gained. We in H.Q. company went down to see what we could do to help, there wasn't a lot. We stopped just short of the river and fired at anything that looked Tedescish (German). One or two of us went into the river to try to rescue some of the wounded. It wasn't easy, bullets buzzed about like bees. The bloke nearest to me had, himself, to be rescued." [21]

As the 9th Battalion fought it out with the Green Devils the 6th D.L.I. were still moving towards the bridge area and could hear clearly the sounds of battle. Lt. (Later Colonel) Fenner found events in full swing when his unit arrived and was soon to learn of his part in the battle:

"We moved across towards Mont Pancali in the twilight. On the way we came across a group of Bren Gun carriers reeking of burnt paint and flesh. They had been caught by Stukas. Just to the west of the road we climbed up to a spur on the Mount. I remember finding empty Thompson gun magazines on the way up. The discarder of these magazines must have been firing and replacing magazines as he climbed. On the top were three dead Germans. One without boots, a Thompson gun and a pile of bloodstained British webbing equipment. We buried the Germans in the slits they had dug and covered them with the earth spoil they had removed. The night was peaceful in our immediate vicinity but we could hear the crackle of small arms fire all round.

We set off next morning through Lentini. As we progressed north we passed lots of our own parachutists who had dropped wide and too far south. We reached a road junction called Dead Horse Corner a mile or two south of Primosole. Here we found dead Paras, British and German. Fighting was going on just in front. It was an unpleasant place full of unpleasant sights and smells. Tony went away to attend the Commanding Officer's 'O' Group (Orders Group, the officers who put the plan into operation). When he returned he told us that the Bridge had changed hands several times. 9 D.L.I. had attacked during the day and after success the Germans had retaken it. 8 D.L.I. were attacking that night. We were to relieve 'A' Company of 8 D.L.I. on the high ground west of the road over looking the river Simeto. We pushed over the forward slope which was covered in a plantation of small trees. I knew most of the officers of 'A' Company 8 D.L.I., having met them during our brief sojourn in Tobruk and on leave in Alexandria. We wished them good luck and settled down to making ourselves at home in our new surroundings. There was a large tent in the Company area. From the evidence of uniforms and empty bottles about the place we concluded it had been a rest camp for Luftwaffe personnel. It was not long before certain members of the platoon had donned German greatcoats and were parading around in them, admiring the padded shoulders. Cries of "Aye aye, spiv" rang around the place! Tony sent me out to contact 9 D.L.I. who were east of the road on our right on a similar forward slope. My first contact was with two soldiers, grey faced with fatigue and stress. Their appearance was descriptive of what they had been through. A forced night move through hostile territory, a daylight attack, driven back by the German counter attack, finally pinned down in the open, subject to shelling by 88mm airbursts. They quietly told me where to find the acting company commander. They moved like automatons. From him I heard the story of 9 D.L.I.'s fight and the loss of friends. I returned to my Company area. We were topped up with rations, water and ammunition but still no blankets." [22]

The German troops had not only selected their defensive positions with great skill but had also been aided by the density of the vineyards on the north bank which made any movement in daylight suicidal and very confusing. Within the vineyards themselves were numerous olive trees extending to a depth of 400

GERMAN ANTI-TANK GUNNERS OF THE ARTILLERY BATTALION, 1ST PARACHUTE DIVISION,
IN ACTION. (*AUTHOR'S COLLECTION*)

yards. Behind the vines ran a sunken road later named by the Tommies as 'Stink Alley' because of the stench from the dead cattle, horses and the dead of both sides, at the time of the attack this feature was unknown to the British. Little could be seen beyond the vineyards and between the rows of vines visibility was limited to ten yards.

During the morning of 15th July, General Kirkman ordered a fresh attack to take place that afternoon with a much heavier artillery support. The assault was to be made by the 8th Battalion D.L.I. and was to be led by Lt Colonel Lidwell. Things looked grim for the 8th Battalion. Lidwell outlined the plan in the presence of Brigadier Lathbury, two Parachute Colonels and Brigadier Curry of the 4th Armoured Brigade, even though he had grave misgivings about it. But he had Kirkman, the Divisional Commander, breathing down his neck, he, in turn, was being urged on by Montgomery to make greater haste and break through the Primosole Bridge and out into the Catania Plain. Despite all his reservations, about the prospects for success, Lidwell was to put the plan into operation.

Lidwell knew full well that this kind of frontal attack was suicidal, the 9th Battalion assault had proved that, but the bridge was holding up the advance of the whole 8th Army and Montgomery wanted it captured regardless of the cost.

Sat listening to all of this was Alistair Pearson, Colonel of the Parachute Brigade, he was dog tired, unshaven and covered in grime from the battle, he could contain himself no longer and in a loud voice the dour Scot exclaimed: "Well, if you want to lose another bloody battalion, that's the way to do it." The two Brigadiers didn't seem to have been annoyed by his remarks but simply asked him how he would do it.

Pearson spoke of a ford about a mile down river which he had used when withdrawing the previous night. The enemy was not in sufficient numbers to cover the whole of the far bank; it being most likely their forces were concentrated near the bridge itself, the delivery of such a left hook would take them completely by surprise. Pearson offered to guide the Durhams across the river and to the bridge, he then told Lidwell: "After that your on your own, I'll cross that bridge and be up that road as hard as I can bloody well go." The attack was then postponed until the night, a decision welcomed by Colonel Lidwell, equally welcome was Pearson's offer of showing the D.L.I. Commander the alternative route across the Simeto.

As Pearson led 'A' and 'D' Companies of the 8th D.L.I. to their crossing point the permanent barrage rumbled ominously in the distance, signal flares occasionally shot into the air causing the long column of men to freeze at intervals until it was realised they were not meant for them.

At 12.50 am the British barrage opened up with a deafening roar upon the vineyards beyond the Simeto as heavy machine-guns raked the entire area. This devastating deluge was kept up without pause until 2 am, when the whole weight of the barrage moved to the northern end of the bridge and was joined by fire from the Besa guns of British tanks.

At 2.10 am A and D Companies crossed the Simeto in single file without any great difficulty, the water was roughly four feet deep except where a shell had fallen and then it doubled its depth, some of the troops disappeared from sight as they walked into them but were soon rescued.

Once across the two companies formed up quickly and made for the bridge - hampered as they were by the closely planted vines. This assault took the enemy completely by surprise, some of the Germans had been killed by the barrage and the main body had withdrawn some 300 yards. Speed was now essential, tracer bullets skipped over the Durham's heads as they rushed the bridge and the night air was filled with their shouts and yells, the few enemy encountered were soon dispatched with small arms, grenades or bayonets.

Both companies established themselves on the Catania road, using a ditch that ran along each side of it for cover. Spandau machine gun fire swept the area, once in position the Durham's view of the area was limited to only a few yards due to the density of the vines, trees and long grasses, they now had to be on the alert at all times to keep the Germans at bay.

The first phase of the battle had been successfully carried out, now it was up to the rest of the battalion, B and C companies to cross the bridge. Colonel

Lidwell had arranged three different kinds of communications to contact the waiting companies in the hope that at least one of them should work. The first was a mortar flare, however in the dark, mortars and mortar bombs had got separated. The second was by wireless, but these sets had been drowned in the river crossing. The last was a carrier with a radio that was stationed at the southern end of the bridge, Lidwell crossed the bridge to find a scene of carnage, the carrier had received a direct hit killing all but one of the four man crew.

Unless Lidwell took the risk of walking up the road to where the Durham's waited the only other possibility of getting a message back was to use one of the Sherman tanks on the other side of the river as a link. He found a tank that was stood with its engine running, there was a lot of firing still going on at this time and Lidwell could not make himself heard, so he climbed onto the tank and tapped the commander of the head. Every hatch on that machine slammed shut and nothing would entice them to open up again. Lidwell walked back to the road when out of the darkness came a figure on a bicycle - a War Office observer called Major Wigram, luckily for him the Durham's were not trigger happy. His arrival could not have been more opportune, he listened to the 8th Battalion CO, turned his bicycle round and took orders for B and C Companies to advance at once.

The breakdown in communications had delayed things considerably and dawn was about to break as B and C Companies left their assembly areas in single file. The troops marched past the wrecked carrier and over the bridge, avoiding mines that lay on the surface. As the leading troops drew level with the blazing farm buildings on the left of the road some wag from D Company shouted: "Push on B Company, there's only a few Ities up front," when enemy machine guns opened up on the leading sections at point blank range. These were no Italians but German paratroops and the Durham's had walked straight into them.

The Durham's scrambled for cover in the ditch running along each side of the road, Lt Jackson led his platoon in an attempt to rush the German gunners but he and his men were cut down before they had got very far. Once more, the Durham's were up and advancing towards their unseen tormentors, the whole of 'B' Companies leading platoon was shot down as the troops pressed forward into the dense vines on either side of the bridge road. In the dark half-light of dawn there began a lethal game of search and destroy as the Durham's and paratroops hunted each other, it was every man for himself in that grim place with the added confusion of being unable to tell friend from foe, no quarter was asked for and none was given.

George Worthington was awarded the Military Medal for his bravery at Primosole and recalls the events that led up to it with typical unassuming modesty:

"I remember before the attack, they came round with the rum ration to give us a bit of Dutch courage. I'd reached that stage in my army life that I thought 'well let's get into it and if I come out fair enough - if I don't so be it.' That's the attitude I took on board at the time and when I came out of the battle, I was informed I'd been nominated for the Military Medal -nobody was more surprised than myself. They tell me I got it because when we'd gained our objectives we were pinned down by heavy fire. Gerry was no respecter of stretcher bearers or whatever, I was all keyed up and went out with other people and started bringing the casualties in. They tell me that under those conditions I had worked with complete disregard of my own safety until everything had been dealt with, it lasted for about three hours, I think. We were pulled back then.

L/Cpl George Worthington. MM. 6th Bn DLI.

There was all these vineyards and pill boxes, it was a hard battle ground favouring the defenders. The only thing to see at night was gun flashes. Some casualties would take it quietly, others would let you know they were there, but that's only natural. We didn't bring any Germans in even though there was plenty laid about, they suffered as heavily as us." [23]

Paratroops would appear without warning and shoot their opponents at point blank range, the Durham's used tactics of stealth and stalked the Germans silently, bayoneting them to death where they lay. The scene was lit up by the flashes from the muzzles of guns and by exploding grenades in the most savage hand to hand fighting the men had experienced. Within twenty minutes both sides had fought themselves to a standstill and the only troops left in the fighting area were the dead and the wounded.

The battalion was now established in a position three or four hundred yards deep to the north of the bridge waiting for the inevitable counter attack. At first light the Germans came and with the first shock over ran two platoons. The Durham's fought for their lives in hand-to-hand combat as one platoon of 'C' Company was forced back over the river. The perimeter held now by the Durham's was only one hundred yards deep and it rested now on the arrival of reinforcements to save a precarious situation.

Pte Hymer crossed the river with the 8th D.L.I., only to be forced back by the terrific volume of fire directed upon them by the Green Devils:

"We went across the river thinking the Italians was holding the other side, there was a big wine place there, but it was German crack troops dug in. We went forward - well they shot the daylights out of us, our packs was dragging us down into the river, the water was red with blood and we had to pull back. Mortaring and shelling was going on all the time." [24]

Pte Reg Pope.
9th Bn DLI.

The 16th July was a day of hard fighting for the men in the bridgehead but they held firm in the face of fierce counter attacks by the Germans. The mortar teams of the 8th D.L.I. set up their weapons and waited for the enemy counter-attack which was not long in coming:

"Primosole was pretty grim, we managed to get over the bridge and took up a position on the other side near a brewery or something. We put up our mortars behind the brewery and the Germans sent their Herman Goering division into the attack, we absolutely murdered 'em. The numbers of dead was tremendous. We were so close when they made this counter attack we had to remove the charge from the mortar shells and fired with just the primary charge. There was no other way of getting such a short range so as to be effective. It was a terrible sight after we'd withdrawn - German bodies everywhere." [25]

Kirkman now decided upon a stronger attack to be delivered by the rest of the brigade, the 6th and 9th Battalions of the D.L.I., as the 8th held their position the 6th and 9th would cross at the ford used the previous night. Once established at the northern end of the bridge the 6th D.L.I. would attack up the left side and the 9th D.L.I. up the right side of the Catania Road to their objective 1,500 yards ahead. The Sherman tanks of the County of London Yeomanry would follow them to exploit the break through. All of this would be supported by the tremendous fire power of 159 pieces of artillery.

The 6th and 9th D.L.I. crossed the River Simeto at approximately 01.30 hrs on 17th July with little difficulty, but the German paratroops were waiting for them and stood their ground until they either killed their assailants or were killed themselves:

Lt Fenner of the 6th Battalion crossed the river with his men and at once launched them into the attack:

"The whole battalion moved silently in single file to the attack. Rum had been issued before we left and was of some comfort in this limbo period where we had little to do but occupy our thoughts with the grim and inevitable prospect ahead. We reached a dry ditch running towards the river and began moving through a battlefield where our parachutists and the Germans had fought. All around the vegetation had been burnt by phosphorus bombs and tracer bullets. Evidence of the fighting was everywhere. The ditch contained many burnt bodies. One completely blackened sat upright staring sightlessly at each member of the battalion as he struggled past in the moonlight. The only sound came from the burst of harassing fire from the Cheshire machine gunners and the bull frogs croaking in the reeds. We paused before the leading Company entered the river, bayonets were fixed, rifles and machine guns cocked. Ben Dickenson, the platoon runner and oldest soldier in the platoon argued with Connel the sergeant, about the need to fix bayonets. He said he had never found it necessary to use one. I cannot remember the outcome of this disagreement but I did appreciate the easing of tension it produced amongst us. Then we were on the move to the river, sliding down the bank into chest high water, again in single file, guiding ourselves by hanging on to a wire stretched between the banks for this purpose. Below the far bank the battalion bore left, then turned to face the enemy, the three assaulting companies in line. So far all had gone well, our objective, a sunken road, was some 500 yards away through the vine yards. It needed a few more minutes to pass before zero hour when someone said "What are we waiting for?" another voice said "Let's get stuck in". Then followed a general move by all the leading platoons up the bank, through the vineyard towards the sunken road. My recollections of what happened after that are confused. Firing began at isolated Germans seen running away, then from the direction of the road came a murderous fire from the Spandaus located there. The gunners were firing past at knee height. The line of infantry kept on going in spite of men being hit until we were struck by heavy concentrations of artillery. Some of this was probably enemy DF (defensive fire) but in the opinion of those who had been shelled by our gunners on previous occasions we were in our own barrage. Ben Dickenson was clear on this point. He shouted "When I get out of this I'll do those bloody gunners". He sounded a bit optimistic, shells were dropping all around, then it stopped, lifted, and groups of men got up and moved on through the cactus hedge into the sunken road. An hour after dawn we saw some Germans coming along the sunken road, about 20, all wearing green face veils, we went for them and shot them up pretty badly, there were screams of 'Kamerad'.There was a lot of shooting, suddenly it was over and we had taken about 8 prisoners, all but two wounded. Mark organised what remained of the Company into a defensive position astride the road. There were elements of two platoons and we started to provide some sort of protection for ourselves by scraping away at the ground with our pathetic entrenching tools. The older soldiers acquired the much more efficient

Lt D. J. Fenner.
6th Bn DLI.

German article and were soon digging in at great speed. The place was littered with German equipment, spandau machine guns, belts of ammunition and corpses. Our prisoners were all parachutists, one spoke good English and told us that three days ago they had been in the south of France! A fierce battle was in progress to our right where the 9th were going in. Apart from the pop of small arms fire, where we were was comparatively quiet. In the first light of the summer's day we dug while the stretcher bearers attended to the wounded lying thick in the vines." [26]

Pte Kerans advanced with HQ Coy of the 9th D.L.I. and immediately found himself in the thick of the action:

"The rest of us went on, Nobby with us, down the side of a big farm building, where a lot of 8th battalion wallahs were dug-in, to the road. We ran across it in a mad dash and through a field to a deep ditch that ran 90° to it. With a C.O. with you there are things done more dangerous than with a 2nd Lieu. Now we were in the thick of bullets and grenades. Some of our carriers had got across the bridge and were going up the road towards Catania. They weren't getting very far, like I say there was a lot of opposition. About forty yards from us two enemy dashed out of a farm building and put something that exploded under one of our carriers. Charlie Sollis and self fired at them two or three times. I don't know if we hit them but they gave up the idea of doing it again. From the other end of our short trench a 'Tiger' fired, I dug myself into the side of the trench until it went away. In a battle like this nobody knows - who's who. There were now less than a score of us. Nobby got the men on a carrier to ask for a 'smoke screen'. This was put down and we ran like the devil the way we had come. We ran back to a deep hollow about 40 yards from the bridge, a bomb hole I think. The bridge was still under constant shell fire. There had been no time for burial parties and there were dead bodies every where. A sunken road was paved with them. As usual I went in with the I.O. and the C.O. at the head of H.Q. Companies' little column.

There were explosions all around me but I went. The floor across was more 'Holy than Godly'. Suddenly I got a painful 'upper-cut' which floored me. A nose-cap from a shell fell almost into my hand. I lay stunned for a few seconds but as my senses returned I realised that this was not the safest place to be and dashed back to rejoin the C.O. and the rest, who by now had returned to the other side of the road. It was not a big cut, I wiped the blood off a couple of times and it soon stopped. The battalion advanced under heavy fire, it was slow going. All day we hung on to half a mile of land every inch of it hard won." [27]

As daylight broke the 6th D.L.I. reinforced their position, casualties had been heavy and the enemy was around them in great numbers giving no sign of a weakening of their will to resist; Lt. Fenner had great difficulty making contact with 6th Battalion HQ and the companies on his flanks, tanks rumbled into action among the Durhams as the infantry of both sides fought it out and the slaughter was great in that small area:

> "All contact with the Battalion HQs and our flanking companies was lost, our radio operators were missing, so Mark set out with his runner and batman to contact the company on our right. We were not to see them for some time. As the light improved we started to explore our new home. We then discovered that large numbers of the previous occupants were still around and full of fight. German Parachutists dressed in their camouflage smocks, with green netting face veils were dotted among the vines shooting at everything that moved. The first hour of daylight was spent trying to cope with this menace by snap shooting and ducking smartly afterwards. Then our Battalion second in command appeared with two tanks. Unfortunately we could not communicate with them. We had no radio, they were completely closed down, having lost too many commanders shot by German snipers when they stuck their heads out of the turrets. They could not see us or our wounded. Our only way of communicating was to jump on the tank and bang on the turret lid with an entrenching tool, the commander would then open it and one could have a chat. Our battalion second in command, a brave man, did this, he was promptly shot through the hip. Rumour afterwards said the tracer bullet was still warm when removed in hospital in Malta two days later. The tanks retired, taking some of our wounded with them on stretchers on the backs of the vehicles. The appearance of the armour must have disturbed the enemy, who started to withdraw in small groups. One such group was seen approaching up the road where we had last seen Mark. Fortunately we saw them first, a quick ambush was prepared from which they were unable to escape, and we caught them in a cross fire." [28]

Sergeant Tom Cairns recalls the merciless fire the men had to endure - as the sixth Battalion advanced into the vineyards during the last hours of darkness:

> "The vineyard is continually swept by enemy fire. Red white and green tracer rips through the vines, scattering their leaves tearing through their roots. Sometimes the bullets find a mark and a man drops, wriggling on the soft, sooty earth. But the companies keep on advancing. In spite of casualties, screams and groans of wounded and dying comrades, they advance towards the sunken road, towards the formidable line of spitting machine guns, they advance so quickly and so determinedly that the forward elements are caught in our own barrage. Several are killed, others drop with smashed legs and ugly shrapnel wounds. And all this in darkness, when control is difficult and voices are scarcely audible against the bursting shells and malicious double barrelled crack of German machine guns. The dawn comes and the Germans are more active than ever, for now they can see. Men are killed and lacerated as they try to move among the vines. Wounded men lay helplessly near the sunken road, make feeble attempts

to move and are shot dead. And the worst of it is the Jerry positions are so cunningly concealed that they defy detection. To move, to disturb a vine, is to ask for a deadly burst of Spandau bullets. The position is intolerable. Some men who cross the road are shot in the back. Others throw themselves on the ground and engage the Germans from the flank. But he had the advantage. He remains hidden and mercilessly snipes from behind the breastwork. No one, not even those wearing the red cross, is safe from the murderous fire. The Second in Command calls for tanks. The Shermans try to cross the bridge and two are immediately hit. The 88 that hits them is destroyed and three tanks roll into the vineyard. But still the Germans hold out. Stretcher-bearers moving among the wounded, are callously shot. One man carrying a stretcher is shot from a distance of a hundred yards. He falls and expires almost immediately. Another has his finger tips shot away while carrying a wounded man." [29]

The Durham's fought their way forward in the darkness, 'B' Company of the 6th Battalion, under Captain Reggie Atkinson, pushed onto their objective - the sunken road, when they came under intense fire, one section being wiped out:

"As we advanced through the vineyards we came under the most tremendous spate of Spandau fire which was most unpleasant. It was rather like walking down a rifle range with everybody firing. Eventually we reached a cactus hedge along a sunken road, which was our objective. The Germans had been dug in there but must have bolted when we got through. Fortunately we found a bomb crater we were able to get into and stayed until morning. The Germans had got back behind the cactus hedge again and fired machine-guns at us. They worked back down the road towards the bridge.

We were in a very strong position to engage them, but we were running desperately short of ammunition. Our tanks managed to get across the bridge, a lot of Germans made a dash for it. We were only 100 yards away and just mowed them down, the rest surrendered, we saw white flags going up all over the place." [30]

The Durham Brigade rushed up their six pounder anti tank guns as the battle raged about them, 'A' Company of the 9th D.L.I. lost a whole platoon and was soon reduced to a compliment of fifteen men. As dawn broke the Germans launched a tank supported counter attack that was broken up by artillery fire. The Durham's casualties were now so severe that tank support was called for, it was not long before Sherman's began rumbling over the bridge crushing the dead in their path. Into the vineyards they plunged, firing their big guns constantly and spraying the undergrowth with their machine guns. The slaughter was tremendous as the German paratroops claimed three more Shermans in this frenzied melée, dawn broke revealing the true extent of the carnage, this field of slaughter was strewn with the broken bodies of dead and dying men, the sight was so

TROOPS OF THE MACHINE GUN BATTALION, 1ST GERMAN PARACHUTE DIVISION,
RAKED THE BRIDGEHEAD WITH HEAVY CONCENTRATIONS OF FIRE

terrible that one German commander arranged a cease fire with the British by
the use of a D.L.I. medic, who had been taken prisoner. Cpt Eric Fassl halted
the battle for a short while to enable the wounded of both sides to be evacuated,
this act undoubtedly saved many lives, as to leave any man lying exposed in such
an area would mean certain death:

"When our medical orderly had understood what I wanted, we both left
cover with me close on his heels. Had we been fired upon he would have
shared my fate. He held a handkerchief aloft and waved it. The British
may well have believed, at first, that we wanted to surrender, for immediately half a dozen flat steel helmets and caps appeared over there and I
had the impression that they had been clearly waiting for this moment.
However they quickly understood what our real intention was and very soon
search parties reached our positions. Then followed some very tense
moments while the first of the seriously wounded men were recovered.
Everyone realised on both sides, that an unexpected move would cause
catastrophe in a matter of seconds. Fortunately no-one lost his nerve and
the business of recovery went ahead. Germans and British called out to
each other to show where their seriously wounded lay. Everything went

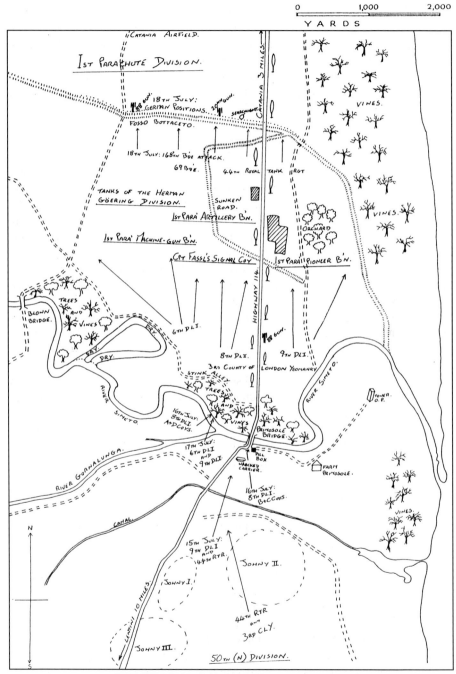

THE BATTLE OF PRIMOSOLE BRIDGE: 14TH TO 17TH JULY.
BRITISH AND ENEMY DISPOSITIONS

well and, finally, two long columns of wounded, some supporting others and all bound up with emergency field dressings, left the battlefield and disappeared into the dusty glowing landscape. We allowed the prisoners to go with them, I asked our British medical orderly to call a few words of thanks to the British and let him leave with the last group of wounded. The flat steel helmets disappeared and we watched the wounded file over the bridge in the midday haze." [31]

The 17th July was a crucial day in the battle for the German troops and a turning point for the British. Other units may have broken in this situation but the courageous men of the D.L.I. stood their ground and gave as good as they got. The Germans had lost nearly all of their anti tank weapons and their commander recognised the hopeless situation they were in, to continue to hold their ground would be suicidal, so it was decided to render the bridge useless by the use of lorries loaded with explosive. All attempts to do this were thwarted. The Shermans were now overrunning German positions and the situation, as far as the Germans were concerned, became hopeless:

The tanks of 'A' and 'C' Squadrons of the 3rd County of London Yeomanry now moved into the fighting area and at once came under heavy machine gun and anti tank fire. Colonel Willis DSO was with the reserve squadron, B Squadron, at the Regimental Headquarters and decided to move forward in his tank to contact the infantry Brigadier. Brigadier Senior DSO made an urgent request that the two forward squadrons be sent to deal with a substantial enemy presence on the left of Highway 114, which was constantly harassing the British troops with machine guns, mortar and sniper fire. Colonel Willis moved forward to make contact with the forward squadrons and came under heavy concentrations of fire. Because of the poor visibility his periscopes offered, he had his head out of the top hatch in order to direct operations when a bullet hit him in the forehead, he died of his wound an hour later.

Major Allan W Grant MC was now called upon to take command, he was with the reserve squadron when he got the call and at once moved forward:

"We were in reserve on the high ground overlooking the river when the Brigadier ordered me forward to take command as Colonel Willis had been killed. I got in my scout car and went down to the river, he was very angry with me because I hadn't gone in a tank. However I went back and returned in my Sherman, there was a great deal of fire going on from the enemy machine gunners. Chris Wrey's tank had been hit by an anti tank shell and had burst into flames burning him badly. Suddenly John Grimwade came up on the air and he said 'there they are the bastards, they're in the ditch.' He fired his tank gun into them making them scatter, C Squadron then started to pursue them in a big way.

I remember one incident clearly, an infantry officer dropped into the spare drivers seat of my tank, he crouched down as he was a very tall man and closed the hatch. He looked as though he was terrified and said 'for christs' sake what happens if we're hit how will we get out?' I replied 'firstly take off your helmet, open the hatch and you'll feel much happier, we do it all the time.' I recall his answer, 'I'm absolutely terrified in this horrible thing, you're a target for everything.' I said 'Well I wouldn't change places with you for anything, you have no protection at all, we at least have armour plate. Things were now hitting us all the time. I saw a bren carrier of the Durham's going along a road by the river when a German popped up and threw a stick bomb at them. They were not having that and spun the carrier round and ran over him. I will always remember his screams." [32]

Lt. D J Fenner and his men took more prisoners and buried the dead as the frantic action of the past hours slowed down:

"We took another 15 prisoners, many wounded, including 2 officers. It was when these men were being searched that we had confirmation that they had indeed been in France 3 days or nights before. Most of them had tickets on them from brothels in Marseilles. The tickets showed the price, the Madam's name, and a place where the soldier pencilled the name of the lady of his choice. Fifi and ZouZou seemed to be popular. Our men soon realised what these tickets meant and both Germans and British started laughing together. This did not seem at all extraordinary at the time. Order was restored when Mark appeared with his men, he had been pinned down by this group of Germans, when they started to pull out he followed, and was pleased to see that we were alert to receive them in the appropriate manner.

The Germans' withdrawal continued. We spent the day patrolling, taking more casualties and tidying up the battlefield. Men who had served in the Battalion since France in 1940, at Gazala, Alamein and Mareth had not seen so much slaughter and destruction in such a small space. The area around the 8th bridgehead and along the sunken road where we and 9th attacked was a shambles, 500 casualties had occurred in our three battalions, representing 1 in every 2 men in the assault. Over 300 German dead lay there, torn trees, smashed guns, tanks and equipment were everywhere. Now little rough wooden crosses made from ration boxes began to appear as we buried our dead. For the survivors began a few hours' respite. We spent the day tidying up the battlefield. There was one grave of 20 men of the Battalion in our company area. Spandau Alley was littered with German machine guns and Parachute equipment. We equipped ourselves with Lugers and German machine pistols. Most of these were handed in later to Battalion HQ as it was "Verboten" to use captured enemy weapons. Our carrier platoon was out forward in contact with the Germans, unfortunately our anti tank guns coming up to join us passed through our line and were shot up by the Germans. A few men survived to get back to us but we lost the guns." [33]

Pte Kerans recalls how he and his mate, Pte Sollis, received a shock, when on the scrounge from an inebriated Goat:

> "We had made some sort of position but had neither food or water. In No-man's-land we could see a farm house. It was less than forty yards ahead. With a Jerry can and Charlie Sollis 'covering me' the two of us warily made our way towards it. It was a huge barn, the floor 6 inch deep in liquid. We tasted it and found it to be Vino. There, wrecked by the enemy, were huge vats with the bungs knocked out. They were all around the wall but not much left in, we only just managed to half fill a Jerry can. Suddenly there was what sounded like a loud snore. We dropped the tin and pointed our weapons at a very drunken goat that was staggering around in the corner. We enjoyed a quiet laugh, refilled our can and set off for home. As we did so others were entering from the enemy side. We did not argue with them, we did not do this killing business just for the sake of doing it." [34]

German resistance at last began to crumble, they had had enough and began to surrender. All along the sector held by the Parachute troops white flags began to appear and the paratroopers came streaming in with their arms raised, encouraged by the men from the north who prodded at them with their 18in. bayonets. In the history of the D.L.I. the area around the bridge is described as resembling 'a regular hell's kitchen'. So it must have seemed to the victors as they surveyed the ground taken, it was littered with smashed weaponry, bloodstained and torn equipment, empty boxes of ammunition, dead German paratroopers, dead British paratroopers and the dead of the D.L.I. It was a scene of terrible destruction, bearing witness to the savage struggle that had taken place. Three hundred German dead were counted and the Durham's had lost five hundred killed, wounded and missing. As the German commander was led away by his escort he was stopped by Colonel Clarke, CO of the 9th D.L.I., who quietly shook him by the hand.

The battle for the bridge was now over but the Germans efforts to destroy it and hold up the 8th Army continued, by noon the enemy artillery had registered the range of Primosole Bridge and one particularly heavy gun fired from positions some miles to the north. The shelling was very accurate and unpleasant, many men were injured, some as they bathed in the Simeto. The rest of the division crossed the bridge, the sights that met their eyes have never been forgotten and the large numbers of dead stand out in the minds of all troops, who passed through the bridge head.

CSM Laurie Whittle crossed the bridge into the fighting area with the 5th Battalion East Yorkshire Regiment and remembers well the large numbers of dead laid about:

> "I was with Battalion HeadQuarters moving up after the rifle companies had gone through and we went over Primosole Bridge. I noticed in the river bed this German who was the tallest man I had ever seen, he must have

GERMAN PARATROOPS TAKEN PRISONER CARRY A BRITISH SOLDIER IN, HIS LEFT
FOOT HAS BEEN BLOWN OFF. (*AUTHOR'S COLLECTION*)

A CARRIER OF THE DURHAM BRIGADE PASSES OVER THE NOW PEACEFUL PRIMOSOLE BRIDGE.
ON THE RIGHT CAN BE SEEN A DAMAGED CONCRETE BLOCKHOUSE THAT WAS HELD
BY THE BRITISH PARACHUTE TROOPS. (*IMPERIAL WAR MUSEUM*)

been about 7 foot tall, laid there dead. Over the bridge we came to what we got to know as 'Stink Alley', it certainly earned its name because there was bodies everywhere, not just ten or twelve, hundreds of bodies. On the sides of the roads in the ditches the Durham's were dug in after repulsing various counter attacks, they were sat there in their slit trenches and instead of sand bags around them they had German bodies - two and three high. They sat there as large as life, with flies buzzing round, in this horrible stench eating their bully beef and biscuits." [35]

Cpl Albert Snowdon of the 7th Battalion Green Howards crossed over into the Bridgehead in a Bren carrier into a scene of utter carnage:

"There was this place called 'Stench Lane' and we had to go down it two or three times a day, you was running over bodies (in the carrier), the D.L.I.'s had been in and just left the German's where they fell. The banks on this lane had men buried in them with their heads and feet showing." [36]

Pte Roy Walker of the 5th Battalion East Yorkshire Regiment looked on aghast at the sight that met his eyes:

"When we went over the bridge in the carriers, we had to run over the German dead to get through, there was so many dead piled up on each side. The Germans had been left where they had been bayoneted - it was terrible." [37]

CHAPTER THREE

THE END IN SICILY
July/August 1943

Primosole Bridge was now firmly under British control but it had been captured far too late, the element of luck needed by Montgomery had never materialised forcing him to abandon his strategy of forcing a breakthrough at Catania. The sea landings were cancelled and the 50th Division was ordered to press forward to the Fosso Bottaceto which formed the southern most defences of the Catania airfield.

On the evening of the 17th July, the German forces were reinforced by the 4th Parachute Regiment, bolstering the badly-mauled paratroops that had fought the Durhams. The Germans now found themselves in vastly superior positions to the ones they occupied around Primosole Bridge, and by the use of these fresh troops plus new weapons taken from British gliders and their weapons canisters, the area around Highway 114 was turned into a death trap for any British units attempting to break through to Catania.

On the night of 17/18th July, the 168th Brigade was to pass through the Durhams with its central axis on the main road. The 69th Brigade would then pass through and in a westward movement capture the railway, screening the left flank of the 168th Brigade in the process.

Lt. Fenner, of the 6th D.L.I. watched as the fresh Brigade passed through his position:

"That night 168 Brigade Companies deployed through the D.L.I. Brigade Bridgehead. (London Scots, London Irish, Royal Berkshires). They were to attack towards Catania. They were very smart, officers wearing the correct pattern webbing equipment, binocular case, compass case, map case, pistol. Our Company Officers favoured other rank pattern equipment. The pouches could be used for grenades, biscuits, tea, compass, and we all carried rifles. My old platoon were draped about with German parachute silk over their torn KD. We looked rather scruffy compared with these new arrivals. It was 168 Brigade's first battle and we wished them well. For some reason, just before the attack began, a Bofors Light anti-aircraft gun fired a burst of tracer to mark the axis of attack for the infantry. This method of indicating to the assaulting infantry the axis had been often used in the desert. It seemed unnecessary under the present circumstances. I am sure the Germans were expecting another attack. This may have confirmed their suspicions. 168 Brigade attack commenced. As the night

GERMAN PARATROOPS OF THE 1ST PARACHUTE DIVISION IN POSITIONS IN THE FOSSE BOTTACETO.
18TH JULY 1943. (*AUTHOR'S COLLECTION*)

wore on stragglers came back saying they had been wiped out. Things obviously had not gone according to plan (do they ever!) However, a lot of ground had been seized and held and the position was now secure enough to allow the D.L.I. Brigade to be withdrawn for "rest". It was 18th July, we had been in action for 9 days. Just before last light we pulled back by platoons over the bridge. I did not like this plan, the bridge was being shelled by enemy artillery and by Nebelwerfers, a large calibre 6 barrelled rocket launcher. It made a noise like a mangle followed by a series of moans as the rockets sped through the air. We had first heard its evil sound at Wadi Akarit in April. Jerry saw us moving and started to clobber the bridge. I led my platoon back through the river (some complained at getting their feet wet!) The rest of the Company followed. The Company ahead of us on the bridge had several killed and wounded crossing." [38]

Pte Forth, of the 5th Battalion East Yorkshire Regiment, was dug in with his mates near a village with a wood to the front. In the wood a German machine gun post was harassing them at every opportunity. It was on the Green Howard's front and would have to be silenced if casualties were to be kept down. Volunteers were asked for:

"We heard there was to be a big frontal attack, I volunteered with four other lads to knock this post out one night. We blackened our faces before we left and all equipment that rattled was taken off or secured. Personal

Pte Harry Forth.
Mentioned in Despatches.
5th Bn East Yorkshire Rgt.
With His Wife Renee

possessions were left behind. The enemy post was well concealed, a deep wooden emplacement. We had to sneak up to it, when we was close enough we lobbed in grenades, one went right into the machine gun aperture, that silenced it altogether. Coming back a Gerry observation post, for their mortars, must have spotted us. He dropped one right in the middle of us and caught me in the leg. The lads behind me caught the lot - killed the four of them. The road was higher than the other ground and a machine gun was firing over me. I could see the tracer bullets striking the road. I thought if they come much lower I could catch it, so I dragged myself to the shelter of the road side and laid low until the early hours of the morning. Then our main attack went in to clear Gerry out of the wood, the infantry passed over me as shells and mortar bombs flew overhead. As the lads passed I could hear them shouting. I looked down and thought I'd lost my leg, the lower part below the knee was doubled back against the upper part. The next I knew a stretcher bearer came, I prayed to the lord to save my leg, I didn't want to lose it in the field, I was numb, the lower part of my body was dead." [39]

Pte Forth was taken to the rear and his condition was so bad a nun was brought clasping her rosary beads. However, his life was spared and his prayers answered, his leg was saved only to give him many years of complications. Harry Forth was mentioned in despatches for his bravery in the field.

During the evening of 17th July, the squadrons of the 44th Royal Tank Regiment deployed to support the infantry of the 69th and 168th Brigades. Before dawn on the 18th all three squadrons rumbled over the bridge: on the westside of the Highway 114 'B' Squadron took up a position with the 6th and 7th Battalions of the Green Howards. 'A' Squadron moved to the east of the Highway and joined forces with the London Scottish and London Irish. Major Whittaker ordered 'A' Squadron forward to assist the troops of 168th Brigade who were now under extremely heavy fire. Harry Gratland was a tank driver that day and when asked what he recalls most clearly said simply: "I remember the terrible heat and the stench of death." [40]

Arthur Soper drove his tank forward into the fight to assist the badly mauled infantry:

"'A' Squadron moved forward to help the London Scottish who were under heavy fire and pinned down in the open. Charlie Hardy, my troop sergeant acting troop officer, moved out to the right flank when his tank ran over a mine which blew a track off, as was usually the case luckily the crew were ok. My tank commander, L/Sgt Wally Warley told me to change direction right and head over to where Charlie's tank lay, the idea being to recover the crew. While executing this manoeuvre we were fired on from a wood behind Charlie's tank, luckily for us the rounds went over our turret. I think the position of the 'angry man' did not allow him to depress his gun enough to register hits much to our relief. We reversed out of harms way and had another go as it was getting dusk. Our second go at retrieving Charlie and his boys was successful and we withdrew as a squadron south of the bridge." [41]

The assault by 168th Brigade was launched into the teeth of the enemy's main defences. These positions had been prepared months in advance by Italian engineers and were now manned by the rejuvenated Green Devils. The artillery barrage made little impression upon the German defenders and when the infantry attacked they were mown down. German troops present talk of the horrific scene before them as machine guns and small arms fire rained upon the attacking force. Lines of wounded and dead lay before the German positions and the cries of the wounded could be heard all night, some of the Germans were so moved by their plight that early next morning they went out and rescued the British that were close at hand. After yet another bloody frontal attack the 50th Division was halted at a point several hundred yards south of the Fosse Bottaceto.

Lt. Fenner was with 6th D.L.I. during their final days in the bridgehead.

"Towards the end of our period in defence in the bridgehead 'C' Company was holding a position 100 yards short of the Fosse Bottaceto. This had been an objective of 168 Brigade's attack on 17/18 July. They had not been able to hang on to it and the high tide mark of their attack was a drainage ditch about 100 yards south of the Fosse. 'C' Company occupied this area during the latter part of our stay in the bridgehead. The layout was like this:

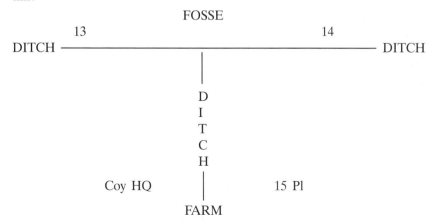

The T shaped ditch was broad, shallow and lined with shrubs. Pits had been dug in the bottom of the ditch to improve protection. Movement above ground forward of the farm was foolhardy. The ditches gave both protection and acted as a means of moving about the company area in some degree of safety. The Germans held the Fosse, a Spandau on fixed lines fired down the main support of the T, mainly by night. Our forward ditch was out of reach of hand thrown grenades but well within the rifle launched grenade range. Movement was possible, with a degree of safety, under cover of darkness, providing one avoided German flares. They used them frequently, we never. Natural bodily functions were attended to after dark or one used an empty bully beef tin.

After lunch one afternoon 13 platoon, except for sentries, were dozing quietly at the bottom of the ditch when we were disturbed by the crash of grenades exploding above us. Sgt. Connel suggested we reply in kind and he set off with the 2-inch mortar man and a Bren-gun team along the ditch to the left and I followed. We moved along the ditch until we were clear of the platoon area. Here the mortar was set up and the mortarman started to lob bombs at the Fosse. At the sound of the discharge some heads appeared on the top of the Fosse and promptly disappeared when the Bren gun opened up. Satisfied with our efforts we returned to the platoon area where Mark, our company commander, had sent a message for me to meet him at his Tactical HQ at the top of the junction of the T. Mark said that Battalion HQ believed the Germans had withdrawn. The company on our right was sending a platoon into a wood to their front. I was to take out a reconnaissance patrol into the Fosse to see if it was occupied. I told him what we had been doing and that the Germans were still there. He telephoned Battalion HQ with my report, which made no difference, we were told to get on with it. Mark warned me to get ready and he set off to brief 14 platoon on what was taking place. I returned with the news to my incredulous platoon and asked for 2 volunteers. L/Cpl. Gibson and Locket said they would come with me. I was most impressed, as I don't think any of us would have given much for our chances. Our plan was simple, we would wear our basic web equipment to take our water bottles, magazines and grenades (water would be very necessary if wounded and immobile in no man's land). We each took a Tommy gun. Connell and the Bren gunners would shoot up the Fosse, we would run like hell, climb up to it to the top and see what happened then. We waited for Mark to return, noted a certain amount of small arms fire and the cry of "stretcher bearers" from 14 platoon area. Tony telephoned battalion HQ, who on hearing the news cancelled my patrol. Meanwhile the platoon advancing on the right had run into trouble. The rest of the afternoon smoke and HE concentrations were put down while efforts were made to try and recover their wounded. Unfortunately because of 14 platoon's close proximity to this operation (and the German positions) several of our shells exploded in the platoon area. We could hear them cursing our gunners. Luckily there were no injuries. Mark, who had been wounded, was in pain, we gave him tea and some morphia. Connel said some of the boys would carry him back if we could wave a (white) towel and put him on a stretcher. We ruled this brave offer out. After Primosole some of our unarmed stretcher bearers were shot while attending wounded. There was a lot of anger in the battalion about this. We got Mark back after last light. He was evacuated to UK and discharged from the army with a permanent limp. Three of us in 13 platoon were grateful to him. Two nights later the company was relieved along with the rest of the battalion. The Germans were still there. Dickie (ex-miner, ex-policeman, ex-guardsman, ex-commando) took over the company. Tony went back to 14 platoon. Dickie commanded the company until a year later. He was wounded and made prisoner in Normandy. He escaped back to our own lines, was then returned to UK with a well-earned MC." [42]

At first light on 18th July the 102nd Anti-Tank Regiment, 2nd Battalion Cheshire Regiment and two battalions of the 4th Armoured Brigade crossed the Simeto to reinforce the bridgehead. With a few minor exceptions 8th Army got no closer to the city of Catania - a mere three miles distant in July. It was not until August 5th that the city finally fell, twenty two days after the 1st Airborne Division took the bridge over the Simeto.

The struggle for access to the open ground of the Catania Plain was to stick in the memory of the men of the attacking force as one of the bitterest of the entire war. Many thought it put Alamein in the shade and the stench of rotting flesh on the banks of the river is still remembered. Even Montgomery referred to it as 'a very bloody killing match.'

Montgomery's dream of a swift victory in Sicily had been halted abruptly and his hopes of a swift advance upon Catania brought to nought.

At Primosole Bridge a small outgunned force of German Paratroops, with no air cover or naval support, had held up the entire 8th Army and so prevented it from rolling up the axis left flank. The 50th Division may not have broken through to the Catania Plain, but their attacks at Primosole Bridge did succeed in drawing all enemy forces away from Catania, leaving the city undefended for five days. Had Montgomery stuck to his original plan of an amphibious landing at Catania he would, at one fell swoop have reclaimed the initiative and gained control of the coastal route to Messina. In this way, the Etna line would have had one of its vital links broken, bringing the campaign to a swift and favourable end for the British.

The most crucial battle of the Sicilian Campaign had been fought by the use of only a fraction of the assets available to the 8th Army, naval fire power and the ample numbers of aircraft at Montgomery's disposal were never fully utilised, thus ensuring that no breakthrough occurred. The official history of the war -

'The Mediterranean and the Middle East' - puts the blame for this failure squarely on the shoulders of the 5th and 50th Divisions. The troops of the 8th Army at that time were seasoned veterans, very tired and at times browned off, but the performance of the lead units on the Simeto was awesome to behold as they doggedly fought their way forward against battle-hardened élite paratroops.

The lack of transport, laid on by the planners and logisticians, was a major factor for the inability of the ground forces to make deep and swift penetrations with their forward units. Because of the mountainous landscape of the Sicilian terrain movement was limited to a few roads already in existence. The enemy knew every turn they took and made maximum use of his detailed knowledge of the interior to harry the invaders at every opportunity. The British pressed forward down these narrow arteries unable to outflank the enemy.

Montgomery now undertook a secondary drive, using 30 Corps. It had been a mistake not to use the full resources at his disposal to launch a thrust to the Catania Plain. His attacks were now dispersed over too large an area and there was no powerful reserve to exploit any break-through. Monty had not adhered to his own rule, when trying to break a strong enemy position, concentration in strength. The usual criticism levelled at him is that he was over cautious. In this case it was the opposite and his only fault here was that the massive combat power of his command was not employed to break the weak coastal sector, where any breakthrough could have penetrated clear to Messina. Monty wrote in his diary on 21st July 1943:

> "My troops are getting tired as the heat on the Plain of Catania is great. He (THE ENEMY) is going to hold the Catania flank against me to the last. The proper answer to the problem is now to reorganise, to hold on my right while keeping up a good pressure, to continue the left hook with 30 Corps using the Canadian Division. I will give 78th Division to 30 Corps and go hard for Adrano and then northwards round the west side of Mount Etna."

The operations undertaken by 30 Corps turned out to be battles fought by the Highlanders and Canadians, neither supporting the other. The Canadians responsible for delivering the left hook from Etna to Leanforte and on to Adrano, were new to combat and lacking in transport. In such mountainous terrain, which fully favoured the defender, it was a lot to ask. Montgomery's new offensive evolved unfavourably, with the Germans putting up savage resistance wherever attempts were made to crack their defences along the northern perimeter of the Plain of Catania. The badly mauled 50th Division was still holding the Primosole bridgehead and a series of attacks by the 5th Division, delivered north of the Simeto with the intention of seizing Misterbianco, met with failure. Some six miles west of the Primosole Bridge was another bridge, named 'Lemon' by the British. The 5th Division was ordered to make a bridgehead north of this feature. As at Primosole, all that was achieved was a tenuous hold on the northern bank of the Simeto. In a number of attacks, by the 5th, extremely heavy casualties were taken as the troops tried to widen their bridgehead.

The Canadians were to have taken Leanforte by the night of 19th July but, because of the skilful delaying actions being fought by the German forces, they did not arrive there until 22nd July. During these events a number of bloody battles were being fought out by the Highland Division. The Highlanders were first to secure the crossings over the River Dittaino and after this was completed, second to capture the village of Gerbini and adjoining features. By 19th July, the Scots were checked at Sferro and unable to cross the Simeto some 2,000 yards south of Gerbini Airfield because of fiercesome resistance. Many men were lost in numerous vicious actions until operations ceased and the Scots took up a defensive posture.

Three days later, the American 7th Army advanced and took Palermo too late to intercept the eastward withdrawal of the enemy's mobile forces. Patton's troops had been used originally as a flank guard to the 8th Army's advance on Messina, but the change of plans now meant they would take on an offensive role. The role of the Axis Forces was now to delay the British and Americans as long as possible by obstructive actions thus aiding the evacuation of troops and machinery. The ground favoured the defenders and each step back shortened the front so that fewer defenders were needed. Both Montgomery and Patton made amphibious landings in attempts to cut off the Axis Forces, but each time the enemy slipped away. By August 16th, many enemy troops had already crossed the straits to the mainland. The Axis Forces conducted their withdrawal with cool ability. In the course of six days and seven nights, 100,000 troops were safely evacuated, together with nearly 50 tanks, numerous guns and 17,000 tons of supplies and equipment.

General Alexander reported at the end of the campaign:

"By 10 am this morning, August 17th 1943. The last German soldier had been flung out of Sicily. It can be assumed that all Italian Forces in the island on July 10th had been destroyed, though a few battered units may have escaped to the mainland."

The allied casualties for the campaign were 5,532 killed, 2,869 missing and 14,410 wounded. Out of a total number of more than 60,000 the Germans evacuated 13,500 wounded 40,000 able troops and lost 5,500 prisoners of war. This means they suffered approximately 10,000 killed.

The German evacuation of Sicily was well organised and was executed with pin-point precision. It was far reaching in its results. The divisions that returned to mainland Italy were fully armed veterans with plenty of fight left in them, as the Allied Forces were soon to find out at Salerno, Cassino and Anzio.

The 50th Division was to find the latter part of the Sicilian campaign a hard slog as they followed up the retreating enemy and when the campaign was over

Monty visited its units giving a hint of things to come. Lt. Fenner has left us a good record of the troops' reactions:

The Advance Catania - Acireale - Riposto 4-12 August

"Several very big explosions took place behind the German lines. The bomb dumps on Catania airfield were being destroyed. This was a pretty clear indication that the German forces would be pulling back. While the 13 Corps to which 50 Division belonged, remained on the defensive, 30 Corps had been active inland and was turning the German flank. We would be leaving our routine of spells in the line, followed by rest periods and bathing in the sea. On 4th August, we followed 8 D.L.I. in pursuit of the departing Germans. We were harassed by enemy 88mm gun fire and Nebelwerfers. One of the Brigade Support Company 4.2 mortar section 3 tonners received a direct hit. The ammunition exploded, the vehicle and crew destroyed. 'C' Company were caught by Nebelwerfer, 13 platoon taking some casualties, most from our new arrivals.

We passed our dead anti tank gunners, killed on the 16th July when they had driven through the forward companies into the German lines in error. None of our dead, at this time, had been buried by the Germans. We discussed this often. In 50 Division, we were most careful to bury all our own and the German dead. Either the Germans were too idle, or perhaps it was deliberate policy to leave our dead unburied so as to depress our forward troops as they advanced. Catania was entered. The locals were busy looting the stores and shops and did not pay much attention to us. The advance beyond Catania was most unpleasant. The road was narrow and either walled or fenced. For some reason we seldom pushed off the line of the road or moved at night. Leading companies were ambushed by the Germans frequently. Losses among officers were severe. The platoon officer would be with the point section, the company commander with the lead platoon. The ambush would get the lot. Machine guns, mortars and 88mm guns were all used. It was one of those operations in which our tanks for some reason or other, never operated. In the early stages, 'C' Company was caught by mortar fire and we lost some good men. Between Acireale and Giarre we lost Sgt. Albert Dunn, MM. I believe he was from Sunderland. He served with the company in France in 1940 where the Brigade had attacked at Arras taking 400 prisoners. He fought in Gazala, Alamein and Mareth. He was killed by a German mine when platoon sergeant of 15 platoon. A brave man and a most happy and amusing character. Tony and Alfie were both hit during this period. The company establishment was 5 officers. We had lost 5 and I was the only one left of those who had landed with the company on 10th July.

Between Acireale and Giarre I was sent out on a contact patrol to a company of 8 D.L.I. The gap I had to cover was very quiet. The area seemed empty of both Germans or Sicilians. Locket, Dickinson and I moved past some buildings when we discovered some very scared Sicilians in a courtyard. The conversation went like this:

Elderly bearded, garlic-reeking peasant ..... Tedeschi?
Me .... Niente
EBGRP .... Americano?
Me .... Niente
EBGRP .... Inglesse?
Me .... Si

I was then embraced by the EBGRP, much to my disgust, and all the locals cheered. This reaction was pretty typical of the attitude of the locals when they first met us. On one occasion they surrounded one of our lead platoons. When the Germans saw the movement they put down a concentration of 81mm mortar bombs which our soldiers recognised as coming and took cover but the locals did not. Our Regimental Aid Post had civilian men and women through it that day. However, back to the patrol. We arrived at the foot of a hill, my information led me to believe 8th D.L.I. were on the top. As we began the ascent we were fired on by a German patrol. It was bursts from a machine pistol and it must have been beyond the limit of accuracy for that, essentially, short-range weapon. We took cover and engaged in a fire-fight with the German or Germans. However, our task was not to exchange shots with the Germans but to contact our 8th Battalion and return to our own Company ASAP. We broke off our engagement with the enemy, climbed the hill and found a company of 8 D.L.I. on the top. The end of the campaign for us was a fighting platoon patrol into Riposto to see if the town was occupied. We entered the town from the east, picked up half a dozen Italian soldiers, but the Germans had left. We returned to our Company area and settled down for the night. During the evening German artillery and machine guns opened up along the battalion front. I think it was their way of letting us know they were pulling out. The next day 69 Brigade advanced through us and on to Messina which they reached on 17th August. It was over.

On 30th August, the 8th Army Commander visited in turn the three D.L.I. Battalions. Monty addressed us in the bed of a dried up river. He congratulated us and said we had fought long and hard under his command since Alamein back in October. We could now have a rest. Meanwhile, the army would be going over to Italy soon. If Monty ran into trouble there he would send for us because, he said, "I like to have 50 Division with me wherever I go." A great groan arose from the soldiery at this remark. He then said "Why, I might be going home." False laughter and cries of "Ha, bloody ha" from the troops. Monty departed smiling among a mixture of

PRISONERS BEING TAKEN TO THE REAR.
SICILY. JULY 1943. (*AUTHOR'S COLLECTION*)

boos and cheers. He must have been wise enough to know what to expect. 50 Division was the longest serving infantry division in 8th Army at that time. It had been in the desert six months before Monty's arrival. Since then it had done all that he asked of it. Among its infantry were some hard bitten, cynical, but lively survivors. They knew what the future held for them. The sort of "General's chat" that may have gone down well with fresh infantrymen, or those members of a less dangerous branch of the army, would have been disastrous. All he had to offer was more of what had gone on before. In spite of this, he came to see us to thank us for what we had done. I am sure that, old soldier that he was, he knew what to expect. He handled it all very well and we respected him for it. We started training hard to prepare for the next campaign. Monty took the rest of 8th Army over to Italy. Early in October we heard the fabulous news that the 50th Division was to return to the UK. One day, later in the month, the whole Durham Brigade embarked on a Dutch ship, SS Sibojak and sailed for home. It was rumoured to be the only 'wet ship' in the convoy and we had to get used to Dutch gin, as that was all they seemed to have to drink. Monty was left behind in Italy. The D.L.I. Brigade eventually, in November 1943, wound up in Cambridgeshire. We went on leave and by the beginning of January we had started to prepare for the future and our role in the forthcoming invasion. We had been led to understand that the divisions who had been training at home for three years would lead the assault. Meanwhile, Monty had returned to the UK to command 21 Army Group and the invasion forces. Towards the end of January our Commanding Officer called us together in our Nissen-hutted Officers' Mess. He said, "As you know, Monty is back running things. I gather he was not happy about some of the divisions earmarked for the assault. He wants one of his veteran formations to lead. The order of battle has been changed, we are to be an assault division to land on D-day." If Monty was aware of it, he had the last laugh." [43]

CHAPTER FOUR

OPERATION OVERLORD
6th June 1944

As late as November 1943, Hitler refused to believe that the Greater Reich was threatened by the opening of a second front in the west. Since the opening of 'Operation Barbarossa' Stalin had pressed for the Allies to save the Soviet Union from defeat by launching a counter invasion of western Europe, but Hitler would not believe it. The port of Dieppe was raided on 19th August 1942, by a force of 6,000, largely Canadian troops, only 2,500 returned to Britain. The aim of this experimental raid, it was later claimed, was to assess the difficulties involved when seizing a harbour for the opening of the second front. Hitler however saw it in a different light, he believed he had inflicted such a defeat on the British it would deter them and their allies from launching a full scale invasion and his confidence was reinforced even more. He believed that the 'Atlantic Wall' would be completed by the Spring of 1943, and that after that date nothing could touch his forces.

In 1942, this assessment of the situation was borne out by the facts, the British were still suffering from the shock of defeat of 1940 and the Americans were not yet adapted to the rigours of warfare. But by the autumn of 1942, the British/American air offensive against the Fatherland was growing in intensity and weight, Kiev had fallen to the Red Army in November 1943, and the British and American forces had gained their self esteem as tried combat troops, and still the 'Atlantic Wall' was not complete. In November 1943, Hitler issued Furher Directive No 51, its main function was to strengthen the defences on the western front of Europe and was to be one of the most important instructions for the Wehrmacht of the whole war. It stated that an 'Anglo-American' landing was expected and that all Panzer and Panzergrenadier Divisions in this area of operations should be reinforced, and that it was only by Hitler's personal order that any formation could be withdrawn.

All ground forces in France and Belgium were commanded by Von Rundstedt, his divisional strength stood at forty six but was soon raised to sixty, ten of these were Panzer and Panzergrenadier Divisions. To the south of the Loire were four armoured divisions and to the north were six more, this strong, mobile and specially well equipped reserve was essential as it was impossible to reinforce the coastal front with a system of fortification in depth at all points. The concentration of Panzer forces was also of importance because the rest of the divisions stationed in the west were totally dependant upon the French railway system should they be ordered to leave their permanent bases, their supply and artillery units were horse drawn and their infantry manoeuvred at marching speed under the threat of attack by the allies from the air. Allied air superiority would severely inhibit any movement on roads or rail tracks.

It was therefore of great importance that the Panzer Divisions, with their rapid off the road deployment capabilities, should be garrisoned near the predicted invasion zone in order to hold the line until the slower moving infantry could reinforce them. The static divisions holding the coast would have protection from allied air and naval bombardment by stout concrete fortifications, these positions would overlook the beaches which in turn were to be wired, mined and littered with thousands of obstacles that had been stripped from areas such as the Maginot Line and the Belgian line of forts.

The idea of an 'Atlantic Wall' was, in theory, very good and its completion would compensate for German inferiority in the air. The Luftwaffe fielded only 300 fighters in France at the end of 1943, on the day of the invasion these would have to hold in check an allied air force of some 12,000 aircraft of all types. But by the time Directive No. 51 was issued the 'Atlantic Wall' was still far from completion.

During the time when Hitler refused to believe there was any danger in the west German troops were more than happy to be posted to the only easy billet in their areas of operations, they ate good food and led a life of luxury compared to their comrades on the eastern front and Italy. The work was not hard and the dangers of actual combat seemed a long way off.

In December 1943, Rommel arrived to inspect the defences, he took over command of Army Group 'B' and the cosy existence enjoyed by the men and officers on the 'Atlantic Wall' came to an end. Rommel inspected the coastal defences, what he saw did not please him and his judgement on the troops stationed there was harsh:

> "Generally speaking the troops are not working hard enough on the construction of defences. They just don't realise how urgent it is. There's still a lot to do, because many a man here has been living a soft life and hasn't thought enough about the battles that are coming, in times of peace men grow lazy and self-content."

Rommel made an unforgettable impression on the commanders of each sector he visited, he was blunt, frank and earnest in his dealings with others and it was not long before the construction of the Atlantic Wall began in earnest as beach obstacles began to spring up, spreading like an ugly growth along the coast of north west Europe.

Robert Vogt was an infantryman in the German Army at that time and worked hard on the new defences:

> "Before 6th June, 1944, we were directly on the coast near Arromanches, planting 'Rommel's Asparagus'. We did all of this at low tide when the sea retreated for several miles. We put in a wooden beam and then, at a

distance of, I'd say five yards, another beam. On top of these we attached a third beam with clamps - all of it was done by hand - and secured with more clamps. We attached land mines to the tips of the beams, all such that, at high tide, the mines were so close to the waters surface that even a flat bottomed boat would touch them and be destroyed.

All this construction went on under great pressure because there was virtually no bunkers at our location, only dugouts. This was the time when Field Marshall Rommel said the famous words - 'You must stop them here on the first day, if you don't stop them here - it's over.' We worked in shifts around the clock, I caught some shut eye that night. We had built two and three story bunk beds in a farm house about 500 yards from the beach."

In April and May 1944, Rommel travelled extensively in Normandy, demanding of his men their utmost efforts. Any open fields inland were dotted with upright tall stakes in order to deter any glider or other airborne landings. Hitler insisted on the 6th May that the defences on the Normandy coast and around Cherbourg be strengthened, the 91st Division was diverted from the 7th Army to Normandy in order to play a defensive role against any assaults from the air. The American troops who were to drop behind the area of Utah Beach would find these German defenders ready and waiting.

On the 9th May, Rommel visited the Contentin Peninsular, Houlgate on the coast east of Merville and on to Caen where he was briefed by senior commanders. In the afternoon he toured the area held by 716th Infantry Division, an area that was to be known to the allies as Gold, Juno and Sword. The concrete casemated naval battery at Longues was visited later the same day and the German commander finished up at St Lo for his evening meal. Rommel now intended to ask Hitler for the transfer of two more armoured divisions to the Normandy sector upon his return to Germany, on a wet and windy morning on 4th June Rommel left in the early hours for home and his wife's birthday.

For many months before the invasion the armies of the United States and war materials in great quantities had been pouring into England. The huge force assembled for this great undertaking, the first US Army and the Second British Army, were placed under the command of the 21st Army Group, commanded by Sir B L Montgomery, who's task it was to secure a lodgement on the continent. The supreme commander of the entire operation was to be General Eisenhower.

The exact date of the invasion was fixed by three considerations: the plan of attack, the tides and the German defences. The ariel photographs of the coast taken that spring showed German troops and French civilians labouring to build gun emplacements and mined obstacles on the beaches. As the Germans intended, if a landing was made at high tide a large number of obstacles would be underwater and invisible and many landing craft would be lost by hitting them. If a landing was made at low tide the troops would have to cross open beaches, 400 yards wide in places, under German fire. Eisenhower and Montgomery took the latter option and to minimise the risk would land tanks ahead of the infantry, the landing would take place just after low tide so the obstacles could be demolished and the landing continue as the tide came in.

Naval considerations demanded that they approach the coast under cover of darkness, however both the Navy and the Airforce needed an hour of daylight for the bombardment of the coastal defences. These considerations fixed the time of the attack at an hour after dawn, combined with the state of the tides, the date of the invasion was now set. On 6th June low tide in Normandy occurred at one hour after dawn, on June 5th and 7th it was just near enough to be acceptable. June 5th was chosen as D-Day, with the 6th and 7th as alternatives if anything went wrong. 'H' Hour, the moment of landing, was to be at 6.30 am at the western end of the landing area, which the tide got to first, and 7.30 am at the eastern end.

The German High Command now knew the invasion was imminent but could not agree whether it would come in Normandy or Calais, this difference of opinion was the result, at least in part, of a deliberate plan of deception by the allies. Having made plans to launch the invasion in Normandy they did everything in their power to convince the Germans it would come at Calais. As the armies and fleets concentrated in the south west of England, dummy army camps and dummy fleets were stationed in the south east. All the normal radio traffic of an army was created in Kent and General Patton, who was well known to the Germans, was brought back to England to command this non-existent invasion force. There was more air activity, reconnaissance and bombing in Calais than in Normandy and all of this seemed to point to Calais as the obvious choice as the invasion point. The British Secret Service was also at work planting the seeds of doubt in a divided German High Command, after the war in German files, about 250 reports were found from the Nazi Secret Service predicting where the invasion would come, they were all wrong but one.

The general intention of the allied invasion was to execute an airborne landing the night before the main assault on D minus one, to land and attack on a five divisional front on D-Day with two American and three British Divisions using various landing craft, in the bay of the Seine, landing follow up divisions later on D-Day and D plus one, and after the lodgement was made to build up the attacking forces by just over one division each day.

The purpose of the airborne landings was to protect the flanks of the main assault group who would land with two US Divisions on the right and the 50th Northumbrian, 3rd Canadian and 3rd British Divisions on the left. In addition to the numerous types of landing craft the might of the Royal Navy was deployed in the Channel and made an awesome spectacle.

For Months before D-Day the great air fleets of America and Britain had marauded across the continent on strategic bombing missions. Their work load increased as D-Day grew closer as they were now required to provide air defence of bases in the UK, protect coastal convoys and the massive concentrations of

ARMOURED VEHICLES PASSING THROUGH A VILLAGE IN THE SOUTH OF ENGLAND

troops in the assembly area, plus when the great day came they had to give air cover to and protect the actual assault. It was essential that British fighter squadrons develop and maintain complete air superiority so that the Germans could not interfere with Allied land and sea operations.

The British Army was to be supplied over the beaches, through minor ports and by the use of pre fabricated ports. One of the latter, code-named 'Mulberry', was to be constructed in the 50th Divisions sector at Arromanches, it was towed over the channel in sections and erected on site.

CHAPTER FIVE

A NEW ORDEAL: PREPARATION

Inside the framework of this broad adventurous plan the 50th Division's allotted task was to storm the coastal defences between Le Hamel and La Riviere, an area code named 'Gold Beach', penetrate as far as Bayeux to the west and the area of St Leger to the east. The 47th (Royal Marine) Commando was to come under the wing of the 50th Division and their given task was to capture the small harbour of Port-en-Bessin, they were to land at H (Hour of landing) plus two hours, head west and take the port from a southerly direction.

Early in 1944, it was apparent that the 50th Division did not possess enough troops to make sure of success, consisting of only three brigades. An extra brigade was asked for and given - the 56th, none of its battalions had been overseas and in the short time that was available to them they trained hard as a reserve unit in one of the assault Divisions, working in unison with the 7th Armoured Division. Other major formations were also incorporated into the 50th's Order of Battle for the invasion - these were; 8th Armoured Brigade, an American Battalion of 150mm self propelled guns, three British artillery regiments, two anti tank batteries and assorted mechanical aids intended to overcome obstacles and defences man made and natural. As D-Day drew ever closer the divisional strength stood at an impressive thirty eight thousand men.

In early November 1943, the troop ships carrying the veterans of the 50th Division had sailed into the Mersey Estuary, the day was wet and misty, yet every man had dreamed of this moment as he sweated under the blazing desert sun or in the hot vineyards of Sicily. American Military Police, smart in their white gaiters and helmets, patrolled the deserted dockside and hidden speakers blared out music of a patriotic nature to welcome home these sun tanned warriors. The sight of the docks brought back many memories for those who had left them in 1941, when the division set forth on its adventures to an unknown land. Many familiar faces were now missing and the first brigade to leave the shores of England, the 150th, did not return, its soldiers now lay in the ground at Gazala or were in enemy hands.

An air of tight security shrouded the arrival of the 50th Division recalls Sgt Max Hearst:

Sgt Max Hearst.
5th Bn East Yorkshire Rgt.

"On the way home we was told to remove all our insignia as no one was to know we was coming, the first thing we saw when we entered Liverpool docks was a big banner proclaiming 'Welcome Home 50th Division'. It was up to Scotland training after that, we had two weeks leave, if you had an 8th Army medal - you couldn't go wrong. There was only about 90 originals left from the 5th East Yorkshires, some were prisoners of war, some were wounded and many had been killed." [1]

Not all soldiers returning home with '50 Div', as the men knew it, were overjoyed about what they had been brought home for. Many felt they had done their share - a lot more than many units - and said so. Pte Forster had been in many bloody actions with the 6th DLI and was not at all happy when he found out what his unit had been brought home for:

"Why does it have to be us, some have never struck a bat, we've been to France, the Middle East and we've been in Sicily. They brought us all the way back for the landing, haven't we done our share? We didn't like that." [2]

Pte George Worthington, MM, served with the 6th D.L.I. and knew what taking part in such a landing could mean, however being picked for such a desperate venture was a compliment in itself and most men took great pride in being a member of the famous '50 Div' - though few would admit this in public:

"We weren't very happy about being used as the attacking troops on D-Day, but there was nothing we could do about it. Everybody was happy about coming home, when we found out what we were coming home for it took a bit of the shine off it. The only satisfaction we got was that Montgomery had asked for our division because he wanted experienced troops and at least we got some leave out of it." [3]

Company Sergeant Major George Warters of the 7th Green Howards looked to the future without enthusiasm for this new venture:

"We were in the South of England on manoeuvres when Monty gathered us all together and gave us a nice speech about how we were going to have the great honour of being among the first troops ashore on D-Day. We didn't take to it very kindly, after three years of fighting we reckoned we'd done our fair wack, we thought we were coming back to be given a break. But Monty's way was to keep you going and going and going, we ended up in an enclosed camp near Southampton and occasionally we would go down to the boats thinking this is it, but it was just training and we would come back. Nobody is ever glad to be engaged in a war, but I do look back with some pride in the fact I was there on D-Day." [4]

Once the division realised that they were to be the spear head of XXX Corps there was no general rejoicing, men and officers were experienced enough to appreciate what this meant and it was with a fatalistic and dogged determination that the troops of 50th Division faced up to their coming ordeal. Training in the new year went on apace, the division had already made one seaborne landing in Sicily and this would be the third seaborne landing for 231 Brigade. However 50% of the men now in the 50th were relatively new and would have to be trained from scratch in this kind of warfare, two weeks was spent working with the assault vehicles and the crews of the 7th Armoured Division, then each assault brigade - 69th and 231st were sent to the Combined Training Centre at Inverary. During April and May four full scale brigade exercises were held on the south coast at Studland Bay and were of great value in integrating the Navy and Army into one cohesive assault force. The final practice for the operation, involving all British assault forces, took place on the 5th and 6th May 1944. No major exercises took place after this date, a breathing space was given in order to allow naval vessels to be re fitted and also to give the Army time to perform specialist tasks such as waterproofing vehicles for the voyage and landing.

Within this mass of organisation and frantic activity was the ordinary Tommy, with his own worries and cares about loved ones left at home, every man knew he may not survive the coming encounter and wanted to make provision for wives and families should their worst fears be realised, Pte Tateson was given a last chance to see his pregnant wife:

"When I was told that I was wanted at Company Office I was puzzled, since I was unaware of any transgression that could have landed me in trouble. It was the middle of May 1944 and the 7th Battalion Green Howard's had just moved to Romsey near Southampton. I was a member of the Signal Platoon, having joined the Regiment soon after its return from Africa and Sicily the previous November. To my astonishment, I was told when I reported that I was to go on immediate leave for 48 hours. As explanation, I was told that we would be moving almost immediately into the invasion assembly area, where we would be completely isolated and allowed no communication with our families. Consequently, a strictly limited number of 48 hour passes were to be allowed. The Signals Platoon had been allocated just one, and "Pronto," the Signals Officer, had specified that I was to be the beneficiary.

Whilst elated at the news I was baffled as to why I had been given preference over the others, much longer serving men, without any suggestion of a ballot. No reason was offered. I had time to reflect on this mystery during my tedious war time train journey to Sheffield, and believe I came up with the correct answer. For a short time previously, letters home had been censored, with the exception of a limited number of 'Green Envelopes.' It was recognised by the authorities that men should have an opportunity of writing a few uncensored letters in which they could write to their wives and families in personal terms which they would not like to have read by their officers. It was a matter of honour and trust that no security matters would be mentioned. I had already used my limited quota when I received a letter from Olive telling me that she was pregnant again and was very upset and worried. I had to use an ordinary envelope when I replied and just hoped that it would not be opened. My letter was a very tender and emotional one and one which I would not have sent through the 'open' post except for the urgency. 'Pronto' never mentioned it to me, nor did the N.C.O.s, who must surely have enquired why I should be so favoured, but I feel that it was because Lt. Wilson had read that letter that he gave me that last chance to see Olive. The Army was not totally without sensitivity.

Knowing that I was very soon to be taking part in the long awaited invasion of France, I was very conscious of the fact that there was a real possibility of my being killed. This meant leaving Olive widowed with a child not yet a year old and another one on the way. It was very difficult to say what one would like to say in such circumstances and I took the course of writing a letter which I left with Olive to be opened only in the event of my death. Apart from an expression of the happiness which our lives together had brought me, I wanted to convey the message that if she should ever want to re-marry she should know that this would have my full blessing. Even in writing I felt I had to say this in coded language which I remember even though I destroyed the letter after Olive died. (We had both read it after my safe return and Olive kept it.) "If at any time in the future you should be faced with a decision affecting your future, and you are concerned as to what I would have thought, I want you to know that whatever would ensure your happiness and the security of you and the children would be what I would want you to do.

It was a sad moment when we had to say 'Good-bye' after that last short leave and Olive was to hear no more of me from that time in May until October when she received my printed post-card informing her that I was alive and a POW. This was just one week before Robert was born" [5]

Early in 1944, new men began to pour into the ranks of the 50th Division, battles fought in Sicily had taken a terrible toll in men and equipment and it was essential that each unit and sub unit be brought up to strength. Pte Cuerdon found himself among his boyhood heroes:

"I joined 50th Division at the start of 1944, one of these unfortunates who was put into a replacement holding battalion. When we were put into 50th Division I was terrified - absolutely petrified on arriving at the 1st Battalion Hampshire's, they were first class fighting men who had been in Sicily and

North Africa, coming back to England spe-
cifically for this invasion. A lot of them were
very highly trained men who knew their job.
We were just twenty two year olds when we
joined this crowd, which in some ways was a
good thing because we had the backing of
good men. I was absolutely scared stiff. We
practised attacks, landings, all this sort of
thing. We were taken down to Ipswich on
training exercises, off the boats - on the
boats, then night exercises week after week.
We were fired on with live ammunition, oh
my god yes, I think Monty was keen on that
sort of thing, I had no idea what we were in
for, I thought we'd go back and have a cushy
time in England." [6]

Pte Peter Cuerdon.
1st Bn Hampshire Rgt.

Pte Stanley Dwyer joined the famous 50th Division in January 1944 and would listen to the tales
related by the old hands with interest:

"In October 1943, I was a wireless operator in a high speed group in a war
office signals based in Egham, Surrey. The section was posted en masse to
two lines of communication groups in Wimbledon. In January 1944, a
number of us was posted to 50th Division Signals in Long Melford, Sussex.
We were living in nissen huts in the grounds of Long Melford Hall. The
unit had recently come back from Italy via Sicily and the desert. After a
couple of weeks we newcomers were very conversant with the geography of
the desert. Every night, when we could not afford the pub, we were up and
down the desert as the old hands 'Gripped' us, as the saying went, about
their exploits.We were told that 50th Division was one of the assault
divisions for the second front and the attitude was that it was going to be
a bloody affair. My attitude was that these chaps had already done 2
assaults, one in Sicily and one in Italy and they were still alive. Having a
father who was very badly wounded in the first great war I realised it was
different in the infantry. We found that their pet hates were Montgomery
and 51st Highland Division. They reckoned that 51st Division took the
credit for 50th Divisions exploits. Also that because of their habit of
plastering their divisional sign, HD, everywhere they were called The
Highway Decorators. Because 50th Divisions sign was TT (Tyne and Tees)
they were known as Town Titivators. Honours even! It was a surprise to
us about Montgomery but they were adamant that he was a rotter.

At Easter 1944, we were sent to the New Forest. We took over a
Canadian camp. My job was to man a high powered wireless transmitter
and receiver in a ready made truck. There was a driver and 3 operators.

The man in charge was also a signalman who it was said, would never be promoted because of his unmilitary bearing. He was also slightly deaf. There was a story told of him that he was on the set at night at Primosole Bridge in Sicily. The next morning he remarked that it had been a quiet night. There had been heavy shelling!

The truck would come ashore some days after D Day and the driver spent his time waterproofing it. For the landing we were to use a 22 Set, this could be carried on the shoulders by canvas straps. We were given a box on wheels and the set was screwed onto a board running across it. The batteries were carried in the well. We spent some time pulling these cross country to get used to it and also linked up to three other similar sets.

About this time there was a series of inspections. First of all was the King's Inspection. The only ones on parade which took place some miles away from the Divisional Signals were us, the replacements. The old hands had skived off. Our Colonel was most embarrassed when the King said to him 'Where are my men of the 8th Army, I came to see them.' A similar thing happened to Montgomery and I was on cookhouse fatigues so I didn't see him either.

For Eisenhower it was different again, everyone wanted to go. We broke ranks at his invitation and sat in front of his Jeep with his curvaceous driver standing behind him. He told a story of two soldiers looking out of a window in the war office as he went by, 'I wouldn't like his job,' said one 'Why not' asked the other, 'No promotion.' This went down very well, also his description of the perks of the job. He described his driver with waving arms to show her curves. If there was a serious side to it I can't remember but all went back happy. It was about this time that stories were heard of lorries chalked no leave, no second front and also of the CSM who marched his company to the station dismissed them and said he was going home. A friend of mine, when we were in Long Melford, had gone on 7 days leave and decided to make it 14, when he got back he was told to go to Scotland Yard who would tell him where to go. He was told to join the others in his mob in the cells till morning. He said it was full of 50th Division including Majors. About the 3rd week in May we were issued with our landing card. As far as I remember it had the code word of the landing beach and time of arrival i.e. Gold Jig/Green H+90. Also the section of the ship we were to occupy.

We were given a talk by the Colonel who told us that the morale of British Army less 50th Division was high. 50th Division was above the Americans. Our morale (Signals) was good. Why he told us this I do not know. Probably airing his knowledge. Some days later we were told we were moving the next day. We had a last night out in the Pubs in Lyndhurst. We went in trucks to a camp near Winchester. It was surrounded by barbed wire and guarded by Americans. In fact they ran the camp though the food was British. We lived in tents and unusually there was a large canvas container containing ice cold water outside. At the end of May we were trucked down to Southampton. We went through an empty shed to a ship in dock, SS Empire Crossbow. Our wireless and barrow went into the hold and we found our berths. We were accommodated in wire beds in tiers of 4. I was on top underneath the galley which was very hot during the day. The time was spent in talking and playing cards, there was no talk, as far as I can recollect, of why we were there. I suppose everyone was occupied with their own thoughts. The weather had been calm and the days sunny. On Sunday before D Day the weather changed. I remember this very well because it was the day the RC Chaplain came aboard to say mass and give general absolution. I remember being very fervent that day" [7]

Pte Tateson returned from his short leave and rejoined the 7th Green Howards to find a flurry of activity as his comrades prepared for the assault, his unit was visited by General Montgomery who left a lasting impression on this young soldier about to go into battle:

"The closed area to which we moved under sealed orders immediately on my return from that last 48 hour pass was in the New Forest, near Southampton. My lasting impression of our driving into the area is of innumerable American tanks and other vehicles parked under the trees at the side of the road, which gave perfect concealment from the air. There seemed to be a great preponderance of American troops in the area where we were situated. It was my first encounter with the yanks and my impressions were, first, of the apparent luxury of their conditions compared with ours, and second, of the inane behaviour of the men. At one point they were lined up for their meal to be dished out to them, and it was rather like a line of farm animals anticipating the trough. They kept lifting their heads and baying, 'Le's go, le's go,' in a plaintive and vacuous manner. I was most impressed though by their washing up facilities, which we shared. In the British Army in those days a single bin full of luke-warm greasy water was all we had to dip our mess tins in, in a rather hopeless effort to clean them. The Yanks had a row of three bins of hot water to be used in sequence, so that the third one remained practically clean and clear. A simple and common sense refinement, but one which made a great difference and seemed to us a luxury.

It was during this period that I came face to face with Field Marshal Montgomery. We were all assembled in a large open space to be shown some of the advanced weapons to be used during the invasion. As a preliminary we were drawn up for inspection by Monty. As there were many hundreds, possibly a thousand there, this was of course a brisk but lengthy affair, but when he came to me he stopped and looked. When this happens, the soldier involved is supposed to look straight ahead, avoiding eye-to-eye contact, but curiosity caused me to look into his eyes. They were steely blue and he gave me a searching, appraising, challenging look which seemed to last for a long time, so that I felt he was about to speak to me. However, he must have decided that I was not really worthy of his attention and he passed on. The inspection over, he took up his familiar position on top of some Army vehicle and called on us to 'gather round.' In an informal manner he then told us, in his characteristic way, that we were going to land in France, knock Jerry for six and finish the war off. There was absolutely no doubt about it - it was all planned and organised. We would just go in, do the job, and that was that. From this distance in time and after all the comic impersonations of Monty, this probably sounds rather corny stuff, but in fact there was something so tremendously impressive, almost hypnotic in his performance, that it did inspire us with a confidence which in retrospect was not at all justified. It was the sheer matter-of-fact certainty of his message that was so much more effective than a high flown 'Harfleur' type effort.

The demonstration of new weapons to be used was impressive. The flail tanks we had not even heard of previously and were an excellent invention. The flail consisted of a rotating bar in front of the tank to which was fastened lengths of chain. These flailed the ground as the tank progressed, exploding any mines - particularly anti personnel mines - thus clearing a path for the infantry through a minefield. There were also the amphibian tanks which could erect a large hood affair above them which helped to give them buoyancy and allowed them, with the help of a propeller driven by the engine, to 'swim' ashore from the tank landing craft. I had mixed feelings about the flame throwing tanks. The demonstration of the huge tongue of flame projected at a dummy pill box was horrifying in its implications. Whilst it was quite irrational on my part, the image of men being burned to death in this ghastly manner seemed barbaric, whereas blowing their guts out with conventional weapons was more acceptable. Such is the comulative effect of the myth of the glory of battle, and the image created by films, that when a man is shot he simply drops dead.

We were sleeping in bivouacs in fields during this period and although most of the details have faded from my memory, I have a vivid recollection of the novelty of reveille being sounded over the Tannoy system and emerging from the bivouac to a beautiful, fresh May morning with the grass heavy with dew and feeling that life was good. The bugle call sounded so clear, almost bell-like in the crystal clear early morning of an English meadow." [8]

The naval force that was to carry 50th Division across the Channel, protect them and land them on the beaches was known as 'Force G'. At the beginning of June Divisional Headquarters was established on board its HQ ship in Southampton Docks as the various brigade groups waited in their separate camps. The greater part of 'Force G' took on their cargoes of men and machinery at Southampton and by the evening of the 3rd June the entire compliment of the 50th Division was afloat, partly in the west Solent and partly lying alongside at Southampton. D-Day was originally set for the 5th June, but bad weather brought about a postponement, finally it was decided it's now or never and that the assault would take place on 6th June come what may. In the early hours of the 5th June this great sea borne force began to move out of the west Solent, through the night of the 5th/6th June this great armada made its way across the channel towards the enemy held beaches. Everything had been planned down to the last detail, 5,333 ships and landing craft were now in the channel, supported by 9,210 aircraft, all taking part in the most complicated large scale operation ever attempted. But the individual soldier only knew of events taking place within sight of the craft he was on, no-one could see so many ships or aircraft, each man was only aware of the fear, hopes and resolution within himself; and so it is only from this view point that the only true impression of this momentous event can be given. This was to be a soldiers battle, the plans had been completed and explained with meticulous care to the men, but once the order was given for the assault to begin the Generals could only sit back and wait as the troops from the rank of Colonel downwards put their plans into operation and launched 'Operation Overlord'.

Pte Tateson felt an air of unreality as the 7th Green Howards at last were ready to leave their mother ship:

"On the first day of June we embarked at Southampton on the 'Empire Mace,' an American ship known as an L.S.I. (Landing Ship Infantry). Slung from the davits were two tiers of L.C.I.'s (Landing Craft Infantry), fourteen in all. These could be loaded with men whilst still on the davits before being lowered into the water. This was a distinct improvement on the scrambling nets which we had used in training on Loch Fynne whilst encamped at Inverary. Those involved climbing down the nets which hung over the side of the ship were fully equipped and in battle order, in my case there was the addition of a large and very heavy wireless set on my back. These '18 sets,' as they were known, were about the size and weight of a case of a dozen bottles of wine. If one went down the scrambling net too slowly, the man above trod on one's fingers, whilst too quick a descent involved the risk of impaling oneself on the fixed bayonet of the man below.

We slept in hammocks, and the days of waiting were spent in eating, sleeping, physical training and studying aerial photographs. These photographs were updated daily and showed all the German defences, gun emplacements, buildings, etc., on the sector allocated to us. One of the features, just off the shore line, showed up as a white oval ring, and in explaining our planned assault and progress this was referred to as the 'lavatory seat'.

We expected to sail on June 4th but there was a postponement due to heavy storms in the Channel. Meantime there were hundreds of ships, as far as the eye could see, assembled in the Solent, and it was quite incredible that there was no sign of the Luftwaffe - not even a single spotter plane. On Monday 5th June there was an announcement over the ship's Tannoy System that we should be sailing that evening for the coast of France. What had seemed somewhat unreal, almost as though we were only engaged in training manoeuvres, now became a reality.

No-one slept much if at all that night, many of us being up on the deck watching the flashes from the coast where our bombers were attacking the coastal batteries. I remember thinking that I ought to be frightened and that instead I seemed to be detached and observing myself as though I were watching a film. The feeling of unreality, the sub-conscious thought that 'this can't really be happening to me' was in some way a calming influence.

Reveille was sounded at 3.15 am and we hastily went for breakfast. This being an American ship, the galley was equipped with the multi-course indented trays which I had not encountered previously. In one indentation was porridge and in another what must have been surely the most unsuitable meals that could have been devised, we were served with minced liver. (We were to see this for a second time after we had been at sea in the small assault landing craft for a few hours.) We were also given a rum ration. For many years after the war I could not bear the smell of rum, since in spite of the thoughtfully provided vomit bags and the fresh sea air, there was a pervading stench of retched liver and rum in the boats as we approached our encounter with Jerry.

At 4.20 am we began getting into the assault craft, and by 5.30 am we had left the ships and were on our way towards the shore." [9]

Pte Stanley Dwyer watched in silence as the infantrymen of the 1st Dorset's were lowered in their landing craft into the waters below:

"On Monday night we up anchored and were away, there was little sleep that night and most of us were up about 3 am. There was a constant drone of aircraft, when it got light we could see the planes. At about 5.30 am the tannoys barked something about assault craft being manned. The infantry -Dorset's - were climbing into them where they lay lashed to the sides. Their faces were startlingly white, all the blood had left them, there was complete silence broken only by one of them shouting goodbye to a friend. Then they were lowered into the sea." [10]

L/Sgt Ken Rutherford was a veteran of the 50th Division and had been in that unit since 1939, seeing action in many theatres of war. Thoughts of his own mortality came to mind:

"Being in the landing craft was very rough, the sea threw us about like a toy boat, a few were sick but not a lot. In our craft it was very cramped but at least we could sit back, I was thinking what would I be doing this time tomorrow, we'd been in so many actions since 1940, I began to wonder whether my chances of surviving this one were good or bad." [11]

Sgt Wills of the 2nd Devons celebrated his sixth wedding anniversary on 6th June, 1944, though not in the circumstances he would have liked:

"Few of us slept well that night and at about 3.30 am we were roused for breakfast, which consisted of almost cold liver and onions and a lukewarm mug of tea. Then we assembled in our pre-determined positions to load into our landing craft.

My LCM, being first off, had to cruise round and round the 'mother ship' until all the LCPs were lowered from the davits and the officers and men had used the scrambling nets to get from the decks and into their allotted landing craft. On board my LCM was the CO and part of battalion HQ, the MO, some stretcher bearers, a few supporting arms personnel as well as the CO's jeep and the RAP jeep.

The choppy sea caused a little sea sickness, helped I suppose by fear, and sitting in front of me was a stretcher bearer called Wally Hodkin who was using a bucket because he had diarrhoea and he was at the same time being sick into a bucket in front of him. The smell was frightful and combined with the action of the very choppy sea several others became sea sick - me too, eventually.

Once all our assault craft were loaded and assembled in flight order we set off for the shore, which could now be seen a few miles away. Most of the sea sickness seemed to terminate then for there was so much of interest going on around us. There seemed to be, within sight, hundreds of small, medium and large assault craft and behind us dozens of large mother ships, some still lowering assault craft, and countless naval ships.

A sneaky little thought crept into my mind, which was 'How's this for a wedding anniversary?' June 6th 1944 was the sixth anniversary of my marriage and I felt I had more fireworks for its celebration than any other living person." [12]

Bombardier Jack Styan was apprehensive as to what the future held; but could not help but be impressed with the view before him:

"There was this massive movement, to me it looked as though you could walk from one boat to another right across the Channel and step off in France, it was so massive, it was a sight I wouldn't like to have missed and yet - I was there but didn't want to be, we was just scared stiff." [13]

On the run in Pte Bowen and his comrades of the 5th B'n East Yorkshire Regiment were so sick because of the rough sea - all they wanted to do was get onto that beach and feel firm land under-foot:

"Reveille was about three-thirty, four o'clock. I washed and shaved and had breakfast and as we came out of the dining saloon we were given two twenty-four hour ration packs containing the usual thing, oatmeal biscuits, tea, sugar and powdered milk.

A high percentage of people, not everybody, was sea-sick. Yes, I was sick. Every day, as soon as I'd had me breakfast, I'd go straight out and throw it up in the scuppers. Some of the Royal Navy personnel had said to me whatever you do, don't do without food; if you're going to be sick, let your stomach have something to be sick on. People were saying, 'I'll be bloody glad to get off this boat,' even though it meant landing on the beach.

It was even worse when we got in the assault landing craft. We had a certain amount of trouble getting on the assault craft because the sea was extremely rough. We got down the netting down the side of the ship. The ship was rolling and the landing craft were bouncing right up in the air and back down again, probably twenty feet... Perhaps that's an exaggeration, but certainly six to twelve feet... And you had to time it so that you could step from the netting on to the landing craft when it came up on a wave. I was fortunate, the thing came up and I sort of stepped off and then went down with it. There were quite a few men who got hurt, mis-timed the jump and fell quite heavily and never got to the shore at all. They were taken straight back onto the ship with broken limbs or dislocated shoulders.

It took about twenty minutes to half an hour to fill the LCA, then they circled round and waited. They had RN speed boats with loud hailers and you could hear all the orders coming over, you know, '4986! Follow me!' Everybody was bellowing and shouting, actually shouting orders to get into position.

Then we started heading in. Of course, I didn't see anything then because you are down in the boat and it's got high sides. You could have climbed up the sides to look, but nobody did. The naval barrage had started by then, it seemed to me as if every ship in the Channel was firing onto the beach.

The landing craft was flat bottomed and it was lifting up in the air and banging down. Everybody was spewing over everybody else. I was keen to get off the damn thing, although I knew I was going into action. I didn't see it as me, an individual, fighting. I merely felt that I was a little tiny person in the middle of a whacking great event that was going to happen. In my mind, all that was happening was that I was on this boat, I was sick, so were all the other people, the front of the ship was going to go down, I was going to get off and I was going to run up that beach. I didn't think anything about firing my weapon or that the enemy would be firing at me. The front of the ship was going to go down and I was going to get off and say 'Thank God.' " [14]

As the 1st B'n Hampshire Regiment headed for the coast, Brigadier Warren was unsure as to their exact landing point:

"What we all felt, and I think this is the most astonishing thing about the Normandy landing, is that everyone was 100% confident that whatever happened to me, anyone else or the Hampshire's, it was to be successful. There was no question of thinking it might not be and I think everybody was quite glad to get on with it because it was like the green light for the end of the war.

We had the advantage of having marvellous models of where we were going to land, and so before we got aboard the ship we were able to brief everybody about the enemy, the models were very good indeed and showed all the intelligence about the enemy, their positions and anything else that was going to be relevant. We knew a great deal about the beach on which we were going to land.

Going in I suddenly realised that with the bombardment there was such a lot of dust, smoke and fire that it was difficult to see where we exactly wanted to land, we knew where we wanted to land but to pick it out was difficult. [15]

CHAPTER SIX

HIT THE BEACH AND RUN LIKE HELL

Great fleets of bombers had been smothering the German defenders with high explosives for some time and at 0510 hours the massive naval force assembled off the coast began its bombardment of carefully selected targets. At an appointed time each enemy position underwent its ordeal by fire, bombs fell on them, naval guns rained shells upon them, followed by a hail of shells and rockets from smaller craft. This huge battering ram, from the air and sea, heralded the arrival of the 50th Division on 'Gold Beach' as it crept in towards the Normandy coast.

The secret 'DD' tanks had been designed to leave their craft some distance off shore and swim to the beach, the rough seas however prevented this and they were landed in the conventional manner. Centaur tanks, mounted in pairs in their landing craft, were mostly delayed or had to turn back because of the rough weather, only two arrived on time on 'Gold Beach'. But the assault went in on time for the attacking brigades who bore the brunt of the hardest fighting that day, the 231st Brigade on the right and the 69th Brigade on their left, plus supporting arms.

Shortly before the infantry landed on Gold beach engineers of the 280th Field Company on 69 Brigades front, and 73rd Field Company on 231 Brigades front, would land and begin clearing the hundreds of deadly obstacles lined along the beach - with the aid of AVRE tanks (FUNNIES). This task was to be performed under a hail of fire from any weapons that had survived the softening up process that still roared over the engineers heads as they approached the shore. The 231st Brigade would also receive assistance from 'B' Squadron of the Westminster Dragoons and the 82nd Assault Squadron RE, to break through the beach defences.

Major Clayton MC, commanded 280th Field Coy and speaks with pride as he recalls how his men performed their duty:

"At 0730 hours, five minutes before H Hour, our craft beached in line in heavy seas and the AVRE tanks immediately started to proceed ashore. All preparations had been completed beforehand for the last tank to tow our foldings boats, but in actual practice this method of getting ashore proved a dismal failure. All rehearsals had been carried out in reasonably calm seas, and it had always been presumed that these conditions would prevail during the assault. The actual conditions however, were quite the reverse to calm, and the folding boats were found to be incapable of standing the buffeting they received in the heavy seas, and most of them either broke in two or capsized and discharged their contents into fairly deep water. All ranks rose to the occasion magnificently, and waded ashore and without further ado commenced clearing their obstacles. Owing to the heavy seas and the following winds, the water had advanced further up the beach than had been anticipated but here the value of the long periods of drill and rehearsal became apparent, as two 200 yard gaps were completely cleared of all enemy underwater obstacles before the tide made further work impossible.

The LCOCUs did magnificent work during this period and even when the tide was at it's highest they still continued towing obstacles and helping in the removal of drowned vehicles. During the whole of this initial period heavy enemy fire was encountered owing to the lack of protection on the flanks. The beaches were being raked by machine gun fire, a number of mortars were also in action and an 88 mm gun was still firing along the beach from an emplacement in the sea wall at LA RIVIERE. Despite this, however, no man faltered in his task, and when the tide made further work impossible, and the roll was called, it was found that eight men had been killed and twenty five wounded including one officer. The LCOCUs had one man killed and four wounded." [16]

Lt Richard Peard MC, landed with 280th Field Coy and was to win the Military Cross for his actions that day:

"Our attacking force was as follows:

Three tank landing craft to land simultaneously on King Sector Red Beach. This was the only time known in history when an Army Officer was permitted to give a Naval Officer an order which he must obey. I was the only one to know the exact spot where we were to land, our Naval Commander landed us exactly on that spot.

On the centre craft was myself, 27 Sappers and one Churchill tank fitted with a Pettard Mortar.

On my left flank was my Platoon Sergeant, 25 Sappers and one armoured bull-dozer. On my right flank was a fellow officer, 26 Sappers and one Covananter flail tank. The Churchill tank was fitted with a 6 inch mortar gun which was to penetrate with its high explosive bombs 14 ft reinforced concrete. The tank carried five such bombs which were very high explosive and very sensitive, also it carried large quantities of high explosives for our later use. Our plan was as soon as we had a small gap wide enough, the flail tank would go up the beach to clear a single path through the land mines for the Churchill to go up to blast the sea wall. This went fine until the Churchill approached the sea wall. Unbeknown to us the Germans had

'HIT THE BEACH AND RUN LIKE HELL'.
A VIEW FROM THE SEA AS TROOPS STRUGGLE ASHORE. THE SKYLINE IS OBSCURED BY THE SMOKE
AND FUMES OF NUMEROUS EXPLOSIONS. (*IMPERIAL WAR MUSEUM*)

cunningly built a gun emplacement behind the end of the wall to fire along the beach with an 88 millimetre gun, this gun hit the Churchill tank a full broadside, there was a brilliant green flash. I am in no way exaggerating, that tank with five Sappers inside completely vanished all but for the engines and turret, but they were blown so high in the air when they dropped they hit the beach so hard they were all buried in the soft sand and nothing could be seen of the tank or the five Sappers, I felt violently sick and my heart sank down to by boots. The commander of the flail tank had detached the flail onto the beach and seeing what had happened to the Churchill he went up close to the sea wall, put his gun muzzle into the slit of the German emplacement and fired twice to completely destroy the Germans.

In the meantime my Sappers were all busy, they were dressed in part battle order with a difference, they had two pouches on their chest with an additional haversack instead of a water bottle, the equipment contained ten made up charges of 3 pounds of plastic explosive in the 5 pouches on each side, in the haversack, on the left hip, they carried bangalore matches and insulating tape, in the right hip haversack, they carried ten made up fuses and detonators. These Sappers were walking bombs and I am very proud to tell you not one Sapper funked his duty by failing to wade ashore, although they could have very easily remained on the tank landing craft. Their task was to fix the plastic high explosive on the centre of the hedgehogs, prime them up then stand with right hand raised, when all were ready I blew a loud blast on my special whistle, they fired up and retreated to the water's edge and laid flat on the sand, there was a loud bang and the first row were gone, there was a repeat action on the second and third rows, then straight on to clearing the debris with a bull-dozer, then more mine clearance for a completely clear path. We accomplished our mission, a 250 yards gap from low water to high water just before the tide beat us.

We re-assembled in front of the sea wall but as soon as we had grouped, the Germans rained mortar bombs on us and three of my Sappers were instantly killed. I ordered my Sergeant to disperse the Sappers along the beach digging into fox holes by using their steel helmets to scrape away the sand but to spread out in fighting positions in case the Germans counter attacked. I thought if not all the Germans in the gun emplacement were killed they could fire along the beach and kill my men so I stealthily crept into the entrance of the gun emplacement and the gun suddenly moved, I froze, but to my relief it was one of the dead gunners collapsing and falling against the gun.

Now the main forces were pouring through our gap. I had been wounded three times, first in my head, then in the knee, the third time a land mine set off by our own bull-dozer which on turning around had just touched the edge of the mine with the track sufficiently to set it off, the driver had been

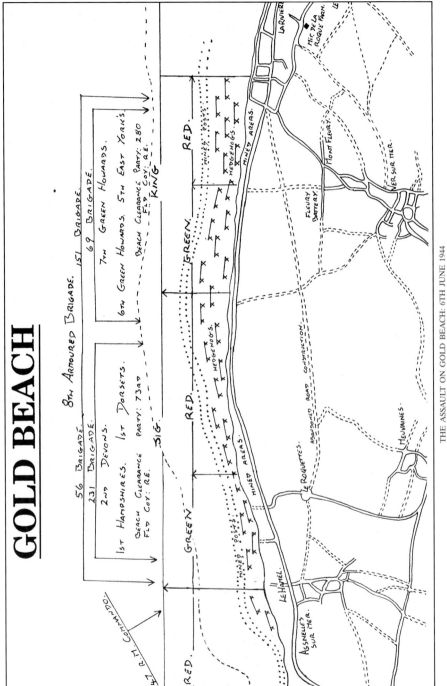

GOLD BEACH

THE ASSAULT ON GOLD BEACH: 6TH JUNE 1944

told to stay still whilst I spoke to my Sergeant to answer his questions, but he thought he could just turn round. I put an arm up to protect my face but a large piece of the metal casing from the mine flew up and penetrated my chest. With the bleeding from my head and chest I was quite a mess.

Shortly after this the R.A.M.C. arrived. A Sergeant and his assistant dressed my wounds, tied a label to my battle dress and said 'it's Blighty for you Sir'. I argued but he was insistent and said 'with a wound like that, if you are not hospitalised you will have gangrene from the red metal the Germans use to make the mines'. So I was forced to leave my Platoon of Heroes." [17]

The 69th Brigade landed on 'King Sector' of 'Gold Beach', between the Dorset's flank and La Riviere, the 5th Battalion East Yorkshire Regiment attacked the area of La Riviere and Ver-Sur-Mer, with the 6th Battalion Green Howards on the right attacking the open beaches. The third battalion, the 7th Green Howards was to land and pass through the beach head at 0815 hours, reinforce the front being forced inland and capture the battery at Ver-Sur-Mer. The 5th B'n East Yorkshire Regiment hit the beach and ran into a hail of fire being directed at them, Sgt Max Hearst remembers the first prisoner they took:

"When we hit the beach it was door down, out and run like hell, I was the seventh man on the right hand side and was carrying the bren, I was supposed to get down and give covering fire. When the barge hit we run out into deep water, two people in front of me totally disappeared, I went in up to my chest and waded out. I was running up the beach behind Major Harrison when he jumped up in the air landed and kept on running. When we got to the sea wall we were under cross fire, mortars and what have you, he said 'I'm hit', he had a bullet through his heel. As he could hardly walk he told me to go down to the waters edge and give his compliments to Captain White and tell him to bring his platoon forward. This Captain White was laid at the waters edge so I had to go down the bloody beach again and tell him, on the way back I picked up a number of wounded and helped them to the safety of the sea wall. I heard a bloke shouting 'stretcher bearer' so I ran over, it was a kid I knew well but he was hardly recognisable, a mine had exploded in his face and it was like a black football. I got him to the sea wall but he died later. We were pinned down and couldn't get over or around, first this Chalkie (Cpt) White went over the wall with pistol in hand and down he went. There was this bloody great gun firing, this RSM got on the backs of a couple of blokes and lobbed three or four grenades through the gun aperture and went through, if anyone was still alive he finished them off, he then came through a doorway out the top firing his sten, as he was firing he shouts 'right lads get over.' Jerry was throwing hand grenades over the sea wall that were bouncing off the shoulders of men that couldn't move, we had a hell of a lot of casualties that way. When we eventually got up onto the top we advanced on our first objective which was a gun emplacement and a tower used for observation, the forward platoon went into the lower part of the tower when our self propelled guns opened fire and blew it down with the platoon still in it. We moved through a corn field in extended order when Sergeant Major Bert Greener said 'Hey Hearsty fan out that way with your bren gun, there's somebody over there, come out you bastard!' All I heard was 'Kamerad - Kamerad!, I went up to see and found a German soldier with two or three dead around him, he was sat behind a spandau holding his arm. I said 'On yer feet' and was none too gentle as I dragged him up, he let go of his forearm which hung limply attached only by a piece of skin, one of the lads said 'nobody can fix that', snicked it off with a knife and threw it away. We dressed what was left of the stump and away he went down to the beach." [18]

Company Sergeant Major Laurie Whittle landed with the 5th B'n East Yorkshires and had to take ashore with him an unwelcome guest:

"As we went ashore enemy fire was still sweeping the beach and men were being killed and wounded all around. Strangely the enemy fire was of little concern to me as I was busily trying to avoid being strangled and drowned by a fellow soldier, during the night crossing of the Channel he decided he could not face the coming battle and shot himself through the left foot. After medical attention he was brought before the CO on a charge of causing himself a self inflicted wound, the CO ruled that he *would* go ashore and that I would guard him at all times to ensure that he did so. I was ordered to get him ashore dump him on the beach and hand him over to the medics for further treatment, I was also to tell them that he was to be court-martialed after evacuation. All went well until the moment we jumped off the landing craft into the sea, I was supporting him with both his arms around my neck, as soon as the salt water got into the wound he started to struggle and dragged us both under water, then I knew the real meaning of fear. Fortunately I was able to disengage myself and drag him onto the beach, there I placed him with the medics and faced the problem of enemy shell fire and rifle fire to rejoin our troops. The view at dawn on that morning is still imprinted on my mind - the sea all around covered in shipping of every size and sort, hundreds of planes above on bombing missions, shells bursting among the ships and the Navy bombarding strong points. The coast line was obscured by low clouds of smoke from the explosions of countless shells, bombs and rockets and the fires that they caused. Above all of this was the penetrating sound of guns and small arms fire." [19]

Pte Roy Walker drove his bren carrier ashore not far from CSM Whittle when one of his passengers became a casualty, Pte Walker drove along the beach to

A CASUALTY CLEARING STATION ON SWORD BEACH. 6TH JUNE 1944.
BOTTOM LEFT CAN BE SEEN PTE ROY WALKER. 5TH BN EAST YORKSHIRE RGT. HIS ACCOUNT OF THIS HISTORIC
MOMENT FEATURES IN THE TEXT. (*IMPERIAL WAR MUSEUM*)

the nearest Dressing Station and dropped his comrade off. As he walked back to his carrier the Beachmaster played merry hell with him for drawing the enemy fire and as he did so a photographer took their picture which was to become one of the classic shots of D-Day:

"Our bren carriers were water proofed with sides on which we fitted ourselves, we made sure we did a good job because we were supposed to float ashore. Once we left the landing craft it worked fine, we were dropped off quite a distance from the shore, I had to keep my foot down hard on the accelerator so that the water didn't get into the exhaust. Luck was on my side once again, I made it landing on 'H' hour, a lot of the poor devils never got ashore, they were mowed down by machine guns, snipers and shell fire, they were just floating in the water. I had a motor bike tied on the back of my carrier and its driver sat in the back, he had his hand over the top of the carrier as he looked through the plates while I looked through the visor, shortly after we hit the beach his thumb was shot clean off. I bandaged his hand with my field dressing, I used his as well but the blood was pouring out. I chased along the beach in my carrier and was stopped by a 'beach master' who bawled at me 'What the bloody 'ell are you doing?' you're attracting enemy fire', 'cos I was going like hell in me carrier.

I told him what happened and had to walk with my mate down to the waters edge where a first aid post was being set up. As I was walking back to my carrier somebody took my photo which was later in all the daily papers. Going back to 'Gold Beach' I picked up a Canadian officer who's ship had been sunk, I had the other lads rifle and he said 'that's great I'll use that - I can't wait to get at those Bastards.'

Snipers was knocking lads off left, right and centre, there was two snipers in a church steeple and we couldn't get 'em out, a tank was brought up and blew the top of the tower off. When they came out it was two women, they were taken to the rear but I don't know what happened to 'em." [20]

With the Yorkshiremen was Cpl Goodman-Tyson:

"I hadn't time to think about being sea sick, especially when I saw the coast, there was hell let loose then. We were a bit frightened really 'cos we didn't know what to expect - we'd been bunged up so much about this 'Atlantic Wall' - we wondered what it would be like. On the landing craft we couldn't see over the sides unless you stood up, but we all kept our heads down. The sailors drove them and dropped the doors as soon as we hit the sand. I was a section commander at the front, we were the first off. There was quite a few shell bursts near the landing craft and the sailor was shouting 'Gerroff the bloody thing - gerroff', he wanted to be out of it and back for more men. The shell fire and machine gun fire was concentrated on the beach. We had orders to get off it as quick as possible, we went hell for leather but a few of the lads was left behind." [21]

The horrors that met the troops on the beach were terrible indeed, Pte Chapman of the East Yorkshires looked around him as his company was trapped under the sea wall:

"Eventually miles off the French coast we were lowered over the side into assault craft, onto a sea that tossed the tiny craft about like corks. Men were so sea sick that they were praying to get ashore, as they staggered out of the landing craft machine guns mowed them down and the dead floated ashore buoyantly supported by their packs. The troops on our flank made it to the sea wall and were pinned there. Nearby was a tank manoeuvring for position to attack a pill box which was preventing our advance, trapped in the sprocket at the rear of the track was the body of a soldier in full kit and great coat. As the tank changed gear from forward to reverse - the soldiers body went up and down like a rag doll. Close to my feet was a body with no face, just the ears and a little bit of flesh at each side blanched white by the salt water. As we crouched there, helpless to move, an occasional German soldier crawled to the sea wall and dropped a hand grenade over the edge. Near the end of the wall was a mass of barbed wire which we managed to cut and clambered off the beach." [22]

The 5th Battalion East Yorkshire Regiment, commanded by Lt Colonel White, landed in it's correct position and on time. The company on it's right flank came under heavy fire as they crossed the beach and advanced inland across mined areas to the battery at Mont Fleury. This battery had suffered an accurate bombardment from the air in the early hours of D-Day and was quickly taken by the infantry, the commander of this position committed suicide rather than be taken prisoner, his men chose to live and were marched off into captivity. The left hand company met much fiercer opposition as it landed close to the sea wall fronting La Riviere, a fifty yard strip had been missed by the softening up bombardment enabling the Germans to pour a withering fire into the ranks of the Yorkshiremen. An 88 mm gun was situated in a casemate at the western end of the sea wall and had a field of fire straight down the beach, this was supported by machine guns. From the moment of landing a murderous fire was directed at the troops and their landing craft and as they fought their way ashore fire also poured upon them from other positions on the sea wall and the houses beyond. Two AVRE tanks that landed here were immediately hit and blew up, killing many men around them, the troops took shelter beneath the sea wall where they were joined by the reserve company twenty minutes later. In spite of the precarious position the troops found themselves in one platoon, supported by a tank, forced their way over the sea wall, through a heavily wired area and began attacking enemy machine gun positions in the houses facing the front. By this time another platoon had reached Mont Fleury and turned north east with tanks in support, they worked their way round the back of La Riviere and began clearing the houses at the eastern end, by 0900 hrs the village had been cleared, forty two prisoners taken and many of the enemy killed.

On the right flank of the 5th East Yorkshires the 6th Battalion Green Howard's fought their way ashore.....

Pte Bill Vickers MM, was in the thick of the action both on the beach and beyond, among the prisoners taken he met again an old adversary and shook him by the hand. However this veteran of 50 Div would see his luck run out - but at least he survived:

> "Lots of the lads were sea sick, I stood up all the way in watching the shore getting nearer, if I'd sat down I knew I would have been sea sick as I had been on other sea trips. The Battleship 'HMS Warspite', cruisers and destroyers were firing salvos at the beach, there was plenty of replying fire coming from the shore as well. There were ships firing their rockets towards the shore and several landing craft were hit by enemy fire as we neared the beach. When our landing craft was far enough in, the ramp went down, I was sixth in line getting ready to jump out, Sgt Hill jumped along with two privates, they disappeared under the assault craft, where they had jumped in was a deep bomb hole and with the weight of all the extra gear they carried, and perhaps the assault craft coming down on them, the three of them drowned. By the time the rest of us jumped out the landing craft had moved slowly forward over the bomb hole, the water was just over my knees, I was soon up the beach and got down behind a ledge

Cpl William Francis Vickers. MM.
6th Bn Green Howards.

of higher ground. Looking around and along the beach we had landed eighty to a hundred yards left of where we were supposed to have landed. To our left a flail tank had landed and as it went up and over this bit of high ground it blew up, one of its wheels came spinning along the beach just missing 18 Platoons Sergeant, George Authwaite, he had a bullet in his thigh and was laid on the beach, he was hit again as we who were left moved inland.

I personally knocked out a spandau machine gun post which was about one hundred yards up from the beach, it was firing across our front at 18 platoon on our right, I was able to get right up close firing my bren gun from the hip, killing two and taking six prisoners. I took them towards where 18 platoon had been moving up in the ditch by the side of the road that ran inland from the beach, six of the lads of 18 platoon were sat or laid there. They had been hit in the legs, I remember two of their names - Eric Charlish from Bedale in Yorkshire and Jack Walton from Middlesbrough. I saw them both after the war, Walton lost a leg as the result of his wounds. I took the six prisoners out to the beach and handed them over to a naval beach officer, one of the prisoners had an 'Africa Corps' sign around the bottom of his sleeve, I shook hands with him and wished him well, then I went back and joined my platoon. All the company officers, except the company commander, had been killed or wounded, as well as Sergeants, Lance Sergeants and Corporals. As we moved inland we lost casualties from sniper fire. One I remember was John Thomas Jackson from Middlesbrough, an old regular soldier who had served in India and on the north west frontier with our 2nd Battalion. By now our ranks were getting thin so I teamed up with another bren gunner - B C Elmer, and on account of his initials he was nicknamed 'before Christ'. As we went up this track we heard this gun firing from the other side of a hedge, just then a Sherman tank came up behind us, there was an officer in the turret so we asked him to put a couple of shots into the gun over this hedge. He asked us if it was an 88 mm, we told him we didn't know, he spoke into the wireless he had on his chest and the tank turned round and went back the way it came, that was the first tank I saw that day - and the last. Charlie went around to a gate at the back of where the gun pit was and I put my bren through the hedge, Charlie or 'Before Christ' opened up with his bren, I fired a full magazine. As I put a full one back in Charlie went through the gate and I forced my way through the hedge, we were on top of them before they could do anything and killed a couple, the rest were wounded, it wasn't an 88 - just a field gun with a spandau in a pit either side of it. We took the wounded through the gate and on to the track leading to the beach, they went without any bother. Then Charlie and I brewed a dixie of tea from the 24 hour packs we had been issued with. Some of our lads came up the track and we moved inland, as we came out of the open ground onto a road a barrage of mortar bombs landed among us. I don't remember much after that, when I came to I was on a stretcher near the beach, I had a shrapnel wound in my upper right arm." [23]

The Grave of Sgt W. A. Hill of Lingdale, Yorkshire KIA: 6th June 1944. Gold Beach Cemetery

As the 6th Green Howard's stormed their part of 'Jig Sector' the clamour and smoke hid from view a great feat of arms that day. Company Sergeant Major Stanley Elton Hollis advanced with his company across the beach and came under heavy fire from a fortified house facing the beach. CSM Hollis picked up a bren gun and fired from the beach using tracer bullets until the gun was silenced, the Green Howard's surged forward, Hollis's company objective was the powerful Mont Fleury Battery which was surrounded by strong pill boxes. His Company Commander noticed that two pill boxes had been by passed and returned with him to see if they were clear, when they had approached to within 20 yards of the first strong point machine guns opened fire from a slit. With his sten gun firmly clasped in his hands CSM Hollis moved to the attack.

"How the two guns firing 700 rounds a minute missed me I don't know, I jumped on top of the pill box, bent down, pushed the sten through a hole and sprayed it around. Then I threw some grenades in, I killed two of the Germans and wounded the rest, there were 16 or 17 of them. I cleared a lot of Germans from a trench behind the pill box as well, we got 35 prisoners that morning." [24]

By his actions CSM Hollis prevented the Germans from laying a heavy fire into the rear of the Green Howards, enabling them to open the main beach exit in that sector. Later in the day the Green Howards reached the village of Crepon, Hollis peered up a lane to see if it was clear:

"I saw two dogs standing in a hedge wagging their tails, I knew there must have been someone behind it. We sent scouts out and found there was a German field gun there" [25]

The 6th Green Howards attacked the enemy position but were stopped in their tracks by the heavy fire, some men were killed and others wounded:

CSM Stanley Elton Hollis. VC.
The Only Man to be Awarded
the Victoria Cross on
6th June 1944.
6th Bn Green Howards.

"I said I would go back with a Piat and try to knock it out, I got in a big patch of rhubarb at the back of a farm house, the Germans had spandaus to protect the field gun. The gun opened up and blew the house down, the company commander said we were to by pass it. We had gone about a quarter of a mile when someone said that two of our bren gunners had been left behind, I went back to look for them and got them out. I went in on the Germans with a bren gun and shot four of them, it was just a case of who ducked first. While I was firing, the two bren gunners were able to get away, I was grazed on the cheek by a bullet." [26]

Later CSM Hollis was at a cross roads as his company moved forward down a sunken lane, a spandau opened up on them:

"Two Germans were dug in at the foot of a tree, I got the idea of how they were firing and I decided that the next time they stopped I would have a go at them. When they did I ran forward and threw a grenade at them, it didn't go off but it made them duck down and I ran in before they had a chance to get their wits about them and shot them both dead. You know I had the feeling all that day that I wouldn't be killed." [27]

For his outstanding bravery and initiative throughout D-Day, CSM Hollis was awarded the Victoria Cross, the only one awarded on 6th June 1944.

Major Jackson landed with the 6th B'n Green Howards to find no opposition and only shallow water. He led his men up the deserted beach and found the Germans waiting for them, mortar bombs cracked around them throwing up showers of sand - while machine-gun fire raked the entire sector. Jackson was hit in the cross fire but it was not only enemy fire that nearly cost him his life:

"As beachmaster, my job was like that of a traffic controller except that my traffic was on foot. I had to see that everyone was directed to their correct positions as soon as they arrived.

The beach was completely deserted as we approached and I remember being puzzled by the comparative silence. Of course, the Allied bombardment was landing far ahead and we could see some of the big shells passing over us, but the absence of any fire directed at us was strange. Our biggest fear concerned the first few seconds when the landing craft doors were opened and we presented a tight, congested target for any machine gunners.

PART OF GOLD BEACH – 69TH BDE SECTOR. 6TH JUNE 1944.
THE DEBRIS OF BATTLE AND THE FALLEN SOLDIERS LITTER THE GROUND BEFORE
THE BARBED WIRE AND A CONCRETE EMPLACEMENT

Because of this we lost a Sergeant, who jumped too soon into the sea when we hit a false bottom. The water there was some eight feet deep, but he thought we had struck the beach. He was carrying so much equipment that he sank straight away and was drowned.

Ironically my fears were without foundation. When we landed the doors opened, we jumped out, but there were no bullets. The beach was apparently still deserted. The water was only about a foot deep and I quickly advanced up the beach, flanked by a radio operator and a regimental policeman carrying a sten gun. At every step we expected to be fired at, but were not. The lack of opposition became eerie.

Then, after about 200 yards, we must have reached a German fixed line. Suddenly they threw everything at us. The mortars took us first and I was hit badly in the leg. My radio operator and policeman were both killed outright by the same explosion. Fortunately, although I could not move, the radio was intact and I was able to keep in touch and help troop movements for a while. The first wave of infantry passed me by, and the next, and after a time the field of fire receded.

I was conscious that my particular D-Day was over and then I realised that the tide was coming in. It was the worst moment of the war for me. I could not move and no one was there to drag me beyond the high tide mark. The water came swirling in until it covered my dead companions. Then it lapped my legs and reached my chest. It was a clear sunny day but the sea was icy cold. I knew I was badly wounded, but not mortally, and it seemed absurd to die like that in inches of water. But then the Sergeant of regimental police, from my home town, came along the beach, saw me in time and carried me to a sand dune, where I lay all day." [28]

The 69th Brigade's reserve battalion, the 7th Green Howard's, came ashore three quarters of an hour after 'H' hour. Lt Colonel Richardson led his battalion across the fire swept beach:

Company Sergeant Major Jack Verity came ashore with the 7th B'n Green Howards and acted as a Landing Officer:

"We dropped into the water up to our chests on account of these obstacles in the water, they were dug into the sand. The sailors would only take you so far, because if they hit these ramps they would blow up. One thing I'll never forget when I was in the water was the strength of the water currents between my legs, one or two of the lads were caught and slipped by.

On the beach a fella said 'keep walking about mate, there's snipers about', I was waiting for the battalion as I was the only landing officer for 'em. I looked back out to sea and saw that flipping lot, it was out of this world to see all them boats and the battle ships firing over us, I didn't see any enemy aircraft. We didn't half get some muck thrown back at us." [29]

Company Sergeant Major George Warters felt he got off lightly compared with other units, he went ashore with the 7th B'n Green Howards and was soon off the beach:

"The crossing was all right but when we had to get into the flat-bottomed craft we were all as sick as dogs. It was dark when we set off for the beach but it was light when we arrived. All hell was let loose. I've never heard such a noise. We were lucky. Where we landed with the 7th battalion Green Howards it was fairly quiet. But we had our friends in the 6th battalion on one flank and the 5th East Yorkshires on the other. They had a very rough time of it but we were able to press straight through. We'd been told not to fight on the beach and we got across quickly as we had been trained to. We lost a few men on the beach and others in the water. There was just a gradual rise up from the beach. The barbed wire had been cleared and we soon got fairly well inland with the tanks. We'd expected more opposition but we must have been lucky. After we had been in action as long as we had there wasn't any particular feeling other that whether or not we would see tomorrow. The officers told us that things were going well and that was good news." [30]

Pte Tateson of the 7th B'n Green Howards had a difficult journey to the coast, having arrived his unit moved quickly inland and became a victim of friendly fire:

"The assault landing craft held about thirty men tightly packed. They were low lying flattish boats and we were seated so that our heads were below the level of the gunwale. We were ordered to keep our heads down as we approached the coast to avoid enemy fire. However, our landing craft was disabled by some underwater mine or other obstacle and it became impossible to steer. One of the other boats was brought alongside, and although it was already fully loaded with a similar number of men, we had to clamber aboard and abandon our boat. We were now exposed to enemy fire as well as being grossly overloaded. From this position I was able to see more of the action, and one image which remains with me is of the rocket ships sending off volleys of rockets, very large numbers in each flight, at an angle of about forty five degrees. Although there is of course no recoil from a rocket, there was, to me, an optical illusion of the ships, or barges, moving backwards as each flight of rockets was fired.

In the confusion of the hordes of other landing craft of various types, and due to the fact that some of the landmarks on which the Battalion commander was relying had been destroyed by the bombardment, we landed about four hundred yards to the right of our planned beach position at 8.15 am, forty five minutes after the leading troops.

The beach was in a state of organised chaos with tanks, guns, jeeps, trucks, personnel carriers, in fact every type of army vehicle. Some had been hit and knocked out; some were on fire. The heather or grass just off the beach was burning and clouds of smoke prevented a view of what lay beyond. Wounded men, including some Germans, were sitting at the top of the beach, and stretcher bearers were carrying others down to the boats from which we had landed. We walked along the top of the beach to reach our intended landing place, which was the road leading inland from La Riviere to Ver-sur-Mer.

Once we reached this road we marched along it and I recall our first meeting with French civilians in a small hamlet, which was probably either La Riviere or Mont Fleury. I remember a hill curving left, with houses on the right, from which people came out to greet us and to offer us drinks of cider. We gave the children some sweets in return.

Although my recollection from here on are disjointed and fragmentary, I recall with the horror I felt at the time an episode involving the tanks. One tank came out of cover to advance across an open field on our left. It received a direct hit, and immediately went up in a sheet of flame. No-one had any chance of getting out. A second tank then broke cover and advanced in the same way, presumably hoping to identify the source of the enemy fire and silence it. Almost immediately it also was hit and similarly became an inferno. Yet a third tank was then sent out only to meet the same fate. The German tanks, or self propelled guns, were so easily hidden in this close country, that it was pretty well impossible to locate them, and three tank crews were sacrificed in vain.

My own role as a signaller was a very minor and passive one. During training at Aske Hall (an off shoot from Richmond Barracks), we had used large cumbersome wireless sets known at "18 sets." These involved two men, one known as the donkey, carrying the set on his back like a large and very heavy great pack, whilst the other man operated the set by twiddling knobs and dials. Shortly before the invasion these sets were replaced by "36 sets," which had fixed crystal tuning and were about half the size and weight, although still heavy. In consequence, each man could operate individually. Throat microphones were used, consisting of two microphone pads, one at each end of a semi-circular sprung metal collar, so that one rested each side of the larynx. The previous "donkey" now became a reserve operator who could also be used separately as occasion demanded. As the latest recruit to the signals platoon this was my designation.

Progress this first day was rapid, but my recollections are very scanty. An incident which has remained very clear however occurred later on in the day when we had covered several miles. Without warning, a salvo of gunfire landed right in the middle of the troops to our immediate left, followed by a second, shortly afterwards. From messages being passed on the radio, I learned that no-one knew who was responsible, except that it was coming from behind us. When a third salvo descended with the most enormous CRACK, my signals training deserted me, and I sent the unauthorised message, "Stop this fucking barrage." By complete coincidence, but to the flattery of my ego, the firing ceased. We later learned that it came from the navy lying off shore, who did not realise that we had advanced so far." [31]

On the right of 'King Sector' the advance was going well, by 1000 hrs the 6th Green Howard's had moved over a mile inland and captured Meuvaines Ridge and were still pushing southward. The 7th Green Howard's pressed forward to Ver Sur Mer and on to Crepon, by 1230 hrs the 7th Battalion passed Crepon and advanced to the bridge over the River Seulles at Creully.

The whole of 69th Brigade pressed forward without pause and fought many fierce actions in the villages and cornfields of Normandy. By 2230 hrs the brigade was well established in positions around the Brecy Coulombs area, with brigade HQ at St Gabriel. By evening the brigade had advanced seven miles inland, only one mile short of its planned objective in the St Leger area.

On the right of 69th Brigade, the 231st Brigade stormed the defences in 'Jig Sector' of 'Gold Beach'. The 1st Battalion Hampshire and the 1st Battalion Dorset Regiments being the assault troops:

Pte Wiltshire was one of a mortar crew of the 1st B'n Dorset Rgt:

"I jumped from the LCA into about seven feet of water, I was the number one of the mortar team and I had to jettison the base plate of my mortar

STRETCHER BEARERS AND WOUNDED FIND SOME PROTECTION BEHIND A KNOCKED OUT PETARD ON THE BEACH. 6TH JUNE 1944. (*IMPERIAL WAR MUSEUM*)

as it weighed over fifty pounds and it would have kept me under. After wading ashore I made a dash across the sand to reach the bank before Le Hamel, eventually we managed to assemble one mortar out of six, the other five were lost. I got the mortar in a firing position but the barrel was full of sand and water because somebody had dragged it along the beach.

After seeing my friends killed and injured around me I thought it would be my turn soon, but I got off the beach after about two hours. The bloodshed was terrible and the Germans were tough fighters." [32]

Pte Minogue was the driver of a Flail Tank which was assisting the 82nd Assault Squadron, RE, who were in turn supporting 231 Brigade:

"I could see that the three tanks in front of us were not doing too well. The first tank had stopped because its commander had been killed, the second tank had been a bit too close to him and had slewed to the right and hit a clay patch on the beach and the tank behind him had taken a hit in the side, which had set it on fire. I saw the crew busily scrambling out. This didn't do a great deal for our confidence.

Fortunately, at that moment the tank commander hit me on the head with his microphone, which was his famous signal to do a 360 degree traverse in the gun turret to break the waterproofing round the turret ring. This gave me an absolutely fantastic view of the whole thing. There was absolutely nothing one could see on the beach in the way of opposition; I mean there weren't thousands of people waiting to fight us off, which is the kind of thing we vaguely expected.

As I began a traverse to the left I saw an odd pillbox here and there, but I wasn't quite sure whether anything was coming from it or not. Then as the turret came back towards the sea I could see the infantry just beginning to come ashore. It was all a bit like a cartoon, a bit unreal. I suppose there must have been a couple of machine guns raking across the beach. You could see infantrymen getting into the water from the small landing craft, some chest deep, some waist deep, and they would begin to run across the beach and suddenly you'd see the odd figure fall here and there.

It wasn't a matter of a whole line of men going down, it seemed as though just one in five, or a small group, might go down. A chap would be lying doubled up on the beach and some people would run past him and then a couple of his mates might get hold of the epaulettes on his battledress and drag him forward to the shelter of the sand dunes.

By this time we had reached the high water mark and we began to flail and I remember hitting the first mine on the first rise of the sand dunes. How many mines we actually flailed I've no idea but when we reached the road the tank commander told us that the tank behind was doing well and was following us along. We turned right when we reached the road and when we reached the first corner there was a dead German there. It was like something from a film. He was young, huddled up and hatless, or rather his helmet had fallen off and he was very, very blond. It seemed so stupid, in a way, that there should be a blond dead German on the very first corner.

Further along the road we were trying to negotiate a bomb crater right in the centre of the road and suddenly the tank began to slide into the crater. We obviously couldn't move and so we got out and by this time the infantry - I think it was the Hampshire's, and the Dorset Regiment - had got off the beach and were breaking through onto the road. Their officers were most impatient about the fact that we were holding up their advance and they cursed and swore in those fancy voices that ordinary soldiers learned to imitate so well, things like, 'I say, old chaps, can't you move that damn thing out of the way?'

Eventually another tank came along and gave us a tow out of this hole and the infantry moved on. Of course they'd been glad of the short rest, because they all got their fags out and had a bit of a breather. Then nobody really knew what to do with us and the rest of the day we were never more than half a mile from the beach and we kept being moved on by military policemen who would come up and say, 'Get this damn thing out of the way.' We finally finished up in the garden of a Frenchman who smoked about forty of our fags in about three hours." [33]

Trooper Lawrenson drove his Flail Tank through the heavy concentrations of wire and mines followed by men of the 82nd Assault Squadron, RE at Le Hamel:

"During the final run in I sat on top of our tank giving a running commentary to the three crew members inside. Cpt. Taylor was on the bridge checking landmarks for the lane we had to sweep through the mine fields. Hostile shelling and small arms fire had started and sixteen LCR's opened fire over our heads. Our tank beached safely with the other flail tank, we blew off our water proofing and dodging between the beach obstacles, headed for the thick wire and sand hills with the other flail slightly in front. We flogged through the heavy barbed wire into the mine field, while the other flail turned right and headed for Le Hamel.

My tank hit a mine which blew off the front bogey assembly and later we found the front driving sprocket had been hit by an armour piercing round. Over 40% of our chains had been blown off, the explosion had damaged the radio so I was sent back through the mine field to find Major Elphinstone who commanded our beaching party. He had been killed and the beach was now under heavy fire from strong points in Le Hamel." [34]

The 1st Battalion Dorsetshire Regiment landed on the left of 'Jig Sector', their main task being to take the high ground overlooking Arromanches, then moving on to occupy the defences of Ryes. By the end of the day they had captured all their given objectives as planned and were firmly established around Ryes, however this was not achieved without suffering heavy casualties in ferocious actions on and beyond the beach.

On the right of the Dorset's the 1st Battalion the Hampshire Regiment pressed forward into a hail of steel and fire:

Pte Peter Cuerdon had a rough landing with the 1st B'n Hampshire Regt, to see his first man killed was a ghastly experience for this young soldier and he has never forgotten his own reactions to the dead of both sides:

"An impression one gets is a sort of dream world, about three or four in the morning we were pretty far out and you could just see the outline of France. Do you know what went through my mind? I always thought I was going to see millions of Germans standing along the beach and firing at us, but it was a quiet morning until it all started. It was the most impressive thing you could wish to see when the battle ships, destroyers and cruisers started up their barrage, the rocket firing assault craft were the most impressive. To hear all of this going over made us think 'It's going to be OK, there'll be nothing left', the noise was colossal, we didn't think about it we were too busy, we put condoms on the ends of our rifles to keep the water and sand out. The shells were whistling over us and I used to wonder where that one was going.

The fire coming at us from the beach was terrific, you could hear it hitting the craft and see it hitting the water. We were hit and the sailors couldn't lower the ramp, so we lost our carrier and had to wade ashore, we ran like hell up the beach. Dozens of men were hit, many Dorset's drowned as they couldn't swim. To see my first man killed was a ghastly sight, it rather upsets one, we ran up these dunes and sheltered in the tall grass and held there waiting for some officers to turn up. We joined up with a young Lt, there was firing all around us, machine guns, sniper and (MULTI BARRELED) mortars (NEBELWERFERS), these were terrible and put the fear of god up you.

Its difficult to describe the fighting as it was so chaotic, we rambled on ahead and got down every now and again. The officers were dammed good though I admired them, we lost quite a few and they weren't much older than myself.

The battalion started to turn right and the ground began to rise, we were looking down on this little town called Arromanches, we couldn't take it from there as there was too much opposition. They decided we should go round the back onto lower ground, that was different as there was hardly any opposition, I think Gerry had decided to get out of it. Attending to our own dead put me right off - it turned my stomach, I thought 'no I never want this again. But when I saw German dead it didn't upset me at all - isn't that terrible." [35]

Pte Holley, 1st Bn Hampshire Rgt, had been in action before and could see the anxious looks on the faces of new men, once he hit the beach he and his comrades came under intense fire from all callibres of weapons and a ferocious melee ensued:

"I had already been in action in the Middle East and I felt like an old soldier, answering questions about what is it like. 'Brakey', one of our reinforcements was not yet nineteen and very apprehensive about going on his first operation. I tried to reassure him.

On our LCA there was a small keg of rum and a couple of bottles of whisky, put there by some unknown person, I never found out who, probably with the intention, good or bad, that we might need a little Dutch courage. One drink was enough for me, in the hope that it would settle a queasy stomach caused by the flat bottomed boat tossing about in the swell. On board we had a naval sub lieutenant who, either from the magnitude of the event or from *esprit de corps* obtained from the rum, felt impelled to stand up and give forth a little speech on the great thing we assault troops were about to do.

Overhead there was the continuous whizz of naval shells homing in on their targets to soften them up for us. We were soon in range of mortars, a weapon we had grown to respect, and we could hear the sharp crackle of machine gun fire. We had the word to get ready and tension was at its peak when the ramp went down. I was with the second in command of the company, a captain, he went out with me close behind. We were in the sea to the tops of our thighs, floundering ashore with other assault platoons to the left and right of us. Mortar bombs and shells were erupting in the sand and I could hear the burp-burp of Spandau light machine guns through the din. There were no shouts, only the occasional cry as men were hit and went down.

To my right I spotted my friend, Laffy, another signaller, crawling on his hands and knees, with the radio floating in the water behind him, attached to him by the long lead from the microphones still on his head. I thought he had been hit and only learned later that he had a relapse of malaria (a legacy quite a few of us had from the Middle East) and had no idea what he was doing. The beach was filled with half bent running figures and we knew from experience that the safest place was to get as near to Jerry as we could. A near one blasted sand over me and my set went dead. (I discovered later that it was riddled with shrapnel.) A sweet rancid smell, never forgotten, was everywhere, it was the smell of burned explosives, torn flesh and ruptured earth.

High up on the beach a flail tank was knocked out. I saw B Company's HQ group take cover behind it as a shell scored a direct hit on them. They were gone in a blast of smoke out of which came cartwheeling through the air a torn shrieking body of a stretcher bearer with the red cross on his arm clearly discernible.

We got to the sea wall, where Spandau from a pillbox to our left flattened us until it was silenced a few minutes later. We got on the road, running as fast as our equipment would allow. A Sherman tank had collapsed in a great hole, its commander sticking his head out of the turret going mad with rage. Past this we turned off the road through a wire fence with signs on it saying 'Achtung Minen'. A long white tape ran straight across the minefield, a corridor repeated twice again before we reached a cluster of trees where we were able to take stock of ourselves. There were six of us left." [36]

Lt Barraclough was in a flail tank attached to 82nd Assault Squadron - RE in 231 Brigades sector, his tank was in the lead as he progressed up the beach and hit an anti tank mine:

"When we landed at Arromanches, I was leading a line of flail tanks, which always headed the set piece attacks, clearing a path through the enemy minefields. As we went up the beach, my tank hit a mine and there was a hell of a bang. Although the tank was totally disabled, no one was hurt. The tank behind me took up the lead and went over the top of a sand dune directly ahead. What none of us knew, and what we couldn't see from our tanks was that beyond the dune was a culvert which the Germans had flooded.

The tank drove straight into the culvert and sank. Two of the crew drowned but the rest escaped only to be cut down by mortar fire. There was only one thing I could do. With Doug Arnold, the tank captain who had escaped, I built a bridge on top of the submerged tank from rubble while under continuous mortar fire. Fifteen years ago, the sunken tank was exhumed and has now become a D-Day memorial. There was never any room for fear except perhaps in the quieter moments. That evening. I learned that my best friend, John Allen, had been killed. As a joke he had painted a cross on his tank turret saying 'Aim here' - and a shell had gone right through the cross. They couldn't even identify which body was which in the tank. That shook me more than anything but I always believed that nothing would ever happen to me - except, I had the worst experience of my life which still gives me nightmares. My tank got a direct hit from an infantry anti tank gun. I was standing with my head out of the turret when suddenly there was a ball of fire inside. The next thing I knew, the gunner had scrambled up onto my shoulders and out. I shouted to the driver to reverse, but he was dead.

I got out of the tank in seconds and then we had to crawl back to our lines through the cornfields. Every time the corn moved our own men would shoot at us, thinking we were Germans. I didn't believe I would get back alive. Next day, with Doug Arnold, I went back to bury my driver. The following day we returned to put a cross on the grave but we couldn't get near the tank. The area had been taped off by the military police. We were told that it was in the middle of an anti personnel minefield - and we had been walking about in it and digging his grave in it without even knowing.

I spent my 21st birthday in the early part of the invasion" [37]

The Hampshire Regiment moved across the beach under a hurricane of steel and were unable to make a swift penetration of the defences, this was due in part to the fact that the RAF bombers had missed their mark and the strong points in and around Le Hamel had been left unmolested by the softening up bombardment. Machine gun fire raked the beach head and 88 shot cracked overhead, slamming into landing craft and tanks. Pressing forward into this fusillade the men of the Hampshire's found their way barred by deep mine fields fronting the enemy defences and each one of these covered by enemy fire. At 0900 hours two companies moved through a gap on the eastern side of Le Hamel and attacked Asnelles from the rear, by 1200 hrs the position was taken, amid the battle civilians walked about the small streets as if they were watching a film being made. Le Hamel fell before the bayonets of the Hampshire's and their supporting armour by 1700 hrs, with Arromanches falling at 1830 hrs after a days hard fighting. This well executed operation was carried out in the face of determined and fierce opposition, all companies suffered very heavy losses.

231st Brigades reserve battalion, 2nd Devonshire Regiment, landed three quarters of an hour after 'H' hour and found things were still very hot on the beach:

L/Cpl Travett came ashore with the 2nd B'n Devonshire Rgt into stiff resistance:

"When we beached we had to jump into the water and it came up roughly waist high. While I was wading ashore, I lost a couple of friends - the beach having been bombed beforehand, had left bomb craters in the water which you could not see. Some people actually walked into these craters and were drowned because of the weight of their packs. There were dead bodies in the water, quite a number, dozens probably. Not necessarily from my own regiment because we went in as a second flight. I think the Dorset's were in front of us, then it was the Devon's, but prior to that the Engineers had been in to demolish these mines on poles, to make room for the tanks to come ashore.

We managed to get to the shore and we had to run up the beach. I think there was a wall at the top of the beach. It seemed to take a long, long time just to get from the beach to the wall. You could see bullets splashing into the water beside you and you could see bullets landing in the sand. We got what cover we could underneath the wall because there was still considerable enemy firepower from pillboxes. It was a low wall and I think it formed part of a road that ran along the top of the beach. There were lots of soldiers with me, everyone was trying to get as much cover as they could. We'd all landed not necessarily in exactly the same spot, but there were a lot of us, anyway, taking cover under that wall. There were officers and senior NCOs but I was only a lance corporal then, so I was well down the list of seniority. I knew the people in charge, some of them were fearless, the only way I can put it. There was the average chap who took as much cover as he could, and there was the other chap who'd say, 'Come on, come on we can get from that wall to this wall, it's all right.' Though you thought twice about it, sometimes. People were being killed because the shelling was still coming from inland onto the beach. In no way could you possibly advance until these pillboxes had been destroyed. So we lay there in our wet trousers, water oozing out of our boots, for what seemed ages and eventually the most troublesome pillbox - it was on our right, I remember - was silenced. That was where I saw my first dead Germans. Gruesome. I thought, really, those chaps had probably been called up for service like myself and had no wish to be where they were, but they didn't stand a chance, not there. They just . . . well, what could they do?" [38]

Trooper Wilson was in the Royal Artillery and had the job of working in a team that laid down steel matting for the vehicles following to use and prevent them from becoming bogged down in the sand, things did not go to plan:

"I was one of the 'roly-poly team', whose job it was to drag out to the shore a huge roll of matting and wire mesh, which was intended to prevent following vehicles getting bogged down in the sand. The 'roly-poly' was about eight feet in diameter, with an axle to which ropes were attached. Most of us stripped down to vest, pants and gym shoes.

We hit two mines going in, but they didn't stop us, although our ramp was damaged and an officer standing on it was killed. We grounded on a sand bank. The first man off was a commando sergeant in full kit who disappeared like a stone in six feet of water. We grasped the ropes of the 'roly-poly' and plunged down the ramp into the icy water. The 'roly-poly' was quite unmanageable in the rough water and dragged us away towards some mines. We let go the ropes and swam and scrambled ashore. All I had on was my PT shorts as I had lost my shoes and vest in the struggle. Someone offered cigarettes all round, but they were soaking wet.

George Chapman in the Bren carrier was the first vehicle off the LCT. It floated a moment, drifted on to a mine and sank. George dived overboard and swam ashore. The battery CP half track got off along the beach, with me running behind. The beach was strewn with wreckage, a blazing tank, bundles of blankets and kit, bodies and bits of bodies. One bloke near me was blown in half by a shell and his lower part collapsed in a bloody heap in the sand. The half track stopped and I managed to struggle into my clothes. Several shells burst overhead and shrapnel spattered the beach. Machine gun bullets were kicking up the sand.

Our survey jeep came off the LCT and went down like a stone, being so overloaded. Our MO's jeep followed and met a similar fate and the driver was just pulled out in time, half drowned. The rising tide helped the LCT lift off the sand bank and it moved inshore, squashing the two jeeps flat.

Eventually a way was cleared off the beach and the battery half track moved inland. I walked along behind it, with the rest of the command post staff, as it crawled along a narrow lane which the engineers were sweeping for mines. Then we came to fields and hedges, two poor stone cottages and our first Frenchmen, two grey stubbled old men who kissed us on both cheeks and jabbered away in the Normandy dialect. The road was crowded with vehicles and infantry moving inland." [39]

Captain Fenner, a veteran officer with the 6th DLI, landed with the follow up waves. By 1100 hrs both reserve brigades, the 56th and 151st, were ashore and although their landing did not meet heavy opposition it was not without incident:

"We beached successfully, the two bow gangways were lowered and we waded ashore in about four feet of water. Beachmasters, RN and army landing officers, met us and urged us on our way. We moved left along the beach past a smashed strong point and its dead crew, up a gap in a minefield into the village. Progress was slow because the Yorkshire Brigade was fighting just to our front and dealing with enemy opposition. Also we were heavy laden with 200 rounds ball ammunition, pick or shovel, 24 hour ration pack, and light weight bicycles!

We followed up behind the Yorkshiremen past the detritus of the battlefield. I met two friends with whom I had had a wild party in Cairo the previous spring after the division had returned from Tunisia. They told me about the fighting on the beach. They were both killed in the next few days. I did not know it at the time but we were in the area where the first and only VC of the day had been won, by CSM S. Hollis, The Yorkshire Regiment." [40]

Lt Jalland was with the 8th DLI, but once off the landing craft events took a turn for the worst:

"The LCI's started going round in tight circles and moved towards the beach circling in that way and eventually, when they were within striking distance, they peeled off one at a time, rammed the prows into the beach and the next LCI's would come next to it and ram in there prows and it worked like a charm. The prow of our boat went into the shingle and the American sailor lowered the ramp and I knew exactly what to do - walk down the gangway onto the beach and get off it as quickly as I could because a lot of shelling was expected. I went down the ramp manfully I hope and stepped into the water, I don't know how deep it was but it was deeper than I was and I went straight to the bottom on my hands and knees. I was aware of the fact that the prow of this LCI kept smashing into the shingle right next to me and I could see it smashing my arms or legs or me if I got anywhere near it. I had these waders now full of water and I couldn't do a thing, my first act was to get rid of the folding bicycle I was carrying, I threw that away, I managed to tear the waders off, I also unfastened my webbing and slipped that off. I eventually landed on Hitler's fortress Europe on my hands and knees, having crawled up the beach, wet through, very frightened and completely unarmed." [41]

Captain Hooper of the 9th DLI found himself in deep water, but to his surprise he floated:

"They'd issued us with some oil skin trousers which came up to your chest, you tie them with a string in a bow. When they dropped the ramps I was standing on the top of the ramp when we hit an underground mine, it exploded and blew the ramp up, I got a hell of a shock in my feet but it didn't effect me, but I never thought as I went down there that the explosion of the mine had made a hole in the sand, when I got in the water I couldn't touch the bottom and started to float, the air in the trousers was compressed up to my chest and I started to get buoyant and I was going over, just then the pressure of the water burst the trousers and let me down again." [42]

The 47th Royal Marine Commando landed in the area of Le Hamel/ Arromanches behind 231st Brigade at 1000 hrs, this separate force was required

GOLD BEACH CEMETERY. 8TH JUNE 1944

because of the already heavy commitments of the 231st in 'Jig Sector', to make a forced march of eight miles through enemy held territory carrying all their weapons, ammunition and supplies, with the prospect at the end of it of a very stiff battle, to take Port-En-Bessin.

The commando landed at their appointed time but three landing craft were sunk on the run in with the loss of seventy men, a number of them did turn up however but had lost kit and weapons, these men re equipped themselves with enemy weapons taken from prisoners. The Hampshire's were still fighting for Le Hemel at this time which delayed gathering the commando together, eventually the marines fought their way towards the assembly area which they found to be occupied by a company of enemy infantry. The attack against this position cost them a further forty casualties before it fell. The now rather depleted commando then advanced swiftly to the small village of Escures to the south of Port En Bessin and occupied it by last light on 6th June:

Pte (SHOCK) Kendrick MM, moved inland with 47 Royal Marine Commando, the fighting along the way was hard:

"Our task was to land and to break out of the beach on to Port-En-Bessin. Our Commando officer, Captain Walton, took us through to a junction on a coast road and told us to dig. We exposed a telephone junction box which connected all military telephones and we blew it up. Later, as we advanced, we had some skirmishes with the Germans. A machine gun opened up on us, injuring some of the lads. 'Shock!' The cry rang out from one of the wounded. As I tended to the lad I realised I couldn't do all the necessary first aid in a prone position, but as I stood up the machine gun opened up again. I could see the bullets hitting the hedgerow but as they came nearer to me the gun must have lifted. Although the firing continued, the bullets were flying about above my head. We put in a flank attack and captured the machine gun and crew. The gunner had a right shoulder injury. I had to treat him. When I'd finished he hugged me. A Scout car with six Germans in it suddenly rounded a bend in the road. We dealt with it. Soon after we heard a horse galloping down the lane. As it came in view we saw it had a German rider. A Sergeant Hooper stepped into the lane and fired his Tommy gun. The horse galloped off with the dead body still on its back. Later we approached a small village. An elderly woman was crying by the roadside. I could see the old lady was wounded in the arm so I tended to her and wanted to get her in the house. While I was trying to get her to understand that she should be in bed she slapped my face! I realised she had completely misunderstood. I had no choice but to give her a morphine injection and carry on. I can almost hear the noise of the fire, see the sky blackened with planes and hundred of ships around us as far as the eye could see." [43]

The town of Port En-Bessin and surrounding features fell at 0400 hrs on 8th June, after fierce fighting. They were then reinforced by men of the 2nd Devon's and supplies were sent through the now open coast road.

CHAPTER SEVEN

THE FIRST BATTLE FOR VILLERS BOCAGE

At last light on D-Day the troops of the 50th Division were six miles inland and patrols from the 56th Brigade were entering Bayeux. The important feature of St Leger was almost within reach.

By first light on the 7th June the allied Armies were found to be firmly established on the continent, not all objectives had been taken but the success of the landing and the grip established on ground already taken gave grounds for satisfaction, with the prospects of greater gains ahead. The sea borne assault was over and the land campaign had begun, on the right the Americans had recovered from a very difficult landing, in the centre the 50th Division had achieved its objectives with the clearing of Bayeux on the morning of the 7th and on the left the 3rd British and the Canadian Divisions were firmly implanted on French soil, but Caen had not yet been taken. On the extreme left air borne troops had secured a bridge head over the Orne and occupied villages to the east of the bridge being held.

The situation the Germans now found themselves in was critical but not totally hopeless, the invasion had been a success but there can be little doubt that the Germans had planned for such a contingency, the next step for them was to contain the bridge head by a speedy deployment of armoured reserves and a strong counter attack to drive the invaders back into the sea.

For the Allies in the bridge head it was a matter of expanding the foot hold being held as rapidly as possible and bring in materials and troops by sea at a great rate each day. The weather came to the enemy's assistance when high seas battered the invasion fleet, making the work of the Royal Navy and Beach Groups extremely difficult and at times impossible. Supplies were held up for days but eventually the build up continued and gathered pace as it did so. The Germans however had great difficulty in moving reserves to the coast as any movement in daylight brought down a hurricane of destruction from the marauding aircraft of the Royal Airforce.

However, by the 7th June, German armoured reserves were on the move, with two of these divisions being very close to or already in the battle zone. Before Caen the 21st Panzer Division defied all attempts to take this old Norman City, their tanks and infantry fighting stubbornly in every corn field and hedge row for each yard of land. To the south and west of 50th Divisions front was the 12th SS Panzer Division Hitler Jugend and beyond the Siene the 2nd Panzer Division was a hive of activity as it prepared to move off. From the Loire in the south the 17th Panzer Grenadier Division advanced to the battle zone and before the 50th Divisions front the Panzer Lehr Division prepared for battle. Little was known at the time about Panzer Lehr, its name means literally 'demonstration division', but it was to become 50th Divisions ruthless and skilful opponent until its destruction in later battles. To contain and eventually destroy these armoured units the allies plan was to allow the enemy no rest by aggressive action, so that the whole of his forces would have to be committed piece meal as it arrived at the front to plug holes in his depleted defences.

The early capture of Villers Bocage was a major part of the Second Army plan for 'Overlord', this was considered to be of great importance as this little French town, twenty miles inland from the beaches, was a centre of communications for the enemy and its retention was essential in his plans to contain the bridge head. The town itself was on high ground and was a junction of five important roads. Overlooking this Norman town were higher features that would become well known to the troops of the 50th Division in their struggle to take the area; to the north east was point 214 standing on a ridge two thousand yards long, to the east stood points 140 and 158 and to the west stood Tracy Bocage.

This bocage countryside was closer than anything the men of the 50th Division had experienced before - with its numerous high hills and deep valleys, tall thick hedges surrounding each small field that were flanked by ditches and narrow meandering roads. These features made the work of tanks extremely difficult and for the infantry it was to prove to be a nightmare. The battle was now to be fought in this mazy bocage country at close quarters, initially the German troops, with their experience of fighting in Russia, had the advantage, but the Allied troops soon mastered the kinds of battle techniques needed to wage war in this terrain. With the failure to take Villers Bocage on D-Day the 50th Division settle down to a lengthy and very bitter period of fighting in which every hedge and field had to be fought for and then held against a very skilful and determined enemy who had the additional motive of knowing that if he failed to contain the Allied landings, devastating warfare would be taken to the heart of Germany.

On 7th June, the 50th Division consolidated it's gains and counted the cost, for some units in the division there were still objectives to be taken and many smaller actions were fought by the troops at the front. The 7th Green Howard's advanced to take a radio station north of Coulombs, Pte Tateson recalls that morning:

"I was wakened at 4.00 am (after two hours sleep) and ordered to accompany an NCO on a forward patrol to establish whether the wireless station had been abandoned. We approached through a cornfield in the semi dark and got within perhaps a hundred yards when we saw smoke rising. I reported this over the radio and immediately there was a burst of

Spandau fire from the buildings. We went to ground, and although I have no recollection of the return journey, we must have got back by crawling through the corn.

The next thing I remember is the crossing of the minefield, I have always retained a clear recollection of this episode. We, or the Engineers, I don't know which, were equipped with mine detectors, rather like the present metal detectors. The man swept the ground in front of him whilst walking slowly forward. Once located, the mines had to be removed and made safe. This was the theory. In practice, three men had their feet blown off before it was realise that the detectors were faulty - probably damaged by sea water.

Our sergeant, Sgt, Potterton, realising that somehow we must make progress, then went forward on his own, without a detector, laying a tape behind him to establish a safe path. If he didn't suffer the same fate as the three before him we had a fair chance of following him through without further casualties. We could only watch him with increasing apprehension as he edged his way forward, and having seen the gruesome results of the previous efforts, admire his cold-blooded courage.

The tension was almost unbearable, and was only slightly reduced when he reached the far side of the minefield and started the return along his taped path. This again he negotiated safely and then led us carefully through without any further casualties. After this first section had got through he again returned and led his other section through. He was awarded the Military Medal for this and other exceptional courageous actions under heavy mortar and machine gun fire during this attack. A VC would have been more appropriate, since his actions in the minefield demanded cool courage without the stimulation of violent action.

The attack on the Station was from two sides, 'C' Company from the east, and 'A' Company, to which I was attached, from the west. The two companies broke through almost simultaneously and about sixty prisoners were taken. My personal recollection of entering the gateway was of passing the body of one of our men who had been killed in the first attack which had been repulsed. He was lying in the gateway with his guts literally blown out and the remains of his 'drawers cellular' adhering to them. I thought how sordid war really was, and how the 'glory of battle' is such a wicked lie. It was a lovely June day and Normandy was lush and green.

We explored the buildings gingerly in case of booby traps amongst the mass of radio equipment and connecting wires. I 'acquired' a Luger pistol (which one of our officers in turn 'acquired' from me a few days later when I rashly tried firing it into the ground). In a ditch surrounding the station I came across the body of a German soldier lying beside his wrecked Spandau machine gun, and realised that it was positioned to cover my approach route through the corn when on that two man patrol earlier that morning. Whether or not he was the one who fired that burst at us I don't know, it was certainly the point from which the fire had come. It seemed to me then that that event had happened days ago, although in fact it was not much more than six hours previously. This was the late morning of Tuesday 7th June, and I had had a total of three hours sleep since the morning of Sunday 5th, a period of about sixty hours." [44]

That same day the 6th DLI formed a mobile column of one squadron of tanks, carriers, anti tank guns and mortars of the 'support' company and 'D' Company on bicycles. The rest of the battalion followed on foot. Captain Fenner was second in command of 'D' Company at that time:

"We had been unable to reach our objective before last light on the 6th. We laagered up and sent out infantry patrols to see if the area was occupied, it did not appear to be.

After first light the column moved and was soon on its objective. The various elements of the column took up the positions that had been selected off the map back at Nightingale Wood near Romsey, this place had been our base before the embarkation and assault. While this was going on we were attacked by some Typhoon Aircraft. They knocked out a carrier. The carrier crew were old hands and were able to bale out before the vehicle was hit. We displayed our recognition signals, yellow smoke and fluorescent panels and no further attacks took place. We were behind the bomb line (the Tilly/Caen Road) and should have been safe from attack by our own Aircraft. We picked up some prisoners including some Flak troops and Tartars. These were small Mongol featured Russians, ex POWs recruited into the German Army, shortly after this the battalion came marching up to the position. Each company headed out to its map selected position. A screen of machine guns was deployed for local protection and the battalion began to dig in. It was smoothly done, as one would expect from a well managed, battle experienced battalion. One of my old Sicily platoon in 'C' Company enquired if I was saddle sore, remarking he preferred to be footsore than saddle sore.

'D' Company moved into battalion reserve. I set out with my team for the Joint Post. The function of a J P was to guard against enemy infiltration between brigades. This particular J P was to be established at Conde Sur Seulle. Here the railway crossed the road that ran SW through Jerusalem X roads. The position was out of sight and about 1200 yards from the remainder of the battalion. The J P garrison was 18 platoon less one section, a carrier section of 3 vehicles and 9 men, and one 6 pounder anti tank gun. This force was to be augmented by a similar force from a Green Howard battalion of 69 Brigade. Both elements of the J P force would have radio communications to its respective battalion HQs. 69 Brigade was an assault brigade and unlike us had had some hard fighting on D-day. I had taken this into account when making the plan for the defence of the J P.

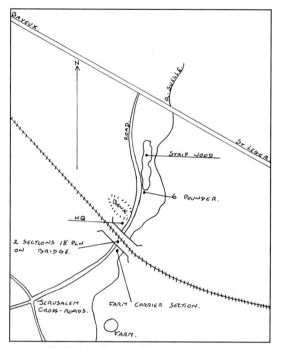

JOINT POST. 6TH DLI AT CONDE SUR SEULLE.
7TH JULY 1944. BY CAPTAIN FENNER 2 I/C 6TH DLI

I assumed the Green Howards would be late or not arrive. Events proved this assumption to be correct.

We were about to move out when we heard some firing, our carriers had ambushed two German motor cycle combinations who had driven into the left flank of the battalions position. The left flank was open because 69 Brigade was still fighting its way forward. We occupied the J P without interference. The two rifle sections of 18 platoon dug in astride the railway line, on the bridge which crossed the road. Passing under the arch of the bridge and to the left was a small farmhouse and yard. Here the carrier section was deployed. Back under the bridge was a bank between the railway embankment and the road. In the gap between the bank and the embankment the HQ was set up. About 100 yards to the North up the road strip wood joined the road, here the 6 pounder was positioned. The gun would be able to deal with any tank coming up the road under the bridge. We began preparing our position. While this was going on there was some shooting on the carrier sections side of the bridge. They had killed a young SS man, a panzer grenadier. But another had got away. One of the carrier crew had been walking up a hedge line when the Germans had appeared. Our mans reaction was quicker, he shot one but the other got away. I

A WOUNDED SS TROOPER MAKES HIS SURRENDER.
JUNE 1944. (*IMPERIAL WAR MUSEUM*)

concluded that this could have been a two man reconnaissance patrol to examine our lay out. Every one was warned to keep a good look out.

We were ordered to send a carrier patrol to sweep SE around Audrieu. Just as it left and was about 200 yards out it was attacked by 4 Thunderbolt Aircraft. They attacked with bombs and machine guns. Fortunately for us they were rotten shots and no one was hurt. Once more we should have not been attacked, we were still behind the bomb line, we had spread a yellow panel on the bridge, and fired yellow smoke. All to no avail, they just waded in.

The patrol was completed with NTR (nothing to report). They returned to base for a brew. Then a Frenchman from a farm just south of our position came to us and reported a party of Germans had passed west to east through his farm. Again our little force was alerted. Battalion HQ of course was informed of our activities. We settled down for our evening brew.

We never enjoyed it. There was an outbreak of firing from the direction of the 6 pounder position, two or three men ran passed the HQ in the direction of the carrier section under the bridge. These were in fact the 6 pounder crew survivors. I stepped from behind the bank into the road and charging down the road towards us was a bunch of angry Germans. I jumped back behind the bank and we all began firing through the hedge that topped the bank. A furious fire fight developed at very close range, one of our number was hit, but we seemed to have succeeded in checking the German attack temporarily. I yelled for the carrier section to come and support us as I lobbed one of the plastic 69 grenades I had in my pouches over the bank. 69 grenades were made of bakelite, they made a big bang but there was no shrapnel, unlike the 36 grenade which fragmented into metal pieces and at close quarters could be dangerous to the throwers.

The Germans stopped firing and disappeared up the road followed by some of the carrier section who had charged round to our support and the HQ party. We ran past an abandoned machine pistol and a pair of binoculars. I surmised later we had probably hit the German patrol commander. At the entrance to the wood we ran into another fire fight at close range. Probably a covering party to secure the withdrawal of the assaulting force. We took 3 more casualties including the brave carrier section commander who was killed. These Germans ran back through the wood. They were shot up by 18 platoon from their position on top of the railway bridge. We found the 6 pounder intact, we also found the 6 pounder commander . He had been walking up the line of the wood when he surprised the Germans·coming the other way. They shot him down, sprayed him as they ran past after the other gunners, whose arrival past our HQ was mentioned earlier. He was badly shot up but was able to walk. We found one wounded and two dead Germans.

Battalion HQs had sent the carrier platoon under Ian Daw to our support. His men swept the wood but the enemy had gone. Our little counter attack had been effective. The German patrol must have come up from the south and passed on a covered easterly route round our position to enter the strip wood from the north. Where they were seen by the gun detachment commander. The German patrol was skilfully handled and the young SS men pressed home their attack. The whole affair could have only lasted a few minutes but it was pretty savage while it happened." [45]

At 2300 hrs on 7th June, orders were received to concentrate a force in the area of Brecy to form a column with the 8th Armoured Brigade and force a passage south into the heart of the Bocage. Its route was to take it, on the morning of the 8th June, across the Bayeux to Caen railway, up the road past Point 103 which dominated the north east of Tilly-Sur-Seulles; then finally on through St Pierre and due south along the main road that led to Villers.

The column was due to move off from the railway line at 1000 hours but was delayed because of accurate anti tank fire coming from the east, the 1st Battalion Dorsetshire Regiment overcame without difficulty the enemy in Loucelles but encountered stiff opposition on the line of the railway between Loucelles and Bas-d'Audrieu. 'B' and 'C' Companies moved out to the right to outflank the enemy holding the villages south of the railway and because it was done quite late in the day it meant the enemy would have to be winkled out of Audrieu that night. In the battalion history this was described as;

"An extremely ticklish and precarious business." [46]

The battle continued into the night and many prisoners were taken, among their numbers were Panzer Grenadiers.

The column was being urged now to press forward to the important Point 103 and early on 9th June 'A' Company of the 1st Dorset's entered Le Haut d'Audrieu and linked up with 'C' and 'D' Companies in Audrieu itself. The whole battalion now occupied a line of villages from Le Haut d'Andrieu to Bas d'Audrieu, meanwhile the armour of 8th Armoured Brigade had taken Point 103 without opposition.

On the right of the Dorset's, at 0650 hrs on the 9th June, the 8th Battalion Durham Light Infantry moved to the south east along the Bayeux to Caen Road, halting one mile behind St Leger. Here the 8th D.L.I. were joined by the tanks of the 24th Lancers, self propelled guns and anti tank crews and their guns. At 0930 hrs this column set off with the infantry riding on the tanks, others followed on their bicycles, though they were of little use as the column did not use the roads but travelled over the rolling cornfields.

After an advance of nearly two miles armoured car patrols reported the enemy near Audrieu Village, these were by passed and the troops pressed on to Point 103. Once in this area the next task was to take St Pierre as the advance could not continue without the capture of this village. At 1745 hrs on 9th June, the Durham men moved forward to the attack, as they did so shells from the self propelled guns of 147 Field Regiment shrieked overhead to explode in the village. The enemy waited until the British troops were almost in the village and then commenced to rain down mortar bombs upon them accompanied by a hail of machine gun fire.

The Durham's took numerous casualties but still pressed forward until they were practically on top of the Germans. In the gardens and streets of St Pierre, fierce close quarter fighting broke out. The battle was short and brutal and in the shock of the assault the Germans fled before these dogged north countrymen, the area being littered with the dead and wounded of both sides. The D.L.I. commenced to dig in as officers ran from position to position preparing the defence for the inevitable counter attack, the Germans that had vacated the village kept up a steady and very accurate stream of mortar bombs upon the Durham's and enemy machine guns made any move in daylight very dangerous.

One or two tanks with the column were hit by long range anti tank gun fire and burned furiously as night fell, the Durham's strengthened their positions that night, the Germans who were still full of fight, prepared to deliver a powerful counter attack with the dawn. At 0615 hrs heavy concentrations of artillery and mortar fire rained down upon St Pierre and the men defending it, the troops braced themselves for the coming ordeal, as the barrage stopped the Germans fell upon the Durham's.

The shock of the assault swept over the first positions as tanks and veteran SS troops poured into St Pierre, heavy defensive fire caused the assault to pause, but the Germans soon reorganised and came on yet again. Frederick Spencer was a nineteen year old Corporal with the D.L.I. and remembers that day in early June only too well:

"During the next few hours we sat it out, exposed to air bursts, moaning minnies, snipers and mortar fire. At night it was standing patrols in the valley on our right flank to prevent infiltration by German patrols. The worst hazard was getting back to the safety of our slit trenches before first light. Our positions were on a forward facing slope and we were harassed each day by an 88 mm SP gun which came forward to fire at us at very close range.

We advanced in extended order in front of a squadron of Sherman tanks. I don't know which was the more disconcerting, the sniper fire from the front or the replies from the tank guns in our rear. The tanks moved through and about 400 yards to our front came under fire from 88 mm guns. I saw at least three blow up, followed by the machine gunning of crew trying to escape. We spent a most uncomfortable time under fire from snipers who had tied themselves into some poplar trees. Some accurate retaliatory fire left several hanging. After dark we were placed among some really thick hedgerows and were told to dig in. As dawn was breaking the sentry pointed out some men 150 yards to our right front. We came under mortar, shell and machine gun fire and German infantry advanced.

'Crouching in our shallow holes we replied with rifle and bren and the infantry ran out of the field on to a hidden sunken road. They tried repeatedly to get at us but we drove them back. A little later I heard the creaking of tank tracks. My heart sank. A Tiger rumbled up the sunken road and stopped at a gap in the hedge about 150 yards away. The tank fired several shells into the bank behind our ditch then moved on and engaged the section on my right. I could hear screams coming from that direction. The tank then moved away and after a spell we were attacked by infantry. I fired the bren and we got them back into the sunken road. During this engagement our two company snipers killed a machine gunner and a man with a grenade thrower creeping along the ditch towards my section. In the sunken road I found a large number of dead Germans." [47]

The 8th D.L.I. were joined by the tanks of the 24th Lancers from Point 103, the first tank to enter St Pierre was hit and burned furiously blocking the road. Two other tanks were hit in the surrounding fields and the rest sought cover in the orchards and hedgerows, the battle roared on with deafening noise as the Germans pressed into the Durham's positions with infantry and armour.

As noon approached the noise of battle subsided and the Germans withdrew, the badly depleted companies of the 8th D.L.I. took stock of their situation. The most forward positions had been abandoned, in the afternoon a platoon and a troop of tanks moved back into the village to deal with enemy troops positioned there.

The Durhams sat tight in their positions throughout the day on the 11th June, at 1900 hrs that evening accurate artillery and mortar fire swept the battered village once again, under cover of this inferno tanks of the 12th SS Panzer Division approached from the east and south east, part of this attacking force by passed the village and made for the Dorsets on Point 103, for a time the 8th D.L.I. were completely surrounded.

The 69th Brigade moved forward at this point to relieve 231 Brigade on Point 103 but ran into the enemy infantry taking part in the counter attack already underway. The 'Tigers' of the 12th SS Panzer launched a ferocious attack on the Dorsets and a bitter struggle ensued with heavy casualties on both sides, 88 shells burst in the trees above the British troops as tanks and infantry fought it out, the men who fought in this area christened Point 103 'Tiger Hill'. The battle continued until 2230 hrs on the night of the 11th June, when the enemy withdrew the Dorsets still held 'Tiger Hill'.

Trooper Fred Ebb was with 61st Reconnaissance Regiment and found himself rounded up with a rag tag group of anybody that could be found to cover some men of the Dorset Regiment as they pulled back:

"The following day was pretty chaotic, the Sergeant Major came round and collected half a dozen of us, it was to give covering fire to some Dorsets that were withdrawing. There was me, the Sergeant Major, the squadron cook, the squadron clerk that was the sort of detachment he gathered up. We took up some positions at the bottom of a ditch with intermittent trees along it. After we'd been there for about an hour a troop of tanks pulled up right behind us spreading out along this ditch line. These Shermans with the short barrels opened fire, they got picked off one after another. Almost as fast as Gerry could reload his gun. One of 'em was right behind us, we heard a dull thud, it was only a couple of feet behind us, two of our lads got hit by splinters. Two seconds after - I've never seen five blokes come out of a tank as quick in my life, it was like a jack in the box. As the last man came out a flame 20 feet high shot out after him. Not long after that we saw some movement and these Dorsets ran across the field towards us.

TROOPS OF THE PANZER LEHR DIVISION IN THE BOCAGE.
10TH JUNE 1944

Our squadron pulled up round the edge of a field, we used to call it going into harbour, we parked the vehicles to give us as much shelter as we could. There was an unfortunate incident, some troops had been out on a fighting patrol, at that time they had a complicated system of passwords that changed at 0100 hrs, these people should have been back hours ago and they didn't have the new password. Our lads opened fire on them and killed one or two." [48]

In and around St Pierre the Durhams refused to give ground and as darkness fell the enemy withdrew leaving behind them a scene of utter desolation and carnage, prisoners taken in this area were found to be Panzer Grenadiers of the 130th Panzer Leher Division.

On 12th June, the Dorsets were relieved by the 5th East Yorkshires of 69th Brigade and the 8th D.L.I. were ordered to withdraw from the St Pierre area as they now occupied a dangerous salient. They left the area with only half the men who went in.

As the spearhead of the 50th Division ground to a halt, the 7th Armoured Divisions pressed forward on the 50ths right flank in an attempt to reach Villers Bocage, the 56th Brigade accompanied them in this thrust. On the 13th June, the 22nd Armoured Brigade entered Villers Bocage and came up against opposition that grew stronger by the hour, the British armour suffered heavy casualties from anti tank and mortar fire and enemy tanks appeared in great numbers. The 2nd Panzer Division had just arrived at the battle front and the British armour had run straight into them.

The narrow streets echoed to the sound of battle as the Desert Rats and 2nd Panzer fought it out, Sergeant Robert Bramwell, MM, commanded a firefly tank - a Sherman with a 17 pounder gun - in three troop, 4th County of London Yeomanry:

> "It was about 10 am when we first heard firing from the town, machine guns and the vicious 'crack' of an 88 mm. That was the first hint anything was wrong. A Tiger came into the village, I think up the road from Longvillers, first it wiped out the artillery observer tanks, these were Sherman tanks with the gun removed to make space from the radio, but equipped on the outside with a wooden gun barrel - poor devils. Then it got most of the Recce troop, the Tiger smashed its way through Villers to the western outskirts on our front, where my colleague, Sergeant Lockwood - also in a Firefly, engaged it with his 17 pounder, he didn't knock it out but he certainly scared it off. Meanwhile other German tanks were attacking 'A' Squadron on the hill. They blew up the leading tank and then the one at the back, which pinned the rest of the squadron down. He then rolled down our line knocking out all the rest, killing or capturing a lot of our chaps - it was a shambles.
>
> Villers was just a large village really with lots of firing going on mainly concentrated on a square near the High Street. Soon afterwards three German tanks came down the High Street, I am sure the one in the lead was a Mark IV, I fired at it and missed. Fortunately a 6 pounder anti tank gun of the Queen's was brought up and they knocked it out, the next tank along was a Tiger, I had reversed back a bit and I could see it through the windows of the house on the corner, so we traversed our gun and began to engage it through the windows, first with HE (High Explosive) which made a terrible mess of the house and then with AP (Armour Piercing), I don't know how many shots we fired but we knocked it out." [49]

The road out of Villers to Point 213 was crowded with Tigers moving forward to reinforce the Germans in and around the village, the situation became hopeless and all British troops in Villers were ordered to withdraw.

Driver T D Hawken, MM, was with the County of London Yeomanry that day but his luck ran out as the enemy closed in:

> "Early in the morning while we were cooking breakfast came the order 'Move at once'.
>
> As we approached the town of Villers we came under heavy shell fire. On reaching the town Lord Cranley left our tank and went ahead to 'A' Squadron by scout car.
>
> Major Carr took over command. We were able to see the Honey tanks ahead being knocked out and the crews being machine gunned as they

Cpl T. D. Hawken. MM.
4th County of London
Yeomanry. RAC.

baled out (this I will never forget). Major Carr on seeing what was happening ordered me to turn right into a field. I drove into the field, straight through the gate and turned around facing the road. We saw a Tiger tank coming down the road. Sgt. Jack Pumphrey called for Harry Ramsbottom who was sat next to me (a wireless operator to Brigade) to come and load the gun.

Harry was able to do this and Jack fired two shots both hitting the enemy tank at close range but they were not powerful enough to do any damage. Wittman traversed his gun, fired, and we received a direct hit and immediately caught fire.

I was able to get out through the co-driver's door when I heard Jack shouting 'Help me with Harry'. Sgt Francis appeared and between us we were able to help them both out. We took cover as best we could behind a large tree and hedge. Jack and Harry were badly burned.

I have no recollection of Major Carr, however, having received a direct hit at such close range, I myself was rather dazed. By this time the German infantry arrived and we were all taken prisoner. One of them pinched my cap badge. I wish he would return it!

A German officer came up in a staff car - a Volkswagen, shouting and raving and then he stopped and fired his pistol, of course we all scattered and then the guards got hold of him and put him back in the staff car. It turned out all his family had been killed the day before in Berlin. He killed six of our soldiers at the back of the column, I was lucky I was at the front." [50]

This action fought by the 7th Armoured Division depended on the capture of Villers Bocage in order to threaten the supply lines of the enemy opposing the 50th Division to the north, this did not succeed and the enemy got the better of the first battle for this small French village, the 7th Armoured were withdrawn after having suffered severe casualties in tanks and men and took their place in the line to the right of the 50th.

This brought to an end the first attempts to capture Villers Bocage and Tilly Sur Seulles, while this was going on, despite the weather, Allied strength was building up in the bridge head, which did not expand as quickly as troops poured into it from the sea. Endless streams of jeeps, lorries, tanks and armoured cars clogged up the little roads of Normandy. This was a volume of traffic these little roads were not constructed to cope with and they were soon pounded to dust.

INFANTRY GETTING A LIFT FORWARD FROM THE TANKS OF THE 8TH ARMOURED BRIGADE.
JULY 1944. (*AUTHOR'S COLLECTION*)

Among all of this bustle and confusion a great force was being concentrated in the bridge head, getting ready for the day it would burst forth across France and Belgium and eventually enter the Reich itself. But this was in the future, the 50th Division had been fighting for nearly two weeks while the main force was still landing and there remained for them no immediate relief from the fatal bocage.

CHAPTER EIGHT

THE DEADLY BOCAGE
(June/July 1944)

The 50th Division was now to enter upon one of the most unpleasant periods in its history, it was here in the bocage countryside that the division was to fight a war of attrition for a month - centred around the general area of Tilly Sur Seulles, Hottot and La Belle Epine. The British and Canadians were suffering heavy casualties but they were achieving exactly what Montgomery intended - the destruction of the German armour, his policy was to pull the Germans onto the British Second Army and fight them in the bocage so the US First Army could carry out their tasks against lighter opposition.

The life of an infantryman, of both sides, in this bloody slogging match was often short. Two armies, each possessing enormous fire power, were locked in furious close quarter combat in the mazy bocage and mere men stood little chance of survival. Tanks blasted the infantry at close range, shells rained down without warning and deadly accurate mortar fire took a steady toll in lives. At times it was impossible to see a man or a machine in the closely hedged Norman bocage; but on the soft summer breezes there could be seen the black clouds of flies and the smell of cordite and charred flesh filled the nostrils. All around were to be found the sad little mounds of earth topped with wooden crosses, a boltless rifle or a steel helmet, marking where some young man had met his end in this verdant countryside. Many dead farm animals littered the countryside, each one grotesquely bloated, stinking and crawling with maggots. Bulldozers buried those in the safe areas but those in the killing zone were a constant torment to troops who lived with the thought that an erupting shell might throw one of these stinking apparitions near them or worse into their trench. This rancid stench of putrefaction was at times overpowering on these hot summer days in the bocage.

The attritional battles of June 1944, ground on without pause, the effectiveness of this tactic can be judged by the fact that Rommel was unable to mount any counter attacks during this time on the British sector and had been forced to squander his panzers. However the Americans were running short of ammunition and had to postpone their planned break out for three days; which meant the British and Canadians had to go on fighting the bulk of the enemy forces for longer than contemplated, and because of the gales in June, three British divisions had to delay their landings, so the British troops already in the bridge head fought on with fewer men than expected.

On 13th June, 69 Brigade was relieved - by the 49th (West Riding) Division after some hard fighting east of the River Seulles and marched off to a rest area in the rear. Pte Tateson of the 7th Green Howards remembers the luxury of the baths at Bayeux:

"The next morning everything seemed peaceful and calm, and a cow was grazing quite close to us. All the civilian farm workers having disappeared, the cow's udders were very distended and we decided we could do both the cow and ourselves a good turn by milking it. One of our number took the task upon himself and a hilarious half hour ensued as he stealthily approached the animal, mess tin in hand. The cow would docilely suffer him to take up position before gently strolling away. Each time this happened the lad was successively cheered on and then greeted with howls of derision as the cow negligently defeated his efforts.

During the brief period in the cow pasture we made ourselves very comfortable in our hole in the ground. We lined it with our capes and installed one of our radios which we illegally re-tuned to the home service. The contrast of our recent experiences with the sound of Vera Lynn singing "We'll meet again" was profound and very moving, however corny and sentimental this may sound now.

On the afternoon of the 13th, the Green Howards handed over to the K.O.Y.L.I.s of the 49th Division and we moved off to the rest area near Conde-sur-Seulles. Here we bivouacked in the orchards adjoining the Manoir de Ghene. The following day we were taken to Bayeux, the first town to fall to the Allied armies, and visited the baths for the luxury of a shower. We also had an hour or so to ourselves and a few of us indulged in the exotic pleasure of visiting a wine bar. Our approach to this period of freedom was not that of tourists admiring the ancient churches and buildings." [51]

In the setting of sunshine, cultivated fields, deep meadows and orchards the 50th Division prepared itself for the next bloody round. On the 14th June, a divisional attack was to be launched, headed by the 231st and 151st Brigades, the 9th D.L.I. advanced upon the village of Lingevres, with the 6th Battalion moving towards the neighbouring village of Verrieres - with the intention of pressing on to Hottot if possible.

The Hampshire's and Dorset's of 231st Brigade were to advance upon the cross roads and surrounding areas of the village of La Senaudiere. Troops were pulled back while the RAF strafed and bombed the orchards near Verrieres and the main road that connected Lingevres and Tilly. The divisional artillery laid down a thundering creeping barrage and at 1015 hrs the troops crossed their start line; this was not without incident for the Dorset's as the barrage came down upon their start line and inflicted heavy casualties on 'B' Company.

The advance went well at first as the troops followed the thundering barrage, but once the inferno had passed over, the enemy met the British with machine gun, mortar and sniper fire, the troops were soon heavily engaged by well dug in veterans who intended to hold onto every yard of ground. Pte Clarke pressed on with the 8th DLI into fierce resistance:

> "The Germans were that strong we couldn't get forward, they were shootin' us up left and right. We was gettin' fresh troops up all the time to make our numbers up - lads with no experience." [52]

All day on the 14th June, the fighting raged as the troops pressed forward taking heavy casualties in the process. Pte Mawson was a dispatch rider with 86th Field Regiment - RA at the time and had to stop for a call of nature and found himself in the middle of a battle:

> "It was like hell let loose and everybody was on edge. I had to relieve myself and I went into the hedgerow and saw an infantryman who said 'Keep down, there's a sniper in that tree. Hold on, I'll get him.' And he did; the sniper dropped like a stone. As I looked over the hedge there was around a hundred Bosch, some sitting, some lying but all dead. I asked the infantryman about them and he said 'We have to make good our losses,' and he never batted an eyelid. Soon after this the chain came off my motor cycle and I was busy with it when someone tapped me on the shoulder. I nearly jumped six feet. It was a German giving himself up! He even helped me with the chain. I told him to get on the back and took him several miles to a prisoner of war cage - I made sure he didn't get shot." [53]

British and German tanks burnt furiously around each objective as the battle reached a crescendo of noise and violence, by evening the situation was stabilising as each unit reached their own destination and made contact with other units involved in the attack. Troops began to dig in and consolidate their positions in the early evening, no sooner had this been done when a vigorous counter attack was made upon the Durhams at 1700 hrs by the Panzer Lehr Division, this was repulsed however and heavy losses were inflicted upon the enemy. To give some idea of the toll taken in such vicious actions here are the casualty figures for one of the four attacking battalions involved in this one day action:

6th Battalion D.L.I.

Killed	Wounded	Missing
25	65	15

On 15th June 69 Brigade moved forward in preparation for an attack on 16th, all three battalions of the 69th were to advance a distance of nearly four thousand yards to their objective which was the main road south of the road Lingevres/ Tilly-sur-Seulles. By the end of the day on the 16th June the 69th were still short of their final objective due to stiff enemy resistance. The leading troops were south of Lingevres but short of the actual village and finished up holding a line south westward towards the River Aure ant Longnaye.

SGT TREVOR INGRAM (LEFT), 6TH BN DLI.
VERRIERES 14TH JUNE 1944. (*IMPERIAL WAR MUSEUM*)

Both physically and mentally this battle of attrition began to take its toll, Pte Tateson of the 7th Green Howards saw his officers and comrades die around him, this had a demoralising effect even on seasoned campaigners like him:

"Almost immediately the Battalion encountered strong opposition. 'A' Company to which I was attached, was on the right of the road behind 'C' Company. There was an enemy 88 mm gun firing directly down the road to prevent any movement of vehicles along it and progress was slow. The two leading Companies came under heavy mortar and machine gun fire and their commanders, Major Bowley and Boyle were both killed. I heard on my radio the signaller accompanying Major Bowley desperately pleading for the Medical Officer to come to the Majors aid as he was dying. Major Bowley was a gentle mannered, civilised person and it affected me to hear so poignantly his actual dying. Major Boyle was also a popular officer but of an entirely opposite personality - extrovert, dashing and courageous to the point of foolhardiness, and a bit of a showman. The sudden loss of these two officers had a terribly depressing effect on us all, and particularly on those who had served with the Battalion all through the Western Desert and Sicily campaigns. We were in a very sombre mood when we settled down for the night.

On coming under fire, the men would go to ground in the standing crops and I was constantly hearing the message that one or other platoon was pinned down. The tanks which were endeavouring to give support lost contact since they had no clear field of vision. On one occasion our section was crawling along the side of a hedge when the chap in front of me disturbed a wasps' nest. The wasps came up in a swarm round our heads; but round his in particular, he immediately came up on his knees and started beating around with his hands in spite of our urgent demands of 'for Christ's sake get down.' Whether he was seen or not I don't know but soon afterwards a burst of machine gun fire rattled through the hedge and twigs dropped on me as we lay motionless. Perhaps it was simply desultory fire at any hedge where we might be lurking, since after a time we were able to press on.

This morning of the 18th, morale was pretty low all round. The heavy casualties of the two previous days had had a depressing effect on everyone and whilst fear seems to be forgotten when everything is happening the dread moment comes when, after a few hours of rest, the word is given that we are to make another attack. Then the stomach sinks and a leaden feeling spreads throughout the body.

By this time the Battalion had lost fifteen officers and over two hundred men. In his subsequent report Colonel Richardson commented that both officers and men were very tired and suffering from lack of sleep." [54]

This attack by the 69th Brigade brought a fierce reaction from the Germans and on the afternoon of the 18th June heavy counter attacks fell upon the Yorkshiremen, the 7th Green Howards and 5th East Yorkshires fell back to the west, Sgt Max Hearst was with the East Yorkshires:

"We took over from the Hampshire's, as we marched in and they moved out everybody was in the open when mortar bombs began to drop amongst us. Blokes were hit by the dozen - mainly Hampshire's. Sergeant Major Bert Greener was hit, we'd started to dig in, Bert and I were sat facing each other with our tin hats touching and a bomb landed behind me - missed me but got him. I said 'are you hit', he held his hand up and you could see through the hole in it, I said 'it's nowt Bert you'll be aright', applied pressure to stop the bleeding and put a couple of field dressings on it. I set off with Bert for the CCS, there was casualties laid everywhere, blokes were pinned under fallen trees, others had been impaled and were screaming - it was bloody chaos." [55]

Pte Mountford was with the 7th Green Howards during this action and like many others his war finished here:

"The extract from the war diary reads - '69 Bde was ordered hastily forward to exploit what was believed to be another gap in the German line around the village of Cristot.' Not a particularly gaping gap - they were waiting for

THE LONLINESS OF THE BATTLE-FIELD. TROOPS ADVANCE THROUGH A CORNFIELD
TOWARDS THE EVER PRESENT ENEMY. 14TH JUNE 1944. (*IMPERIAL WAR MUSEUM*)

us - Panzer Lehr Bayerlein Grenadiers in fact. Some of them were the same troops we fought in North Africa.

We became hopelessly pinned down in a shallow ditch alongside a hedge which we had just scrambled through with what was left of two rifle companies. All the same nobody surrendered until our Colonel did.

After being disarmed, we were marched past a line of panzer tanks, no wonder the stuff that was fired at us was on the heavy side, then across a field and there was the main road across our front which we had been ordered to take, I might say without artillery support or the backing of any vehicle - armoured or otherwise.

Marching back from the front we found to be a bit hazardous as some of the German drivers tried to 'skittle' us as they passed. Overnight was spent in a farm yard with their medium artillery blasting away in the next field." [56]

Pte Tateson, also of the 7th Battalion, remembers the traumatic feeling generated as he became disarmed and completely vulnerable after the excitement of combat:

"I have a recollection of coming across an abandoned machine gun post with a dead German soldier lying covered by a blanket, I turned back a corner of the blanket covering the dead man's head. There was no blood on his face but a very small hole in the middle of his forehead. Foolishly I stood there gazing at him and thinking that somewhere in Germany his relatives had still to be told that he no longer existed; his face was of a narrow triangular type with a small mouth and his hair was dark and lank. The picture of his face remains clear in my mind after all these years, I covered his face again and moved on with a feeling of shame for having intruded.

As night fell there were four of us in an advanced position near to the wooded country to which the enemy had withdrawn earlier that day. Our group of four consisted - so far as I can be sure - of Sgt. Potterton, Ted Russell, myself and the C.O.'s batman who was acting as company runner. Sgt Potterton told us that he 'didn't know where the hell Major Spark had got to.' He told us to stay put under cover of a ditch whilst he went off to arrange for more ammunition. He did not return and it soon became obvious to us that under cover of darkness the Germans had put in a heavy counter attack and that in fact we had walked into a carefully planned trap. They were all around us, tanks on the road to our rear and German voices shouting in the woods close by. There was heavy and constant firing all around but mostly from the rear and we realised that we were completely cut off. Ted Russell now being the senior N.C.O., told us to ditch our equipment, including the wireless sets, and this we did. The intention was that we should try to filter back through the enemy to our own troops. Whether we could have got out is very doubtful; after reading Col. Richardson's account I should say impossible. However, matters were decided for us when, hearing Germans approaching our scanty cover Ted leaped up and surrendered.

The psychological effect of being taken prisoner is an almost complete numbing of the senses, we were lined up with our hands on our heads by men with Schmeiser automatics and it went through my head that they might be going to shoot us out of hand. The dulling effect of anti climax however meant that this thought simply left me with a detached feeling almost of curiosity rather than fear. From prolonged intense excitement leading to near exhaustion we now experienced a complete lowing of the senses, even that of self preservation. When dumping my kit I had recovered a leather writing wallet containing a photograph of Olive and her letters to me and simply slipped this inside my battledress blouse. Now, with my hands on my head, the wallet slipped down and fell to the floor. I stooped and picked it up, in so doing risking an instant burst of fire and a quick death." [57]

While the enemy concentrated their efforts upon 69 Brigade the 2nd Essex Regiment and 6th D.L.I. attacked Tilly-Sur-Seulles, and by last light commanded the approaches to and the area around the village - it fell the next day. Tanks and artillery supported the troops closely during this action and suffered the inevitable casualties.

Trooper Dewar was a gunner in a Sherman tank of the Nott's Yeomanry:
"A small French girl, in a village we liberated, gave us a tame live rabbit which I called Abdull. He was our lucky mascot and lived in the turret on my great coat. Captain Fern saw what he said were Germans with horses through his binoculars, he ordered us to fire high explosive shells at the farm. I loaded about 20 shells and Abdull scampered into the side sponson as empty shell cases fell upon the turret floor. Nitro Cellulose fumes from

the gun are inevitably inhaled filling the lungs unpleasantly. We proceeded firing our sponsons at various Germans observed running. [58]

Bombardier Jack Styan of Batttle-Axe Coy, RA, was caught up in a night barrage and recalls with vivid clarity the sight of his first casualty:

"One night the tanks moved into a field beside us, the Germans must have had the range and started shelling like mad. I heard one of our lads cry out and I went over to him, he was sat against a wall with his legs stretched out. I went to pick him up and his body just parted in the middle, I just put him back, that was the first real casualty I had seen." [59]

When Tilly finally fell to the 50th Division the sight it presented was one of utter desolation, shells and bombs had battered it beyond recognition leaving a pitiful sight for the victors. This was to be, for the troops of 50 Division, the first of many such towns and villages to be well and truly obliterated in the process of liberation. The enemies grip on Tilly had been prised loose and the heavy casualties suffered was the price paid, the whole division had suffered 673 killed, 3,072 wounded or maimed, with 1,236 missing, only 505 of the latter were accounted for later. But the viscous killing match was not over by any means as the enemy waited at the next village - Hottot.

The troops of the 231st Brigade attacked Hottot early in the afternoon of the 19th June in pouring rain, the attacking companies moved forward over the difficult ground under a storm of mortar bombs and bullets. The village was held in strength by the Germans but the attackers pressed forward until it was reached, that achievement brought a most violent reaction from the enemy who counter attacked in force with panther tanks and drove the Hampshire's back. Later in the day the 2nd Devon's forced their way back into this smouldering heap of ruins - repelling several determined counter attacks to maintain their precarious hold. During the night 231 Brigade were forced to retire and the Germans moved into Hottot once more. Lt Blackmore was with 'A' Coy, 1st Hampshire's:

"The attack on Hottot started in pouring rain, which began before noon. The start line was neatly marked with white tape, and the enemy gave it (and us) a terrific plastering with his mortars. We pushed forward under a heavy barrage with our Brens fighting a staccato duel against the faster b-r-r-r-p of Jerry's Spandaus. In the din it was difficult at first to know which was his artillery and which was ours, but one soon realised where the 'receiving end' was when we reached a sunken lane, evidently well pin-pointed by the enemy. Several men in 'D' Company (the leading forma-tion) were also held up in this lane. But the place was decidedly too hot for comfort; so we climbed up the bank and dashed across the next field through a hail of mortar bombs and bullets, luckily without any casualties. We shoved over a lot more artillery than the enemy; he seemed to rely more on his mortars.

We got to close quarters with him at a farm. One of his Panther tanks came rumbling forward right up to our position, firing everything it had. With great presence of mind, one of our anti-tank gunners caught the Panther amid - ships, but not before it had managed to get one of our Shermans belonging to the Sherwood Rangers who were in support. Both caught fire but the Sherman crew managed to get out all right. The 'brewed up' tanks, now well ablaze, began to attract heavy mortar fire, and although 'A' Company were still supposed to be in reserve, we moved forward towards the farm where Major J Littlejohns (commanding 'D' Company) had set up his headquarters.

No sign of the rain stopping after ten hours. Everyone is tired and wet, we have moved forward nearly a mile from La Senaudiere, with Hottot just another thousand yards ahead." [60]

After the failure of this attack the division settled down to an unpleasant period of close contact with the enemy, the snipers paradise that was the Norman bocage took a steady toll of men even when no major action was being fought. Constantly the British pressed the Germans to keep the pressure on, mortar bombs and shell fire came down without warning and both sides suffered casualties daily, many good men lost their lives in this static warfare.

On the 8th July. 151st Brigade was to be found in the general area of Tilly, the 231st Brigade was north of Hottot, 69th Brigade was south of La Belle Epine and Senaudiere and on their right was the 56th Brigade. On this day the battle for Hottot was taken up again as the 56th Brigade pressed forward with the intention of getting across the main road west of the village, enemy troops and tanks were concentrated in this area and the attacking troops of the 56th were met by heavy machine gun and mortar fire. During the afternoon the troops reached their objective, but even as they prepared new positions heavy tanks were rumbling forward to take part in the counter attack, by the evening the two leading battalions had been forced to withdraw north of the road. The 56th Brigade attack had brought the divisional front closer to the main road but the Germans were determined to take back the ground lost, at 0600 hours the next day nearly thirty enemy tanks, with three companies of infantry spread out between them, attacked the 2nd Essex Regiment and in the melee eight German tanks were knocked out and many of their infantry killed as the counter attack was repelled.

With the 56th Brigade so far forward it now fell to 231st Brigade to complete the move and take Hottot itself, at 0700 hours on the morning of 11th July, a massive barrage fell before the troops as they waited on their start line, it rumbled forward at a very slow pace as it was necessary to allow the infantry a steady pace of advance in this close bocage countryside, the creeping barrage was to halt at agreed points to allow the infantry time to mop up resistance and maintain the agreed timetable.

A BRITISH INFANTRY PATROL IN THE BOCAGE.
JUNE 1944. (*IMPERIAL WAR MUSEUM*)

The lead troops, the 1st Hampshire's (on the right) and the 2nd Devon's (on the left), were supported by the Sherman tanks of the Sherwood Rangers, flail tanks, flame throwing tanks (crocodiles), mortars and machine gun fire, their objective being the village of Hottot and the high ground beyond. In the tradition of the bocage, and Hottot in particular, the fighting for this much disputed village was bitter in the extreme, tanks blasted away at each other, the cruel flame throwers spewed out their venom in great arcs of fire as the barrage rumbled forward and the infantry fought it out in the ditches and hedgerows:

Pte Peter Cuerdon was with the 1st Hampshire's at Hottot:

"Hottot? My god that was a terrible place to be, it's dreadful country to fight in, all bocage and perfect for Gerry who was on the defensive. We went from field to field, this was the place we spent the longest time - about three weeks, we couldn't shift 'em out of Hottot. As they started to bring up armour we saw some Tigers, we were dug in in a big field and a Tiger came to our front, there's nothing more eerie than the sound of a tank grinding and clanking it's way towards you, we put our heads down pretty sharp. He stopped quite close and two of these chappies got out to have sandwiches or something and then they suddenly pulled out much to our relief. There were times when even an infantryman thought the better of things, if you fired a shot in the evening you would find it triggered off the other side to do the same and you ended up in the middle of a major confrontation for nothing. There were a lot of occasions when you kept quiet, gallantry wasn't always the best thing. Typhoons came over and blasted Hottot to try and shift Gerry, the poor devils we took prisoner always looked very dejected, half starved and very young." [61]

The battle increased in intensity as noon was passed, the noise was terrific and unceasing as each side pounded the other with mortar and artillery fire. The Hampshire's in particular had suffered heavily as they pressed forward against a determined enemy, but their tenacity paid off and in the early afternoon their lead troops entered Hottot. At this point two incidents occurred that were to have tragic consequences, the men had been fighting through the heat of a very hot day against very fierce opposition, at the point of achieving their objective shells from their own artillery came down upon them inflicting more casualties on the surviving troops. Their positions on the Hottot Road also took a pounding as Typhoons screamed out of the sky mistaking them for the enemy, bombing and strafing these unfortunate men. Lt Colonel Howie went forward to find out what was happening as no radio contact with the companies could by made, as he directed the forward troops he was killed. Lt Blackmore has cause to remember that terrible day well:

"We began the attack on Hottot at 0700 hrs., starting off with a hand to hand party in the orchard. I got the leading section of 7 Platoon near the southern end under covering fire without much trouble, and then Jerry gave us everything he had at point blank range.

At this stage Horace Wright, who was in the adjoining field, crawled up to give me further orders through the hedge, and while he was talking I had the uncomfortable sensation that my backside was being made a target for Spandau fire. From his position in the ditch on his side of the hedge he couldn't see the ground being churned up behind me, whereas I was uncomfortably well aware of the fact! Luckily the gunner was a bad shot.

For a while things were somewhat hectic, but Private R Robins did a good job single handed with a Bren gun, charging into a heavily defended post and silencing it, after which we had things our own way. The enemy now began to surrender, and fourteen of them came out - two or three of whom were boys of about eighteen years or so, but fierce fighters for all that. I counted seven enemy dead in the orchard, and there were also several badly wounded Huns who seemed glad enough to be put 'in the bag' after their ordeal.

After a brief pause to regroup, 'A' Company then advanced and reached its first objective (known as 'Orange') without meeting anything worse than moderately heavy mortar fire. But after we had consolidated the position, hell was let loose on us by mortars and 88 mm shells for two or three hours, causing further casualties among the company.

In the afternoon we moved forward again and reached the outskirts of Hottot at about 1530 hrs after getting through some really heavy mortar fire. Here we dug in, there were woods to our left and right and the houses of Hottot itself could be seen about 500 yards to our immediate front. Tanks from the Sherwood Rangers - complete with flails and flame-throwing Crocodiles - were now in close support. Then at about 1600 hrs., I heard the drone of approaching aircraft - our Typhoons were coming over.

The engines of the nearest aircraft roared as the plane began to dive, but with a feeling that quickly changed from one of relief to horror, I realised that our RAF friends were attacking our positions! Not altogether surprising because the whole picture was very confused, our tanks being in close combat with the enemy's. The first rocket came down with a mighty roar and I felt a somewhat queasy sensation in the pit of my stomach as the rocket exploded in a wood about seventy yards away. The Typhoon in question banked for a second attack when one of our tanks managed to fire a yellow identification signal just in time to warn the pilot. He rose steeply and flew on without firing. Then a Panther tank opened up on our right flank and moved towards us, but another of our Typhoons spotted it and attacked immediately. There was an ear splitting explosion and the Panther rocked sideways then halted abruptly while red and orange flames rapidly engulfed it and set fire to its ammunition. Another tank was also hit judging by the flames that rose from a near by copse, but it was now becoming impossible to see anything clearly through the thickening smoke.

Despite a prolonged and accurate bombardment we hung on to our forward positions with our right flank dangerously exposed. During much of the time there was a lot of confused firing in our rear and it seemed as if the enemy were launching some kind of counter attack from the woods south of the Chateau de Cordillon. We heard later that they had done so twice but with limited success, against the 1st Dorsets, who were able to prevent them from making any serious penetration.

After nightfall 'A' Company was given orders to withdraw, which we managed to do in orderly fashion and without further incident, passing silently within less than 200 yards of the enemy who made a great deal of noise digging in. However they didn't hear us and we got back to a position some 250 yards north-east of the Ferme de la Briajere. Although most of us could cheerfully have fallen asleep standing up - we were pretty tired - it was irritating to yield the ground that we had won at the cost of severe casualties." [62]

By the end of the day the 231st Brigade held a line just north of Hottot with the enemy still in possession of the village. On the night of 18th/19th July, the German troops withdrew from the 50th Divisions front leaving the ruined village of Hottot empty.

The enemy withdrew in good order leaving in their wake mines and booby traps in profusion, through this carnage followed the 50th pressing the enemy constantly. This brought to an end a bitter and bloody phase in the divisional story, no set piece battles, no swift blitzkrieg assaults, only a bloody slogging match to hold the German armour in one place and destroy it. The 50th was being bled white in the bocage and the man power situation was becoming critical. In the Normandy battles the division had suffered 4,476 casualties - officers and other ranks, companies were below strength and the green recruits taking the place of veteran soldiers were not in sufficient numbers to totally compensate for the troops lost in this blood-letting.

Albert Carman was called up in November 1943, at the age of 18, he was among a draft of new troops that joined the 50th Division at the end of July 1944. As a young lad he had read of the exploits of the men of 50 Division and never dreamed he would become part of such a prestigious unit:

"We landed at Arromanches and marched to Bayeux, the action had moved inland and you could hear the ominous rumble of gun fire in the distance. The best way one can describe our feelings is to say we were very apprehensive. At Bayeux we went to a reinforcement holding unit, one waits there while units need reinforcing. In my case it happened to be the 6th D.L.I. who were part of the 50th Division. I'd read about them when they were fighting in North Africa when I was only 15 or 16, I never thought I'd be part of them.

They were great lads, a lot of them were veterans, I felt quite honoured to be with such experienced people. A lot of these chaps were older than me, when you're 18 someone who is 25 or 26 is old. Us rookies would be talking together and the older chaps would be talking knowing that we would be listening - they would be saying 'remember old so-and-so? Aye lost his leg didn't he', they were only saying this just to frighten us to death and of course they succeeded. But they were very good - took you under their wing, they were good lads." [63]

CHAPTER NINE

THE FALL OF VILLERS BOCAGE AND ON TO OLD FAMILIAR BATTLEFIELDS
(July to September 1944)

The allied forces that had fought so hard in Normandy were now ready to break out in a movement that would carry them to the borders of the Reich, in order to understand the 50th Divisions role in this act it is necessary to outline the broader picture of events now taking place. On July 18th, the 8th (British) Corps made a large scale attack south east from Caen, it was preceded by a gigantic air assault by Bomber Command and the U.S. Air Force. The grand scale of these operations and the destruction they wrought will never be forgotten by those who witnessed them. In tight formation rank upon rank of bombers flew over Caen, dropped their bombs and wheeled about for home, in the British bridgehead and on the enemy side the ground heaved and trembled as each new load of high explosive detonated on this undefended city, the stink of cordite filled the nostrils and the air was thick with brick dust as each building was raised to the ground. 1,100 British heavy bombers, 1,600 Flying Fortresses and Liberators, 600 British and American medium bombers and 1,200 fighter bombers rained down 8,000 tons of high explosives in two hours.

Even so all did not go well with the attack and it was away to the west with the American First Army that the ball was set in motion on the 25th July, supported by another vast air armada they struck south along the West coast of the Cherbourg Peninsula and in gloriously sunny weather swept through Le Mans and on in a great northerly arc to Argentan. Pressing south to meet them came the British Second Army advancing to the general line Vire Conde-Sur-Noireau/ Falaise, here was formed the infamous Falaise pocket in which a whole German army was slaughtered by the bombs, tanks and artillery of the allied forces.

The Second Army launched its offensive on July 30th, on the right flank was VIII Corps - newly refitted and rested after its costly attack south east from Caen, in the centre was XXX Corps consisting of the 50th, 43rd, and 7th Armoured Divisions; and in line eastward stretched the units of the XII Corps, the I Corps and the Canadian Corps. In this drive south to meet the Americans the 50th Divisions role in events can be divided into two parts; firstly the capture of the

A SGT SNIPER OF THE 5TH BN EAST YORKSHIRE RGT
CLEANS HIS RIFLE WHILST HIS COMRADE CATCHES UP
ON SOME SLEEP. JULY 1944. (*IMPERIAL WAR MUSEUM*)

Amaye feature - advancing to Villers Bocage; secondly the advance to Conde-Sur-Noireau.

Against slackening opposition the troops of the 56th and 231st Brigades pressed forward to the high ground in the vicinity of Anctoville and Feuguerolles-Sur-Seulles and were firmly entrenched here by the 1st August. On 2nd August 69 Brigade, in the face of small arms fire only, attacked and captured an important hill to the west of Villers Bocage - known as the Amaye feature. This was followed by the capture of Tracy Bocage which stands on the high ground just outside the town of Villers. These new positions were shelled constantly by the enemy for over twenty four hours.

The advance to Tracy Bocage and the southward pressure being applied on the left by the 59th Division tightened the Allied grip on Villers Bocage, on the morning of the 4th August the final enemy 'Hate' (bombardment) came down on the 1st Dorset's - a farewell from a departing enemy. 'C' and 'D' Companies sent out patrols which took many prisoners and in the afternoon a patrol from 'C' Company under Cpl Boydell, reached the outskirts of Villers Bocage. Permission was given for them to press forward and Sgt Moss led a patrol into the town itself, the scene was one of utter carnage, British and German burnt out tanks and lorries littered the streets - bearing witness to the savage struggle that had taken place here between the 7th Armoured Division and 2nd Panzer Division. Each street was raised to the ground after incessant poundings by the RAF and Allied artillery, quietly the dazed troops picked their way through the demolished buildings - always mindful of booby traps on this bright and sunny August day. The name of this town had become a household name in England as the viscous battle for its possession had rumbled on and, at long last, it was in the hands of the 50th Division, just under two months behind schedule.

On August 5th the whole of the 50th Division was relieved and moved out of the front-line; this was their first break from the front since they landed on D-Day and what a welcome experience it was. For the next two or three days the men could relax as new recruits swelled their ranks, elsewhere the attack was in full swing as the Americans forced a passage through the Avranches bottleneck, virtually cutting off Brittany from the rest of France and forming the Falaise Pocket by thrusting their armour eastwards. To the east of the pocket a route still lay wide open through which a German withdrawal to the line of the Seine was still a possibility, Hitler however had other ideas and, determined not to yield a yard of ground, ordered a counter attack to the west from the Mortain area in order to cut across the American lines of communication and emerge on the west coast. On August 7th four Panzer Divisions struck out towards Avranches and the 2nd SS Panzer Division recaptured Mortain, here the counter attack ground to a halt as the massive air power of the allied Forces came into action and strafed and bombed the advancing German armour, over one hundred German tanks were destroyed in the battle. By August 12th all hopes of a breakout by the Germans had evaporated, but by that time the American outflanking armour was in the process of completing its great wheel; capturing the town of Alencon and pressing on northward, with the British moving towards Falaise to meet them. And so the jaws of the pocket had been steadily closing as the Germans wasted their energies on a doomed counter attack, ordering such an action Hitler had sealed their fate and cancelled out any hopes of a sound withdrawal from the Normandy campaign.

On August 6th the 43rd (Wessex) Division captured Mount Pincon opening the way southward to Conde-Sur-Noireau, the seizure of this town would eliminate a vital point in any enemy withdrawal to the north. The 7th Armoured Division was ordered forward at once with the 50th Division following up; the armour however found the going harder than expected in this enclosed countryside and once more 50 Division found themselves in the front-line on August 9th.

Over the southern slopes on Mount Pincon the road from Le Plessis Grimault falls gradually for nearly four miles until it reaches St Pierre La Vieille on the road to Conde. On either side of St Pierre stands two hills - on the western side is point 229 and on the eastern side point 266. From here the road runs over higher ground to the north of the village of Proussy and down into the valley at Conde.

The 50th Division advanced on the 9th August into stiff enemy resistance, the 151st Brigade - supported by 13th/18th Hussars attacked south through Le Plessis; their own barrage whined overhead exploding on the enemy positions and shell fire, mortar bombs and machine gun fire harried the attacking Durhams. They pressed their attack home to a point two and a half miles north of St Pierre and at 1400 hours 69 Brigade passed through them making slow progress because of the desperate rearguard actions being fought by the Germans. Lt Colonel Hastings of the 6th Green Howards commented on the enemy:

> "The Germans met in the last fortnight had been quite different from those of the coastal divisions. They came mainly from 12th SS Hitler Jugend and the 130th Panzer Lehr Divisions and were, on the whole, young men who had been brought up as Nazis and were prepared to die rather than surrender; these were determined fighters." [64]

After a mile the advance ground to a halt, as the 69th Brigade consolidated its position it came under heavy fire from 88's and heavy calibre artillery. The plan for the next day was for the 5th Battalion East Yorkshire Regiment to continue the attack with the object of capturing St Pierre and point 229; the only forming up place however was under direct observation by the enemy gunners and it seemed the 5th East Yorkshires would inevitably suffer heavy losses before the attack got underway. As daylight broke on the 10th August luck was with the Yorkshiremen - the area was covered in a dense blanket of fog concealing both infantry and tanks as they prepared to move off.

At first all went well as the Yorkshiremen and supporting tanks overran the enemy outpost line - taking many prisoners and killing many Germans. Two companies tried to storm point 229 but were met by a hail of high explosive from

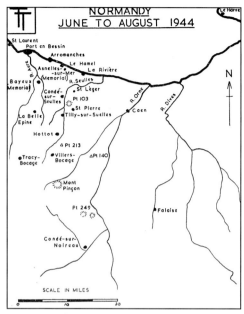

NORMANDY: JUNE TO AUGUST 1944

tanks and self propelled guns on the crest. Each time the infantry attacked they were hurled back with heavy losses - finally being halted short of both objectives.

At 0830 hrs the next day, August 11th, 231st Brigade renewed the attack on point 229 and St Pierre, again early morning fog hid the attackers from sight at first, all three Battalions fought numerous actions that day against an enemy who would yield not one yard of ground willingly. In the hot sunshine and by the force of their own persistence the infantry pressed forward until by last light the Dorset's were just south of the town with the Hampshire's fighting in it.

The next day, August 12th, at 0600 hrs the Devon's and Dorset's pushed on and by 1000 hrs had penetrated two miles south of St Pierre creating a long salient into the enemy positions. Both flanks were now wide open and the forward companies found themselves being shelled by heavy calibre guns from three directions, as the light began to fade the Germans launched a counter attack with a battalion of infantry from west and south. Blazing vehicles lit up the area and the enemy were often silhouetted against the flames making easy targets for the defenders who met the Germans with a spirited defence; after suffering very heavy casualties the Germans broke off the attack. While 231st Brigade had been holding their salient 151st Brigade had taken points 249 and 262 and during the night of 12th/13th August the 7th Green Howard's finally threw the Germans out of St Pierre breaking enemy resistance north of Conde. Just one week after the advance had started British units entered Conde.

The commander of XXX Corps sent the following message to the commander of the 50th Division:

Main HQ 30 Corps
DO/915
Aug 44

Commander, 50 (Northumbrian) Division

I would like all ranks of 50 (N) Division to realise how much their efforts of the last few days have contributed to the general plan for the encirclement and destruction of the German Army.

The road VIRE - CONDE and to the East has been one of the main German supply routes and recently the enemy has done his best to use it for the withdrawal of the large forces west of our present area.

It was vital that this escape route should be closed and the task was given initially to 50 (N) Division.

During the last week the Division has been fighting down towards CONDE from MONT PINCON. Although the country was suited for defence, and although the enemy was fighting stubbornly, all the attacks launched by 50 (N) Division have been successful and many prisoners have been taken.

Owing to the scarcity of roads deployment was difficult, yet the Division never faltered and we can now say that the escape route through CONDE is closed to the Germans.

I cannot give you higher praise than by saying that the most experienced battle fighting Division in the British Army has once more lived up to its high reputation.

Well done, 50 Div.

(Sgd) B C HORROCKS,
Lieutenant-General,
Commander 30 Corps.

Operations by the Allied Armies had by this time been going well and 50 Div.'s advance to Conde had been their contribution to the general effort, by August 19th the trap had been well and truly sprung as the Polish Armoured Division, operating to the south of Falaise, met the Americans in the area of Chambois. The final escape route from the Falaise Pocket had been closed and the Allied Forces now began the systematic destruction of the large enemy forces trapped within it.

TROOPS LOOK ON INTO THE KILLING ZONES AS HIGH EXPLOSIVE IS RAINED
UPON THE TRAPPED GERMANS. FALAISE. 1944

During those sunny August days of 1944, the scale of the destruction that came down upon the Germans was beyond the comprehension of most men who witnessed it, though what the soldiers could observe was at once fascinating and terrible beyond words. In the green fields and along dusty lanes and roads the greater part of the German Seventh Army were slaughtered. Inside the pocket German battle groups fought frantically to break free from the allied grip, while troops not engaged in any action could merely wait in crowded roads and lanes.

The Allied Armies forming around this trapped army divided the enemy held areas into zones, each zone would be covered by one unit, i.e. Corps artillery, an armoured brigade and so on, until every zone was covered - these were termed 'the killing grounds'. Once the shooting started a storm of high explosive was poured into the area day and night without pause, whole columns of motor vehicles unable to move were blown apart along with numerous horse drawn transports trapped in country lanes. As allied pressure forced the pocket to contract the congestion became worse and the slaughter more concentrated, the roads became choked with dead men, horses and blazing vehicles forcing the lines of troops into the fields, where they were mercilessly strafed from the air and from the ground. The scenes of carnage that were witnessed here were the worst most men had seen and the fields became like the roads - impassable.

The men who served with the 50th Division were taken aback by the scenes that greeted them as they pressed on; Pte W. M. Hewitt of 6th DLI had never seen anything like it:

"The Germans had a lot of horse drawn transport, men and horses were laid all over the place, just blasted to pieces. Behind the hedges there was rows of big guns that hadn't been used much. The rocket firing Typhoons were terrible, they must have had a demoralising effect on the Germans." [65]

Pte Reg Pope pressed on with the 2nd Cheshires:

"They had a terrible bashing there, I've never seen anything like it. It was just suicide for the poor devils - there was no way they were going to get out of there. Their artillery was horse drawn and the aircraft just blasted them from the air - it was pure carnage there's no doubt about it." [66]

Pte Jim Betts of the 5th East Yorkshires recalls the appalling scenes as his unit advanced:

"There was dead horses and men, smashed carts and tanks scattered all over the place - it was a terrible thing to see. As Gerry tried to get away the rocket firing Typhoons caught up with them - it made me cringe. As we moved up we found what was left - hundreds of dead Germans." [67]

Bombardier Jack Styan remembers seeing terrible scenes of slaughter in the killing zones:

"You could see our bombers flying over in box formation, loads of 'em going into Germany to bomb way up in front of us so we could get a push through. The roads were littered with burnt out wagons, tanks and trucks, I remember looking into one of the burnt out tanks and saw a foot - the sole of somebody's foot and it was white, the remainder of the body was charred black. It was one of those terrible sights you can never forget." [68]

By the last days of August it was clear the Germans had lost France and the remnants of the badly battered German Forces streamed eastwards. Nearly three months of the bloodiest fighting had produced the turning point of the war in Europe, Paris was in friendly hands again and the Allied Armies pressed forwards liberating villages, towns and cities as they went. As Pte Hardy, of the 5th East Yorkshires, and his comrades entered one farm yard the fleeing enemy were still lobbing shells over to deter their pursuers and the events of that day left him deeply scarred:

"As we moved forward we saw all the dead horses and men laid about, wrecked transport and tanks were everywhere. We stopped at a farm house, this was the worst part of my experience during the whole war I think. There was a young girl there, she was only about twelve and had a brand new coat on - she looked real smart and was very excited to see us all. I hadn't left my carrier as we hadn't been there above ten minutes when Gerry sent some 2-10's over - she was killed in the explosions. I can always remember her after all this time, I often think if we hadn't been there she wouldn't have been killed. But I can always remember that girl coming to our carrier all fussy and pleased to see us. That did me in worse than anything else." [69]

Pte Norman Hardy
5th Bn East Yorkshire Rgt.

After the Falaise disaster the remaining German forces disengaged the bulk of their units and headed for the German frontier, the flying bomb sites between the Seine and the Dutch Frontier were abandoned plus the unfortunate troops still isolated in the Channel and Atlantic ports. Urgently needed reinforcements had to be found from other theatres of war and from occupied countries as the German Forces regrouped along the Rhine.

The victorious British and American Armies were now prepared for the pursuit towards Germany, within the compliment of the Second British Army was XXX Corps (including 50 Div.), who were in the van. Between the 25th and 28th August the 43rd (Wessex) Division, who were the lead troops of XXX Corps, forced a crossing of the Seine at Vernon. On the 28th the Corps received orders to press on and its units began to cross the Seine and advance to the Amiens area, on the right leading was the Guards Armoured Division; with the 11th Armoured Division on the left. The order was for these units to press on with all haste regardless of the flanks, the 50th Division was to follow the armour mopping up any local resistance and protecting the Corps left flank; The advance began at first light on the 29th August.

On August 31st Amiens was taken, the 6th D.L.I. drove straight into the town in the wake of the 11th Armoured Division and mounted guard over the main road bridge. The welcome the troops received was at first restrained by an uncertain population, but by the evening it was obvious the British were here to stay and the celebrations spilled out onto the streets.

The story of the 50th Division that now unfolds is mainly one of long distance driving interspersed with enthusiastic welcomes given by grateful citizens as their towns and cities became free for the first time in four years. There was without doubt fighting to be done but it was on a small scale and not continuous, the murderous actions that had been fought in North Africa, Tunisia, Sicily and since the invasion seemed a long way off. There was no real front, isolated groups of enemy troops were taken into captivity, woods had to be cleared and bridges taken. During these short actions men lost their lives, there is a special tragedy and poignancy in such deaths, the 50th Division had travelled a long hard road for this moment.

A MIXED COLUMN AWAITS THE ORDER TO MOVE OFF.
(IMPERIAL WAR MUSEUM)

On September 1st the 8th D.L.I. moved to Picquigny, a small town on the River Somme to the north of Amiens, in order to secure the bridge over the river. As the D.L.I.'s carriers approach the town the Germans were in the process of leaving, the lead carrier was blown up as it made for the bridge. As the Germans pulled out across the river a storm of mortar bombs and shell fire came down upon the Durham's making them keep their heads down as the enemy blew the bridge. The Durham's and the machine gunners of the 2nd Cheshire's now moved into positions that gave a commanding view overlooking the far bank of the Somme. The Germans formed up in orderly fashion under cover of some woods by the river and prepared to withdraw, however the ground over which they would have to pass was flat and open and completely dominated by their opponents.

At 1700 hours the machine gunners of the Cheshire's saw crossing their front a target the like of which they had never seen before, a column led by a staff car, followed by horse drawn transport, followed by infantry. The machine gunners waited until the column was completely exposed and proceeded to sweep it with heavy waves of fire for thirty minutes. The staff car and its occupants were enveloped in flames, the horses legs gave way beneath them as bullets tore through their bodies and the luckless infantry were mercilessly slaughtered. The enemy transports moving over this open ground suffered the same fate as they left the relative safety of farm buildings, the infantry of the 8th D.L.I. poured mortar bombs into the area while anti tank gunners made the most of these excellent targets. Artillery observation officers were now well forward and it wasn't long before the guns of the 74th Field Regiment rained down shell fire upon the retreating Germans - playing havoc with them. 5 Platoon kept up a constant fire on the retreating Germans and as they did so 3 Platoon crossed the Somme and gave invaluable help to the 9th D.L.I. building a bridgehead across one of the smaller bridges that had not been destroyed.

Many small actions such as this were fought at various points along the advance, by the evening of September 1st elements of the 50th Division had taken over Arras from the Guards Armoured Division. It was here on May 21st 1940, the 50th had fought its first major action against the German Army, for those who had survived the long haul since those far off days it was a time of thankfulness and sadness. Thankfulness that they had been lucky enough to come through such hard times and sadness at the thought of long lost friends that had come to France with such high hopes as young green recruits.

The final phase of the advance began on the 3rd September with the move into Belgium, the welcome the troops received here was even more tremendous than the welcomes given to them in France and the advance became a triumphal procession. Crowds of cheering civilians lined the streets and brought columns to a halt as they swarmed over the vehicles and tanks. Gifts of beer, fruit, cakes, matches and kisses from young women were pressed upon the grimy Tommies and left with them unforgettable memories of the generosity and hospitality of the Belgium people. Sgt Ken Rutherford remembers those happy days:

> "We were the first to enter Alost, it was great passing through the town - just as if we were in the Lord Mayors Show, the people were so pleased to see us. They found their bottles of wine and flowers and cheered us through the streets - it was wonderful." [70]

The 50th Division pressed on in their dust covered transports across France and Belgium against light opposition and were welcomed as the conquering heroes they truly were, but the enemy was not yet beaten, only regrouping and gathering his strength for one last futile stand against the irresistible weight of the Allied war machine as it forced its way toward the borders of the Reich.

CHAPTER TEN

LAST BATTLES AND DISBANDMENT
(September to December 1944)

On September 7th 1944, the headquarters of the 50th Northumbrian Division received word it would soon be required to force a crossing of the Albert Canal; this being one of the last great water obstacles before the Dutch frontier. The crossing was to be made at either Beeringen in rear of the 11th Armoured Division, or at Gheel. The 69th and 151st Brigades moved to Hersselt in preparation for the crossing, the 231st Brigade stationed at Antwerp returned to the 50th Division again at this point.

The 69th Brigade was the first to move forward in preparation of the assault to come as it was now essential that two routes be opened over the Albert Canal. The Guards Armoured Division on the right of the 50th had secured a crossing, while on the left the 11th Armoured Division had met determined opposition and failed to get across. It now fell to the 50th to make a bridgehead south west of Gheel with as much speed as possible. The lead battalion would be the 6th Green Howards followed closely by the 7th Green Howards.

The main Gheel Road Bridge had been blown by the Germans but it was not known for sure if the bridges east of it had met the same fate. If no bridges were left standing the troops would have to cross by boat, the crossing place would now depend on the news brought back by reconnaissance parties, but wherever it may be the new bridgehead would have to cover the main Gheel Road which was vital for future movements.

Lt Colonel Exham went forward personally with his Intelligence Officer and the officers commanding 'C' and 'D' Companies, to reconnoitre a possible crossing place on the canal should this become necessary. From the roof of a house near the canal he had a good view, the canal was thirty yards wide at this point with a very high and steep nearside bank, but it was judged possible to launch boats despite this. As the officers scanned the far bank parties of Germans could be seen moving about.

Reconnaissance parties reported back to Brigade Headquarters that they had found all the bridges to be destroyed and that they had come under accurate mortar and Spandau fire when they had approached the canal. On hearing that all bridges had been blown the Brigade Commander confirmed his order for a night crossing, the bridgehead must include the village of Het-Punt on the Gheel Road in order to give protection to any subsequent bridging operations.

'H' hour was fixed at 0130 hrs on the 8th September, 'C' and 'D' Companies of the 6th Green Howards would make the assault with 'A' Company standing by to give covering fire if necessary. One Mark II assault boat was allotted to each of the companies making the crossing, plus three reconnaissance boats (Clay gives the latter figure as six). The battalion was to cross one thousand yards east of the road at Het-Punt, then turn north west to take and hold a bridgehead covering the site of the original bridge. Surprise was essential and to this end no barrage would precede the attack, with any luck the initial crossing would be made swiftly and in silence before the enemy realised what was happening.

During the evening heavy rain fell steadily as the troops prepared for the crossing, unfortunately it stopped just before the men moved off and was succeeded by bright moonlight. The infantry of 'A' and 'B' Companies carried their assault boats up the steep bank of the canal and wondered what would greet the sudden appearance of such an easy target in the moonlight. Over the top of the rise they went and plunged down into the water - still no reaction, the enemy was not alert and the crossing took place without a shot being fired. A cable was laid across the canal and the long and drawn out job of ferrying the troops across the river began; all four companies of the 6th Battalion did not get across until 0445 hrs.

This lack of opposition was not to last long as the Germans became aware of what had happened, 'D' Company had advanced in the dark to their objective and in doing so passed several enemy positions without realising this and became isolated for a time. Machine gun and mortar fire was directed upon the Green Howards from the houses in Het-Punt and during the morning their Commanding Officer - Lt Colonel Exham - was wounded.

Early in the day the 7th Battalion passed over into the bridgehead to reinforce the badly mauled 6th Battalion, during the 8th September the position held firm and by 0700 hours on the 9th the 5th Battalion East Yorkshire Regiment had concentrated just south of Gheel in preparation to cross west of the main crossing place at Het-Punt, and in so doing squeeze the Germans from the other flank.

On the night of the 9th September at 2100 hours the troops formed up with their assault boats under cover of the large bank south of the canal, it was bitterly cold and rain was falling as darkness descended at 2130 hrs. The tired, cold and wet infantry dragged the boats up the bank and out across the bare sandy ground that lay before the canal. The only sound to be heard by the sweating Tommies were their muffled curses, the splashing of the boats in the water and the constant hiss of the rain. 'D' and 'B' Companies crossed unobserved by the enemy, but when the reserve companies began to cross the enemy at Het-Punt came to life and rained down small arms fire upon the East Yorkshires as they landed.

A RIFLEMAN LOOKS FOR ENEMY SNIPERS FROM A RUINED HOUSE

At 0100 hours the Yorkshiremen attacked Het-Punt setting buildings on fire, taking twenty two prisoners and liberating a group of Green Howards who had been taken prisoner. 69th Brigade was now across the river and had established a bridgehead, opposition in this sector faded away allowing prisoners and wounded to be ferried back across the canal.

Late in the afternoon of September 8th 151st Brigade made ready to make a crossing in the vicinity of Steelen, the initial crossing was to be made by the 8th Battalion D.L.I., once they were established on the far bank the 6th D.L.I. was to pass through them and take Gheel itself. The crossing was to be made in silence until enemy positions were pin pointed, 296 Battery, Royal Artillery would then be on call to lay down defensive fire where needed.

As 'A' Company crossed the canal they were greeted by machine gun and mortar fire that increased steadily in intensity causing many casualties, including the Coy Commander Major Chris Beattie who died of his wounds on 9th September.

Pte Reg Pope was with the machine gun and mortar platoon of the 2nd Battalion Cheshire Regiment who took up positions on the bank of the canal:

"We dug in on top of this bank, on the other side was a big plateau, there was Gerry tanks, lorries and infantry near a farm half a mile away. That was the first time I'd seen a good clear target for machine guns and mortars, we had a perfect view of the target and got onto it firing direct at Gerry, we just blew them to pieces, it was no problem blowing them to bits." [71]

At 5.30 p.m., under cover of smoke, 'D' Company crossed the canal meeting less opposition than had 'A' Coy. They quickly formed up on the bank and attacked a farm house from which machine gun fire was being directed upon them. CSM Bill Brown was wounded in this fight:

> "Assault boats were at the Albert Canal to meet us, these were collapsible wood and canvas boats and heavy to carry down the bank. We could see boats sinking and blokes being shot by machine guns. Later I was standing talking to a section commander in a sunken road when an enemy machine gun opened up, it looked like flashing lights going past me and I fell onto the sunken road. About three men were killed and my guts were oozing out. I said to this young officer who hadn't been with us long 'give us your hand and grip as tight as you can', he took my hand and I was conscious all the time, I thought if I loose consciousness I will die. They put about four field dressings on me, put me on a stretcher and the two stretcher bearers carried me down the road. The German machine guns could have opened up on us but they didn't." [72]

The German machine gunners swept the Durham's positions and accurate mortar fire descended upon them, the Germans were well concealed along the road embankment and in the hedgerows and they proceeded to take a heavy toll of the 8th D.L.I. An anti aircraft gun kept up a constant stream of incendiary shells in the area setting fire to buildings and lighting up the bridgehead, by the light of these flames and by the clear light of the moon the Germans attacked in open formation. They were met by the fire of a dozen bren guns but still they came on, some got to within twenty yards and began to throw grenades into the Durham's positions, but as suddenly as the attack had started it petered out and the Germans withdrew taking their wounded. The rest of the night was relatively quiet, a new bridge had been completed and the battalion casualties were seven officers and twenty two other ranks.

By 0700 hours on the 9th September the 61st Reconnaissance Regiment crossed the folding bridge and moved through the positions being held by 8th D.L.I., they patrolled vigorously and were soon prevented from any further advance by enemy resistance. As the 6th D.L.I. prepared to cross the bridge, which was under heavy fire mainly from air bursts, it collapsed leaving the infantry to cross in any assault boats that had survived the earlier crossing. In the bridgehead itself the fighting increased in intensity and scale as the troops crossed the canal, by 11 am the bridge had been restored by the sappers who worked under heavy fire and the carriers and anti tank guns of the 6th D.L.I. began to cross into the bridgehead.

There was no violent reaction immediately from the enemy and the 6th D.L.I. pressed on to Doornboom mopping up light resistance on the way, prisoners taken during the day were from German Air Force Units, 4th Fleiger Ersatz Regiment, 572nd Grenadier Ersatz Regiment and 101st Grenadier Regiment. They reported the reinforcement of Gheel by about three hundred troops, it was obvious the enemy was pulling together a mixed bag of units to hold the 50th Division on the line of the canal. The rest of the 9th September passed quietly and as darkness fell only 'B' Company reported any shelling.

On the 10th September all three battalions of the 151st Brigade were in the bridgehead, the 6th Battalion pressed on to Gheel with the 9th Battalion moving up on their right flank. As the 6th moved off an enemy counter attack fell upon their right flank overrunning the forward platoons of 'A' Company, this desperate situation was only saved by the arrival of a section of carriers who's task it was to stem the enemy advance.

Shells screamed over the attacking Durham's and the whole area was raked by German machine gun fire as the 6th pressed on. Tiger tanks were spotted in the area and a squadron of tanks of the Sherwood Rangers moved into the fighting area and joined the battle which was raging furiously.

The 6th D.L.I. forced their way into Gheel, ejecting the Germans house by house, yard by yard and street by street. This viscous fight saw little quarter given by either side as the Durham's moved from place to place, the people of the area showed them where the Germans were hiding in houses and in cellars, if they did not come out at the first call they were not given another chance and died in a hail of grenades or machine gun fire.

The enemy artillery fire on Gheel increased in intensity and at 2000 hrs a counter attack fell upon the 6th Battalions right flank and the enemy, ever watchful of weakspots, infiltrated between the forward companies of the left flank. The 6th found their position more and more difficult as the enemy moved in and around the now much weakened companies which were in great danger of being cut off from the rest of the brigade.

On the left the 8th Battalion had moved up to protect the left flank of the 6th, only not before the enemy had been able to exploit a gap between the two units; the 9th Battalion on the right had managed to beat off all attacks and remained under extreme pressure.

All morning on the 11th September the battle in Gheel and along the fronts held by the 8th and 9th D.L.I. continued as the Durham's and Germans fought it out. Pte W.M. Hewitt was with 'A' Company, 6th D.L.I. when a German counter attack cut off him and his comrades.

"We entered a town called Gheel after a lot of heavy fighting, Gerry counter attacked and drove us out of the place. The platoon I was with was well forward, I had this wireless set and all I could get was flamin' music - this was with it being a built up area, we had no contact at all with the rest of the battalion or brigade. They had been forced to pull out leaving us there, we were still there when the Germans moved in. We hid away for two days in a house still occupied by civilians, the son of the family came upstairs and asked us if we would move into an empty house across the road, there was only nine of us left. We entered the empty house and went up into the loft,

A BREN-GUNNER OF THE EAST YORKSHIRE REGIMENT FIRES
FROM A ROOFTOP. (*IMPERIAL WAR MUSEUM*)

about half an hour later the Germans came and took us prisoner. I don't know if it was the civilians who had told them where we were." [73]

At 1400 hrs orders were received to withdraw the companies from Gheel but it was to prove very difficult to get these orders to men who were only a matter of yards from the enemy and in some cases nearly surrounded. Pte Carman was with 'C' Company in Gheel when they were forced to pull back to the outskirts.

"We were in the front window of this house looking up the street, almost opposite us was a hospital, I think it was a catholic type of place because there was nuns going in and out with casualties. We knew Gerry was only a hundred yards up the road to our right. One of our three tonners came passed us; we thought 'hell - he shouldn't be going up there but by then of course he'd gone past. We heard the squeal of brakes and a Gerry patrol came out of this side street. We saw the driver get out of his cab, put his hands up and they marched him off, we couldn't do a thing about it.

During the night Gerry counter attacked, we pulled back and dug in just outside of Gheel, he re-took the bridge we had just come over - in other words we were cut off. There was machine gun fire flying all over the place and the shelling was bad, for us that had not long ago been in England it was very hair raising, it made you grow up over night. After two or three weeks when another lot of reinforcements arrived we felt we were old timers." [74]

During the misty morning of 11th September the German troops could achieve no more and began to withdraw from the bridge head, this proved to be a risky business in broad daylight and as the enemy tanks revealed themselves the British armour punished them severely. The machine gunners of the Cheshire Regiment found easy targets in the withdrawing German infantry, as the enemy went to ground the machine gunners advanced in their carriers and blasted the Germans where they lay at point blank range. Many Germans were killed and wounded in the slaughter and the bullets left the ground like a ploughed field such was the rate of fire.

Throughout the bridgehead on the 11th the tank and infantry battles continued to be fought out in a bitter struggle for survival; both sides suffering heavy losses. In the evening the first paratrooper was taken prisoner, he revealed that the 2nd Parachute Division had arrived in lorries from Germany to reinforce the counter attacks now being delivered. On 12th September the Germans resumed their desperate attempts to break into the bridgehead but were held off by the hard pressed Durham's, more prisoners were taken from the Parachute Division.

During the evening of the 12th, both 69th and 151st Brigades were relieved of the heavy burden they had shouldered for so long by the 15th (Scottish) Division, both brigades pulled back over the Albert Canal for a well earned rest. The next morning it was reported that the enemy had had enough and pulled out of Gheel and back across the Escaut Canal.

And so the bitter and bloody battle for Gheel came to an end, the situation had swung first this way then that in a most confusing manner, often with small groups being cut off to continue the fight on their own. This was a battle which required junior officers and NCO's to use all of their initiative and resourcefulness, because of this and the undoubted fighting qualities of the men of the 50th Division the bridgehead had held firm, finally wearing down the enemy and forcing his withdrawal to the Escaut Canal. The enemies main intention and focus in this fight had been to crush the bridgehead and in so doing to open up the flank of the Beeringen bridgehead further east that was held by the Guards, but units that could have been deployed against the guards at Beeringen were systematically destroyed by the 50th Division at Gheel in three days of bitter fighting. It speaks highly of the fighting qualities of the troops at Gheel that when the Scottish Division attacked on the 13th September they were able to pass through the town without firing a shot. With the fall of Gheel a phase ended for the 50th Division and a new one was about to begin.

In England a large airborne army had been assembled and General Montgomery had been awaiting an opportunity to use it - that time was now at hand. The boldness of his plan would only be matched by its far reaching consequences should it be successful, it would be known as 'Operation Market Garden' and would culminate in the grim struggle at Arnhem. 'Market Garden' was intended to make a rapid thrust due north to the shores of the Zuyder Zee - splitting

Holland in two and so isolating the many thousands of Germans in Western Holland and cutting their line of retreat to the Reich.

This bold plan involved the crossing of several water obstacles plus three major rivers - the Maas, the Waal and the Neder Rijn (Lower Rhine). The main crossing points were to be seized by parachute troops in the largest airborne operation ever seen and in this way allow a free passage for the land troops as they rushed forward.

Three airborne divisions would take part in this operation, the 101st US Airborne Division would seize the canal and stream crossings at Eindhoven, Zon and Veghel, the 82nd US Airborne Divisions objectives were the bridges over the Maas at Grave and over the Waal at Nijmegen, while the British 1st Airborne Division took the bridges over the Neder Rijn at Arnhem.

For the troops on the ground the main thrust was to be delivered by XXX Corps with VIII and XII Corps guarding the flanks of the advance, the airborne troops would form a corridor for XXX Corps to rush down - this force would consist of the Guards Armoured Division, the 43rd (Wessex) Division and the 50th (Northumbrian) Division. They were to advance to Arnhem and join the bridgehead formed by the 1st Airborne. The role of the infantry Divisions was to hold the ground taken by the armoured spear head and guard the flanks against attack. If this daring stroke was successful the Siegfried Line, which ended North of Aachen, would be out flanked securing powerful armoured forces on the edge of the North German Plain; This was one last opportunity to end the war in 1944.

On the 17th September the troops of 151st and 231st Brigades were holding positions in the bridgehead over the Escaut Canal through which the armoured spearhead was to pass; From above came a rumble which developed into a roar as an astonishing array of aircraft towing gliders passed over their heads as the Airborne Army sped off to its objectives. The troops gazed up from their slit trenches as the sky filled with aircraft thundering forward.

The Guards Armoured Divison began its move out of the Escaut bridgehead at 1430 hrs, a thunderous barrage fell before them heralding the advance into Holland. The Guards soon ran into determined and effective opposition and the first nine tanks were knocked out by German gunners. The 2nd Devon's and 1st Dorset's of the 231st Brigade were called upon at this point to move up behind the guards and clear the woods on the left of the main road as it was from here most of the opposition was coming. At the end of the day on 17th September the battle ceased for twelve hours, with the Guards Armoured Division six miles south of Eindhoven and the Americans four miles to the North of the city, the programme for the ground forces was already falling behind schedule.

At first light on the 18th September, as the armour pressed on the Dorset's took over the town of Valkenswaard. It was a relatively quiet day on the divisional front apart from a counter attack on the 9th D.L.I. who still held the Escaut bridgehead. The armour continued to advance slowly and by noon had passed through Eindhoven. On the 19th British forces advanced northward passing through the American bridgehead at Zon, Veghel and Grave and came into contact with enemy forces at the southern ends of the Nijmegen bridges and between the Rivers Maas and Waal; just west of the Reichswald Forest.

The American Paratroopers had met with great success at Nijmegen and shortly after their jump had destroyed the 1st and 2nd Battalions of the Para Training Regiment Hermann Goering at St Oedenrode and Zon, other objectives had been taken without a fight. The road and rail bridges at Nijmegen were protected at their southern ends by pre war concrete emplacements and it was not until the 20th that these vital objectives fell to the Americans and the Guards Armoured Division. At this time the last and most important bridge still remained untaken - that over the Neder Rijn at Arnhem, here the British Airborne were resisting ferocious counter attacks.

The successful operation at Nijmegen was the cue for the 69th Brigade to join the battle and press forward, the route was jammed with vehicles of all kinds and it was not until late on the night of the 21st September that the brigade arrived at its destination. The Germans now put into operation a plan to assist the SS troops locked in battle with the British at Arnhem and prevent XXX Corps from pressing on to relieve the airborne troops there, the plan was to cut the main route forward by launching a number of counter attacks upon the British flanks.

On September 22nd, two German infantry battalions and a regiment of tanks attacked and cut the main road at Uden, eight miles south of the bridge over the Maas at Grave. To the north of this breach was the 5th East Yorkshires and to the south the 6th and 7th Green Howards, 69 Brigade had been cut in two by the counter attack. Moving up with the 69th Brigade was the 124th Field Regiment, RA, who now found themselves cut off from their Commanding Officer, but batteries were soon in action supporting the 101st American Airborne holding crossings in the area of Oedenrode. The following day the Germans attacked Veghel further south, in an attempt to strengthen their grip on the road, here they were met by fierce resistance from American infantry supported by British artillery and tanks and were driven off with heavy losses. This action resulted in a temporary opening of the road and enabled 69 Brigade to unite once more and advance to Nijmegen where they took their place with the defenders of the bridgehead over the Waal. Sgt Max Hearst was with the 5th East Yorkshires when they crossed over the river:

> "We crossed the bridge and took over from the Yanks, our forward platoons were engaging Gerry. When we approached the bridge there was a lot of dead American Paras laid about. Here we met the German storm-troopers, you know the death or glory boys, they were firing at our lads, one or two of our boys that were good marksmen were picking off these Germans. We dug in both sides and held the position for a number of days. Frogmen

came up the river to blow the bridge but they were spotted in time and shot in the water.

I was sat in a slit trench having a drink when a plane came over, I said 'look the poor buggers on fire!' That was my first sight of a jet fighter." [75]

The threat to the main road however was far from over as the Germans scraped together tanks and infantry from slender resources that were now very thinly spread. The task of the 50th Division was now the protection of part of the Uden - Vehgel Road - the lifeline of the Army, the two remaining brigades and three reconnaissance units found themselves fighting off German attempts to cut the road on the 23rd, some miles south of Veghel. Major W J R Scott of Newcastle who was with the 9th D.L.I. remembers an incident involving the Corps Commander Lieutenant General Horrocks:

"When the road was cut, we found ourselves on the wrong side of the cut. General Horrocks was forward with us and couldn't get back to his headquarters. Our 'B' Echelon was on the other side of the Germans, but one of our dispatch riders got through to us. General Horrocks sent for him, and asked him how he had managed it. The man said he had used the back roads. The General thought for a moment. Then he asked 'Can you get me back?' 'Yes, sir,' said the dispatch rider. The general climbed into his jeep and with the dispatch rider leading the way, he went through with a section of carriers. They got through and the general was over the moon. He went round thanking and shaking hands with everyone." [76]

By the evening of the 24th September the road was still threatened by the enemy, the 50th Division was reinforced as 131st Infantry Brigade, 7th Armoured Division and a regiment of tanks were placed under its command. These were committed to the battle the morning of the 25th. Pte J H Clarke, 8th DLI, was moving up behind the armour when he was ordered to take a couple of high ranking officers on a reconnaissance patrol of the road ahead:

"I was a carrier driver for the mortar platoon Commander Captain Rory O'Conor, 8th DLI, we had moved up behind the armour with very little contact with the enemy until we came to a halt with Germans in front and on our right flank. I was ordered by company HQ to take a couple of Officers on a recce of the area, I think one was 151 Brigade Commander and the other from 50 Div. HQ. During darkness that night we got orders to move forward along a straight narrow road, making as little noise as possible. After about a mile we ran into an ambush - German infantry were strung out along the road side ditch. Mine was the lead carrier and received a grenade in the engine compartment knocking out the engine. After a sharp exchange of small arms fire and grenades we were able to spin round the remaining carriers and withdraw." [77]

The American and British units attacked the enemy in unison, the opposition was stiff and it was not until the 26th that the road was finally cleared - marking

A DEAD GERMAN PARATROOPER ON THE BRIDGE AT NIJMEGEN

the end of the enemies main attempts to cut this vital artery. The next few days were relatively quiet for the 50th Division, most of its time being occupied with guards, patrols and moves from position to position.

The 69th Brigade, now under the command of the Guards Armoured Division at Nijmegen, on September 22nd was holding positions on and around the bridge and saw for the first time jet aircraft as they dive bombed the structure with little effect. Sgt Max Hearst watched with his mates at this unusual sight:

"This was our first sighting of a jet aircraft, somebody said 'why he's going too fast to do any good'. It was here and gone so quickly." [78]

The first major task undertaken by 69 Brigade was to capture the village of Bemmel, north of the river and east of the main road. On the 24th at 1630 hrs the troops of the 5th East Yorkshires began the attack over flat country side crisscrossed with ditches. Before them a furious barrage thundered and the supporting Guards tanks found the going rough - as did the poor infantry, by dusk the enemies outpost line had been overrun but 'A', 'B' and 'D' companies failed to break into the village.

At first light on the 25th Major Harrison led 'C' Company, supported by tanks and a short bombardment, into the village. The troops winkled the enemy out of each building and by 1400 hours the village was firmly in the hands of the Yorkshiremen, forty enemy dead were counted and Eighty prisoners taken. Sgt Max Hearst was enjoying the local hospitality that evening when one of the inhabitants of Bemmel became very agitated:

"I was sat at the side of the road near a huge chateau and a church, it had gone nice and quiet, we were talking and a couple of locals came out and

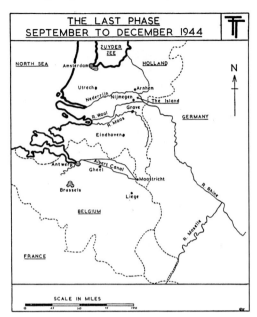

THE LAST PHASE: SEPTEMBER TO DECEMBER 1944

gave us a drink. One old chap came up to us talking excitedly in Dutch, he kept saying 'Allemande', we didn't understand he meant Germans. He kept pointing so we followed him to a cellar entrance at the Chateau, 'Allemande, Allemande' he kept saying. Some of the lads got their stens at the ready and the door was kicked in - 'Come out yer bastards!' was shouted. The answer was a burst of automatic fire, we ducked for cover. Someone said 'We'll give you up to three to come out - at three there was no Kamerad so we lobbed grenades in. After the explosions the lads waited a while but there was no sound. We finally went in and found quite a few SS troops laid about - they'd rather die than surrender. One of the lads saw a movement among the bodies and finished 'em off." [79]

Pte Roy Walker of the 5th East York's fought at Bemmel and recalls a close shave with one bovine inhabitant:

"The thing that stands out most in my mind about coming up the corridor was all these aircraft coming over. They filled the sky, we saw all the white parachutes opening as they jumped. That was a lovely sight to see, it gave us confidence when we knew we weren't on our own. We went over the pontoon bridge and guarded the main bridge that night - Gerry was throwing shells at us.

The last battle we fought was at Bemmel just outside Nijmegen, it was held by SS troops, it was a hard fight and we lost quite a few lads. I remember going in the church in Bemmel and up into the Belfry to observe the enemy to our front with our officer and Johnny Dolan. The thing that struck me was a cross with our Lord on it - hanging by one chain, the rest of the church was in ruins. We killed the last pig in Bemmel, Johnny Dolan had been a butcher in Civvy Street and had this pig in the cellar of a farm house, he said we would go back after dark to kill it. We returned later and I was supposed to hold a candle while John killed it, when the pig saw the light in the dark cellar it charged at me knocking me over - it went mad, I left after that. John said 'leave it to me Roy, I'll get it' - which he did and we had pork for lunch the next day, he made a brawn for the officers." [80]

L/Sgt Ken Rutherford remembers Bemmel as "Being constantly under fire by Jerry's heavy guns, the village and the surrounding area were thick mud and filthy." The enemy was not reconciled to losing this tactically important village and the 5th East York's suffered heavy shellfire day and night.

To the east of Bemmel was the village of Halderen, the tall chimneys of its many factories were being used as observation posts by German troops, on the 26th September the 6th Green Howard's were ordered to take it. The opposition was so strong they did not reach the village but the 7th Battalion on the left had better luck reaching all of their objectives. Throughout the day on the 27th brigade attacks continued against unwavering opposition, enemy tanks were brought up to fire on the troops and 88's covered the roads preventing any tank support.

The paras to the north at Arnhem had by this time been withdrawn, the attempt to reach them had failed and the main objective of Market Garden - to cut Holland in two and turn the Rhine defences - had not been achieved. The effect of this failure was, for 69 Brigade, dramatic. It transformed a sharply resisting enemy force into an aggressive one as tanks and infantry, that had been in operation against the paras at Arnhem, became available to attack the bridgehead over the Waal. On the 28th operations at Halderen were halted as the 69th Brigade re-grouped and braced itself for the storm about to break.

The 29th September saw the Luftwaffe in the skies again, a mark of the new confidence felt by the enemy after their victory at Arnhem, the Nijmegen Railway bridge was hit by a parachute bomb tearing a forty foot gap out of its structure and on the same day human torpedoes damaged the foot bridge. The troops in the bridgehead found their only line of retreat temporarily closed and their lines of communication threatened. The only complete division north of the river at this time was the 43rd (Wessex), the 69th Brigade and the 5th Guards Brigade were placed under its command for the coming battle.

The first counter attack fell upon the 5th East York's on 30th September but the enemy could not break through the hail of machine gun and artillery fire. On 1st October a much stronger attack fell upon a broad front, intending to push on to Nijmegen while crushing the bridge head, seventy tanks and an infantry division pressed home attacks against 69 Brigade, the 5th Guards Brigade and the 43rd Division. It soon became apparent that the main assault was directed to 69

TROOPS MOVING UP THE LINE. WINTER 1944. (*IMPERIAL WAR MUSEUM*)

Brigades front and at 0500 hours the full fury of the German counter attack struck the three weary battalions. Behind the deluge of shells and mortar bombs came the tanks infiltrating between companies and forcing the Yorkshiremen to give ground. By 0700 hours the attack was in full swing, defensive artillery fire was called upon to engage infantry and tanks causing heavy damage and casualties.

In this inferno the Green Howards held fast all day giving as good as they got until relieved by the 5th East York's and a squadron of the 13/18th Hussars, this relief force began their advance at 1800 hours, arrived at 2300 hours and not a minute too late, the Green Howards were hanging on by the skin of their teeth. Sgt Max Hearst was one of the relief party:

"We went back up the line near Bemmel, the Green Howards were being pulled out and as they left the relieving company was on the road, Gerry never missed a trick like that and started to pound us with everything he had. It was bloody pandemonium! There was all sorts of stuff flying this way and that. The heavy guns in our rear were called up to lay down a creeping barrage, when it came it frightened me, I was in a dug-out and I thought by 'ell I wouldn't like to be on the receiving end of that. We got cut up pretty bad with shrapnel and machine-gun fire and had lots of casualties." [81]

The Green Howards deserve praise particularly for their days work here, they sat amid this storm for eighteen hours, taking the worst the enemy could give them as one tank and infantry attack succeeded another, all the time being subjected to heavy artillery fire. Through all of this they held on until relief came and achieved here a feat of arms to be proud of. Captain Gus Mason remembers the fearsome shellfire:

> "We were told that the Germans had no armour. The acting adjutant had a premonition that something was going to happen. On his own initiative he stood the battalion to at 4 a.m.
>
> It was a good thing he did, because at 5 a.m. they attacked. They came in with everything they had. We stuck where we were and fought them off. Eventually we were relieved. Even they couldn't move, it was so hot.
>
> Practically all the rifles in our battalion were smashed to bits by shell fragments because the men had left them on the trench parapets. The 69th Brigade went back across the Nijmegen Bridge. It was very hot going. The sentry boxes were like shells with lids." [82]

The 69th Brigade was now joined by the remainder of the 50th Division which took over the eastern sector of the bridgehead. The 231st and 151st Brigades relieved the battered 69th and on the 4th October attacked the village of Halderen with the intention of improving the line, as usual the opposition was stiff but the village fell on the 6th October.

The troops in the bridgehead now settled down to a period of static warfare, for the 50th Division this was to be their last operation in the second 'Great War'. This period was to be relatively quiet and was to last all of October and most of November, the name given to this area between the Neder Rijn and the Waal was 'the Island' as it seemed to be surrounded by water, the men of 50 Div. came to know it well.

At night the great bridge at Nijmegen had an eerie appearance as searchlights continually swept the water, this combined with a continuous smoke screen gave the area an atmospheric glow that shrouded the iron structure. Notices advised you not to tarry long as all the approaches to the bridge were under observation by enemy gunners.

The 50th Divisions battalions were all now well below strength, many officers and NCO's had been lost in the past months and the man power situation in the army as a whole was becoming acute. For the forward troops life was hard in the extreme and any period of rest was welcomed, Pte Pope of the 2nd Cheshire's was often up the line:

> "The winter of 1944 was very cold and their was lots of snow, we were pulled out after a couple of days as we had been in action since D-Day. The Americans took over from us but our rest was over all too soon and we had to go back and relieve them." [83]

Sgt Max Hearst of the 5th East York's had adopted a dog as a mascot:

> "We had our HQ in the cellar of a café, it was at this time my dog had pups - we called one Tilly and one Bocage. Tilly got blown up by a shell in an orchard. We were pulled out of the line and went back to Nijmegen for a rest and when we had to go back up the line I got lumbered with driving a bren-carrier. We got orders to mount up and I'm shouting for the dog but couldn't see it, I pulled forward and even above the noise of the engine I heard the yelp. I stopped and pulled her out but she was no good. We went back up the line." [84]

Pte Jim Betts was also with the 5th East York's and took advantage of any little luxuries that became available:

> "We were in Elst (NORTH-EAST OF BEMMEL) and went in a truck to this big jam factory that had been knocked about - we were scrounging for sugar and jam, mortar bombs and all sort of stuff were dropping on us here. In the surrounding fields we shot wounded cattle and our butcher came along and cut them up. My god it was a hard life." [85]

When troops did find themselves in the rear sports events were organised to keep their spirits up, baths could be taken and cinemas visited, but the highlight of social events was a dance held in Nijmegen attended by over two hundred people.

October passed and November wore on, the 50th Division were still on 'The Island' and the weather grew progressively worse. On November 29th the Division was relieved and pulled back into Belgium and so ended the fighting for 50 Div.

By the end of November rumours about the 50th's future circulated among the men, there was much speculation especially about the prospect of the divisions return to England, a piece of news that would have been music to the ears of the long serving men who had come through so much since 1940. The only definite news was that the 21st Army Group had to be reduced by one division because of the lack of quality recruits and the axe was to fall on the famous 50th Division.

News was confirmed that the 50th was indeed to be sent home - this would not apply to all troops and company commanders were asked to draw up nominal rolls split up into four categories; men who were fit to be posted to rifle companies in another division, men who needed to be retrained as infantry, those who would return to England and men who were able to perform garrison duties.

This was a difficult task for commanding officers, along the way they had seen many men fall by the wayside and a number of 'old hands' still served in the division. Quite a lot of men had not been with the division more than a few months but there had developed a strong sense of comradeship within each unit as troops crouched together under intense shell fire, or moved forward on patrol before the ever present enemy. These men had seen death in the waterlogged positions on the 'Island' and had shared hardship and deprivation, when such a bond has been forged one does not part from ones companions lightly.

The front line troops of 50 Div. had fought in the second 'Great War' in which thousands had died and for each one of them there had been the ever present fact of mutilation, dismemberment and death. During the bitter struggles of 1944 the 50th had lost 65.9% of its officers wounded and 16.5% of them killed. Among the 'other ranks' 50% had been wounded and 8.7% killed. One thing that so often came up in interviews with veterans of all units was a weariness of spirit and the slow and dreadful realisation that with each action the odds against survival became slimmer and slimmer, but most men stuck it out beside their comrades and pressed forward into the most viscous fire supporting and caring for each other and at times giving their lives for their friends.

A war correspondent wrote:

> "The cheerfulness and good nature of the British soldier in the most trying of conditions is now so much commonplace that it is no longer noticed. I want to notice it here with moved admiration."

These men had lived in a world dangerous beyond our comprehension and had witnessed scenes of carnage beyond description, these were not just cheery souls smiling their way through a fairly unpleasant experience, they were often at the limits of strain and fatigue and the effort of carrying on and thinking of others required a will of steel and devotion. The human spirit exposed was truly magnificent, but it must never be forgotten that the steel enclosed within it was forged in hell.

Pte Roy Walker had served with the 50th for three years and had this to say regarding his time as a fighting man:

> "We had some good times and we had some bad times - it wasn't wasted, it was an experience. I met some great friends - mates, it was a sad time when I lost some of them but I just carried on, I never saw any lad turn back, they had a job to do and went forward. The only thing I used to think of was well it's your turn next, we had so many replacements after actions. It was like that all through the war - it will be my turn next, we had a sergeant Jimmy Lister with us - a real nice lad. Well he had a premonition he was going to be killed, the NCO's had to go out on a recce, before he went out Jimmy gave his watch and all his money to his carrier crew and said 'I won't be coming back.' He never did come back, his body was found the next day - riddled with machine gun bullets. He'd been in action many times before - it wasn't new to him." [86]

Pte Jim Betts said of his service:

> "I look back upon the war as six years wasted, the best years of my life wasted, even though it was a war that had to be fought, if it hadn't I don't know what would have happened - if Gerry had got over here" [87]

FRONT LINE INFANTRY. WINTER 1944

Pte Harry Forth:

"I had no hatred of the Germans, they had a hard job to do and so did I, the ordinary Wermacht soldier was like you and me - the SS troops were different altogether. This was a war that needed to be fought." [88]

The bond formed by the front line men was strong and remains so after so many years, George Worthington MM:

"The bond of comradeship formed with the lads who served is just as strong today, I don't regret my part in the war, it was something that came along and fortunately I made it and stayed the distance. We always go down to London on Remembrance Sunday and when we go abroad we visit the cemeteries." [89]

Sgt Bob Gibson, MM:

"I was mates with lads I'd slept along side of since 1939, before the war we used to go to camp on our own civvy mortar - bikes. Once you've lived with those chaps you are like brothers - more than brothers, you can depend on each other. I knew all the officers and they knew me and knew I'd do what was right." [90]

Sgt Max Hearst looked forward to a return home, but for him and many others the war would always be with them:

"I was glad to be out of it at last - I'd seen so many of my mates killed, one lad had both legs blown off at Gazala, for years after I would wake up hearing his screams." [91]

Other men in the division who were being sent to other units were not so pleased about the present changes, and although they wanted to carry on to the end with their beloved 50 Div., being sent up the line to a strange unit, and possibly being killed serving with that unit was not a welcome thought. Slowly but surely the 50th Division was dismembered, but not all the officers were happy about things. Major Peter Martin felt this a shameful way to treat the troops of one of the most famous divisions Britain had ever produced:

"People began to wonder if we were going home - there were rumours from the clerks at Battalion HQ. I was told this is exactly what is going to happen, we would be reduced to twelve officers and one hundred and nine other ranks and sent home to train surplus RAF and naval recruits as infantry for the Rhine crossing. The reason: 50 Div., had not only done its stuff, but its standard of training was getting shaky, and it was time someone else bore the burden. This was fine except that from my own company only myself, my 2ic and about twenty men would be left. All the rest would be dispersed around the place and retrained as infantry, this was a betrayal! We pleaded with the CO to lodge an objection to say we were quite happy to go on fighting providing we could be kept together. We didn't want to be relieved - we didn't want to be sent back to England.

There was tremendous jubilation in the company at the thought of going home, little did they know - poor chaps - what lay in wait for them, one awful day in February, wearing the badges of many different units, off they went. Some went straight to battalions in the front line, some to holding units, some to the Far East. It is something I have never forgotten. The shame of the CO allowing this to happen has been with me for the rest of my life, I know a great number got killed in the final battles of the war - that was unforgivable." [92]

The numbers of the 50th Divisions complement slowly dwindled, last farewells were made and the men were addressed by 30 Corps Commander General Horrocks and Monty - who awarded gallantry medals and said their final parting words. Horrocks commented: "The TT boys will be much missed by everyone."

On December 14th 1944, the remains of the 50th Division sailed up Southampton Water and disembarked at the same spot they had sailed from on June 6th. From here it was back home to train young men in the art of war. What stories these new recruits must have listened to in the barracks at night, tales of Arras and Dunkirk, travels to Cyprus and Iraq, the fight at Gazala and Alamein and of the Desert Fox, on to Tunisia and Sicily and finally the storming of the

Normandy beaches and the battles up to Nijmegen. These men received no mere technical training but heard the truth from men who had seen it all first hand and who were proud to wear the double 'T' shoulder flash.

The majority of troops in the Second World War existed simply to keep the infantryman in action, and as such there was a great divide between the two. The infantry were a self conscious minority who lived in a world which is as different from this known world of ours as if they inhabited another planet. The rifleman fights without promise of reward or relief, beyond each river is a hill and beyond each hill a river, and this for weeks and months at a time with no comfort, safety or a bed to sleep in. This is how they fought and died, the record of the 50th Division is one of appalling suffering, endurance and true comradeship. No man, no matter how he may talk has the remotest idea of what an ordinary infantry soldier endures. Front line combat troops are an exclusive set and if they wish to be regarded that way, it is their privilege.

SICILY: 1943

FOOTNOTES

The following abbreviations apply regarding these first hand accounts.

Iwm: Imperial War Museum
Tiwa: Taped Interview With Author
Msta: Manuscript Sent To Author

1. Pte. N Hardy. 5th B'n East York's Reg., (Tiwa), 1990.
2. Pte. R Hymer. 8th D.L.I. (Tiwa), 1991.
3. Pte. J H Clarke. 8th D.L.I. (Tiwa), 1991.
4. Pte. H Forth. 5th B'n East York's Reg., (Tiwa), 1990.
5. L/Sgt. K Rutherford. 5th B'n East York's Reg., (Tiwa), 1991.
6. Montgomery. El Alamein To The River Sangro. P90-91.
7. Major K. C. Harrison. 5th B'n East York's Reg., (Msta), 1994.
8. Message To All Troops: July, 1943.
9. Pte. E. Kerens. 9th D.L.I. (Iwm: 86/61/1).
10. Pte. R. Smith. 1st B'n Parachute Reg., (Msta), 1991.
11. Pte. Priestley. 1st B'n Parachute Reg., (Iwm).
12. Cpt. Gammon. 1st B'n Parachute Reg., (Msta), 1992.
13. Major R. Bohmler. 1st B'n F.J.R.S. (Msta), 1992.
14. Pte. Priestley.
15. Colonel D. J. Fenner. 6th D.L.I. (Iwm - 84/2/1).
16. Pte. Kerens.
17. Ibid.
18. Lt. D. Cole. 2nd B'n Inniskilling Fusiliers. (Msta), 1991.
19. Lt. Col. J. Frost. 1st B'n Parachute Reg., Co. (Msta), 1994.
20. Pte. R. Pope. 9th D.L.I. (Tiwa), 1991.
21. Pte. E. Kerens.
22. Colonel D. J. Fenner.
23. Cpl. G. Worthington. Mm. 6th D.L.I. (Tiwa), 1994.
24. Pte. R. Hymer.
25. Pte. Reg Pope. D.L.I. (Tiwa), 1994.
26. Colonel D. J. Fenner.
27. Pte. E. Kerens.
28. Colonel D. J. Fenner.
29. Sgt. T. Cairns. 6th D.L.I. (Msta), 1992.
30. Cpt. R. Atkinson. 6th D.L.I. Interview: 1957.
31. Cpt. Eric Fassl. F.J.R.S. (Msta), 1990.
32. Major A W Grant. MC. 3rd County of London Yeomanry. (TIWA) 1997.
33. Colonel D. J. Fenner.
34. Pte. E. Kerens.
35. Csm L. Whittle. 5th B'n East York's Reg., (Tiwa), 1994.
36. Cpl. A. Snowdon. 7th B'n Green Howards. (Tiwa), 1991.
37. Pte. R. Walker. 5th B'n East York's Reg., (Tiwa), 1991.
38. Colonel D. J. Fenner.
39. Pte. H. Forth.
40. Harry Gratland. 44th RTR. (Letter to author.) 1997
41. Arthur Soper. 44th RTR. (Letter to author.) 1997
42. Colonel Fenner.
43. Ibid.

BIBLIOGRAPHY

Clay. E.	'The Path Of The 50th'. Gale And Polden. 1950.
Cooper. M.	'The German Army: 1939 To 1945'. Macdonald And Jane's. 1978.
Montgomery. B.	'El Alemein To The River Sangro'. Hutchinson. 1948.
D'este. C.	'Bitter Vistory: Sicily 1943'. Collins. 1988.
Lewis. P. J. and English. I. R.	'Into Battle With The Durhams'. London Stamp Exchange. 1990.
Arthur. M.	'Men Of The Red Beret'. Hutchinson. 1990.
Whiting. C.	'Slaughter Over Sicily'. Pen And Sword. 1992.
Whiting. C.	'The Poor Bloody Infantry'. Paul. 1987.
Liddel-Hart. B.	'History Of The Second World War'. Cassell. 1970.
Howarth. P.	'My God Soldiers: From Alamein To Vienna'. Hutchinson. 1988.
Brook. S.	'Montgomery And The 8th Army'. Bodley Head. 1991.
Ellis. J.	'Brute Force'. André Deutsch. 1990.
Mitcham. S. W.	'Hitlers Legions'. Leo Cooper. 1985.
Barker and Rust.	'A Short History Of The 50th Northumbrian Division'. 1966.
Rissik. D. Major.	'The D.L.I. At War'. Brancepeth Castle, The Depot Of The D.L.I. 1953.
Mollo. B.	'The Sharpshooters'. Historical Research Unit: Kent And County Of London Yeomanry - Royal Yeomanry Rgt. 1970.
Crookenden. A.	'The History Of The Cheshire Rgt. In The Second World War'. Chester: W. H. Evans. 1949.
Graham. A.	'Sharpshooters At War: 1939 To 1945'. Regimental Association. 1964.
Synge. W. A. T.	'The Green Howards: 1939 To 1945'. Richmond, Yorks. 1952.
Cyril. N.	'The London Scottish: 1939 To 1945'. Clones. 1952.
Blight. G.	'The Royal Berkshire Rgt: 1920 To 1947'. Staples. 1953.

APPENDIX 'A'

50th Northumbrian Division

Honours And Awards: 10th To 18th July, 1943.

Abbreviations Used In The Text:

DSO: Distinguished Service Order
DCM: Distinguished Conduct Medal
MC: Military Cross
BEM: British Empire Medal
MM: Military Medal
MID: Mentioned In Dispatches

BAR: If a bar was awarded it means the individual has been awarded the same gallantry medal for the second time. This was worn on the ribbon of the original award.

151ST INFANTRY BRIGADE

NAME	AWARD	DATE OF ACTION	DATE GAZETTED	UNIT
MAJOR. R. G. ATKINSON	MC	16th/17th JULY	23/12/43	6th D.L.I.
L/SGT. J. CONNEL	DCM	13th JULY	18/11/43	6th D.L.I.
L/SGT. C. R. CRITCHLEY	MM	16th JULY	21/10/43	6th D.L.I.
PTE. H. DUCKWORTH	MM	13th/17th JULY	18/11/43	6th D.L.I.
LT. D. A. FRENCH-KENOE	MC	17th JULY	18/11/43	NORTHAMPTONS: ATT'D TO 6th D.L.I.
CPT. R. GALLOWAY	MC	10th JULY	23/12/43	6th D.L.I.
LT. D. A. LOVERIDGE	MC	17th JULY	21/10/43	SUFFOLK RGT: ATT'D 6th D.L.I.

151ST INFANTRY BRIGADE
(Continued)

NAME	AWARD	DATE OF ACTION	DATE GAZETTED	UNIT
PTE. R. ROBINSON	MM	16th/17th JULY	21/10/43	6th D.L.I.
PTE. D. H. SABAN	MM	17th JULY	21/10/43	6th D.L.I.
L/CPL. G. WORTHINGTON	MM	16th/17th JULY	21/10/43	6th D.L.I.
CPT. C. L. BEATTIE	MC	16th/17th JULY	21/10/43	8th D.L.I.
PTE. G. T. GOODWIN	MM	16th JULY	21/10/43	8th D.L.I.
CSM. J. R. HANNAH	MM	15th/16th JULY	21/10/43	8th D.L.I.
LT. P. G. HAMPSON	MC	16th/17th JULY	21/10/43	8th D.L.I.
SIGNALMAN P. J. HORTON	MM	15th/16th JULY	21/10/43	50 DIV SIGNALS: ATT'D TO 8th D.L.I.
LT. COL. R. P. LIDWILL	DSO	15th/16th JULY	21/10/43	KING'S LIVERPOOL RGT: ATT'D 8th D.L.I.
SGT. J. J. LEE	MM	NO SPECIFIC DATE GIVEN	23/03/44	ARMY CATERING CORPS: ATT'D 8th D.L.I.
CPT. J. A. LEYBOURNE	MC	16th/17th JULY	21/10/43	8th D.L.I.
CPT. D. A. NEALE	MC	15th/16th JULY	21/10/43	8th D.L.I.
SGT. F. MITCHINSON	MM	15th/16th JULY	21/10/43	8th D.L.I.
L/SGT. D. J. RICHARDS	MM	16th/17th JULY	21/10/43	8th D.L.I.
CPL. W. D. SCRIVEN	MM	15th/16th JULY	21/10/43	8th D.L.I.
CPL. F. SPINK	MM	16th/17th JULY	21/10/43	8th D.L.I.
L/CPL. G. F. SHEPHERD	MM	15th/16th JULY	21/10/43	8th D.L.I.
CSM. S. WARDLE	MM	15th/16th JULY	21/10/43	8th D.L.I.
SGT. C. J. W. MACKMIN	MM	16th/17th JULY	21/10/43	8th D.L.I.
L/SGT. P. DALEY	MM	15th JULY	21/10/43	9th D.L.I.
LT. W. J. H. MUIR. MC.	BAR TO MC	9th/10th AND 17th JULY	21/10/43	9th D.L.I.
L/CPL. S. S. ROSE	MM	14th/15th JULY	21/10/43	9th D.L.I.
CSM. F. THOMPSON	DCM	17th TO 19th JULY	21/10/43	9th D.L.I.
L/CPL. C. B. SIMPSON	MM	17th JULY	23/12/43	9th D.L.I.

NAME	AWARD	DATE OF ACTION	DATE GAZETTED	UNIT
SIGNALMAN T. P. BOYD	MM	16th/17th JULY	21/10/43	50 DIV SIGNALS: ATT'D 151 BDE.
L/CPL. A. COCKETT	MM	16th JULY	21/10/43	50 DIV SIGNALS. ATT'D 151 BDE.
DVR. S. SEARLE	MM	16th/17th JULY	21/10/43	50 DIV SIGNALS. ATT'D 151 BDE.
L/CPL. H. BLEAKLEY	MM	JULY/ AUGUST	23/03/44	50 DIV SIGNALS: ATT'D 151 AND 168 BDE.
CPT. K. H. WHITAKER	MC	15th/16th JULY	18/11/43	SOMERSET. L. I. TROOP COMMANDER: A/TK GUNS. 151 BDE.

168TH INFANTRY BRIGADE

NAME	AWARD	DATE OF ACTION	DATE GAZETTED	UNIT
CPT. H. R. R. ATWOOL	MC	16th/17th JULY	UNKNOWN	1st LONDON SCOTTISH
LT. J. H. GILLAN	MC	15th/16th JULY	21/10/43	1st LONDON SCOTTISH
PTE. A. P. PROCTOR	MM	16th/17th JULY	21/10/43	1st LONDON SCOTTISH
PIPER. T. J. BRIGHTMAN	MM	17th/18th JULY	21/10/43	1st LONDON IRISH
CPT. W. E. BROOKS	MC	17th/18th JULY	UNKNOWN	1st LONDON IRISH
CQMS. W. HUNNEX	BEM	17th/18th JULY	UNKNOWN	1st LONDON IRISH
SGT. J. T. MADIGAN	MM	17th/18th JULY	21/10/43	1st LONDON IRISH
LT. A. E. CRAMPTON	MM	17th JULY	23/12/43	1st LONDON IRISH
CPL. C. BLAIR	MM	17th JULY	18/11/43	1st LONDON IRISH
PTE. P. ADAMSON	MM	JULY/ AUGUST	UNKNOWN	10th ROYAL BERKSHIRE RGT.

69TH INFANTRY BRIGADE

NAME	AWARD	DATE OF ACTION	DATE GAZETTED	UNIT
L/SGT. E. A. HOOD	MM	18th JULY	21/10/43	7th GREEN HOWARDS
LT. C. G. SMITH	MC	14th JULY	23/12/43	7th GREEN HOWARDS
CPT. L. HERBERT	MC	17th/18th JULY	21/10/43	6th GREEN HOWARDS

69TH INFANTRY BRIGADE
(Continued)

NAME	AWARD	DATE OF ACTION	DATE GAZETTED	UNIT
PTE. J. BAILEY	MM	15th JULY	21/10/43	5th EAST YORK'S.
LT. COL. R. B. JAMES DSO BAR	2ND BAR TO DSO	12th JULY	21/10/43	COMMANDING OFFICER - 5th EAST YORK'S
	(KILLED IN ACTION - AUGUST 1944)			
PTE. H. FORTH	MID	17th JULY	UNKNOWN	5th EAST YORK'S
LT. COL. D. G. JEBB	DSO	17th/18th JULY	23/10/43	7th GREEN HOWARDS

ROYAL ARTILLERY

NAME	AWARD	DATE OF ACTION	DATE GAZETTED	UNIT
SGT. H. H. ASTON	MM	14th JULY	21/10/43	124 FLD RGT. RA.
L/BDR. E. W. ARMIGER	MM	14th JULY	21/10/43	124 FLD RGT. RA.
SGT. F. W. HOPKINS	MM	16th TO 19th JULY	23/12/43	124 FLD RGT. RA.
GNR. H. J. PHILLIPS	MM	14th JULY	21/10/43	124 FLD RGT. RA.
RSM. A. J. SHARP	MM	14th JULY	21/10/43	124 FLD RGT. RA.
GNR. R. SNELLING	MM	18th JULY	23/12/43	90th FLD RGT. RA.
LT. COL. THE HON. G. C. CUBITT	DSO	10th TO 15th JULY	21/10/43	COMMANDING OFFICER: 98 ARMY FLD RGT. RA. (SURREY AND SUSSEX YEOMANRY)
CPT. G. H. PEILE	MC	16th/17th JULY	21/10/43	98 ARMY FLD RGT. RA. (SURREY AND SUSSEX YEOMANRY)
LT. L. L. PIKE	MC	14th TO 18th JULY	21/10/43	98 FLD RGT. RA. (SURREY AND SUSSEX YEOMANRY)
MAJOR G. C. WELLS	MC	17th JULY	23/12/43	90th FLD RGT. RA.

ROYAL ENGINEERS

NAME	AWARD	DATE OF ACTION	DATE GAZETTED	UNIT
MAJOR C. A. O. COMPTON	MC	15th/16th JULY	21/10/43	505 FLD COY. RE.
CPL. G. Y. RUSSEL MM	BAR TO MM	16th JULY	21/10/43	505 FLD COY. RE.
PTE. F. HAMBLETT	MM	10th JULY	23/12/43	1st WELSH RGT: ATTD 34 BEACH BRICK
CPT. L. F. HARD	MC	10th JULY	23/12/43	1st WELSH RGT: ATTD 34 BEACH BRICK

R.A.M.C.

NAME	AWARD	DATE OF ACTION	DATE GAZETTED	UNIT
PTE. J. G. HALL	MM	JULY/ AUGUST	23/03/44	149 FLD AMB.

APPENDIX 'B'

'THE FALLEN': 50TH NORTHUMBRIAN DIVISION

Sicily: 13th To 18th July, 1943

SYRACUSE WAR CEMETERY

AUSTIN, Rfn. ARTHUR HENRY GEORGE, 5345381. 1st Bn. The London Irish Rifles, The Royal Ulster Rifles. 18th July, 1943. Age 26.

AUSTIN, Tpr. JOHN HORACE, 7886982. 3rd County of London Yeomanry (Sharpshooters), R.A.C. 13th July, 1943

BAKER, Gnr. ALBERT GEORGE, 1112718. 98 (The Surrey and Sussex Yeomanry) Field Regt., Royal Artillery. 13th July, 1943. Age 35.

BEAZLEY, Gnr. FREDERICK WILLIAM HENRY, 987907. 98 (The Surrey and Sussex Yeomanry) Field Regt., Royal Artillery. 13th July, 1943. Age 23.

BEATTIE, Rfn. HENRY, 7021571. 1st Bn. The London Irish Rifles, The Royal Ulster Rifles. 18th July, 1943.

BEECH, Pte. HAROLD, 4918820. 7th Bn. The Green Howards (Yorkshire Regt.). 18th July, 1943. Age 25.

BELL, Pte. HENRY, 4455469. 6th Bn. The Durham Light Infantry. 12th July, 1943. Age 29.

BENNETT, Gnr. GEORGE HENRY, 940587. 102 (The Northumberland Hussars) Anti-Tank Regt., Royal Artillery. 13th July, 1943. Age 24.

BERNSTEIN, Pte. JACOB, 4751190. 5th Bn. The East Yorkshire Regt. 13th July, 1943.

BLADES, Pte. ERNEST, 4345010. 5th Bn. The East Yorkshire Regt. 16th July, 1943. Age 25.

BROWN, Cpl. ALAN, 4396737. 7th Bn. The Green Howards (Yorkshire Regt.). 17 July, 1943. Age 31.

BRUTON, Pte. WILLIAM HENRY, 4070502. 9th Bn. The Durham Light Infantry. 17th July, 1943. Age 40.

BUDGEN, L. Sjt. PHILIP HOWARD, 7891594. 3rd County of London Yeomanry (Sharpshooters), R.A.C. 14th July, 1943. Age 35.

CHAPMAN, Capt. JAMES HAY, 143393, M.C. 6th Bn. The Durham Light Infantry. 13th July, 1943. Age 21.

COX, Pte. NORMAN ALBERT GEORGE, 5350414. 2nd Bn. The Cheshire Regt. 14th July, 1943. Age 21.

DARCH, Sjt. NORMAN BRIAN, 7906125. 'A' Sqn., 3rd County of London Yeomanry (Sharpshooters), R.A.C. 13th July, 1943. Age 33.

DERBYSHIRE, L. Cpl. WALTER, 4862844. 7th Bn. The Green Howards (Yorkshire Regt.). 15th July, 1943. Age 28.

ELSON, Pte. JOHN DONALD, 5350431. 2nd Bn. The Cheshire Regt. 14th July, 1943. Age 21.

FROST, Pte. ROWLAND, 4393634. 7th Bn. The Green Howards (Yorkshire Regt.). 17th July, 1943. Age 23.

GARRETT, Pte. PATRICK, 4453374. 9th Bn. The Durham Light Infantry. 15th July, 1943.

GIBSON, Pte. THOMAS, 6854955. 2nd Bn. The Cheshire Regt. 14th July, 1943. Age 30.

GOOSEY, Pte. WILLIAM HENRY, 4862230. 2nd Bn. The Cheshire Regt. 14th July, 1943. Age 27.

HARDY, L. Bdr. THOMAS HENRY WILLIAM, 977867. 102 (The Northumberland Hussars) Anti-Tank Regt., Royal Artillery. 14th July, 1943.

HARRINGTON, Sjt. ARTHUR WILLIS, 4391904. 6th Bn. The Green Howards (Yorkshire Regt.). 14th July, 1943. Age 24.

HARRIS, Sjt. CHARLES LEONARD ASTON, 7890148. 'A' Sqn., 3rd County of London Yeomanry (Sharpshooters), R.A.C. 14th July, 1943. Age 35.

HENDERSON, Tpr. WILLIAM, 7936625. 'A' Sqn., 3rd County of London Yeomanry (Sharpshooters), R.A.C. 13th July, 1943. Age 33.

HONE, Lt. DAVID ARTHUR, 176312, M.C. 5th Bn. The Northamptonshire Regt., attd. 7th Bn. The Green Howards (Yorkshire Regt.). 14th July, 1943. Age 24.

HORNBY, Pte. HAROLD JOSEPH, 4128415. 2nd Bn. The Cheshire Regt. 15th July, 1943. Age 22.

HORTON, Cpl. ROBERT ALLAN, 4348003. 5th Bn. The East Yorkshire Regt. 13th July, 1943. Age 28.

HOWARD, L. Sjt. HARRY WILLIAM, 5932815. 7th Bn. The Green Howards (Yorkshire Regt.). 14th July, 1943. Age 33.

HOWELLS, Pte. WILLIAM, 5122665. 9th Bn. The Durham Light Infantry. 16th July, 1943. Age 34.

HURMAN, Gnr. PETER REGINALD, 920449. 74 Field Regt., Royal Artillery. 13th July, 1943. Age 23.

INCE, Gnr. WILLIAM, 964524. 74 Field Regt., Royal Artillery. 13th July, 1943. Age 26.

LANE, Pte. MATTHEW, 4399285. 7th Bn. The Green Howards (Yorkshire Regt.). 14th July, 1943.

LISHMAN, Cpt. STANLEY, 4460624, M.M. 6th Bn. The Durham Light Infantry. 17th July, 1943. Age 27.

LONG, Dvr. GEORGE, 2138413. 235 Field Park Coy., Royal Engineers. 13th July, 1943. Age 22.

LOWTHER, L. Cpl. JOHN JAMES, 4468532. 6th Bn. The Durham Light Infantry. 13th July, 1943.

LYNCH, Pte. JOHN, 3461291. 9th Bn. The Durham Light Infantry. 18th July, 1943. Age 33.

MACKIE, Gnr. JAMES LIONEL, 1099863. 74 Field Regt., Royal Artillery. 13th July, 1943. Age 36.

MATFIN, Pte. MATTHEW, 4399285. 7th Bn. The Green Howards (Yorkshire Regt.). 14th July, 1943. Age 23.

MAYLAND, Sjt. THOMAS ROLINS, 2039494. 235 Field Park Coy., Royal Engineers. 16th July, 1943. Age 28.

MOORE, L. Bdr. WILLIAM ARCHIBALD, 933559. 74 Field Regt., Royal Artillery. 13th July, 1943. Age 25.

MORRIS, Sjt. THOMAS HENRY, 4859897. 9th Bn. The Durham Light Infantry. 12th July, 1943. Age 24.

PILBROW, Bdr. JOSEPH HENRY, 855217. 74 Field Regt., Royal Artillery. 13th July, 1943. Age 28.

RAWSON, Tpr. REGINALD, 7938053. 3rd County of London Yeomanry (Sharpshooters), R.A.C. 13th July, 1943. Age 22.

REYNOLDS, Sjt. ROBERT VICTOR, 4618054. 5th Bn. The East Yorkshire Regt. 13th July, 1943. Age 23.

RILEY, L.Bdr. DAVID BRYNMOR, 894538. 98 (The Surrey and Sussex Yeomanry) Field Regt., Royal Artillery. 13th July, 1943. Age 33.

RIXON, Sigmn. JACK, 4348753. Royal Corps of Signals, 50th Div. Sigs. 15th July, 1943. Age 24.

SAUNDERS, Gnr. ALAN BENJAMIN ROBERT, 877147. Royal Artillery, attd. H.Q. 50th Div. 14th July, 1943. Age 26.

SISTERSON, Gnr. JAMES WILLIAM ALLENBY, 322229. 102 (The Northumberland Hussars) Anti-Tank Regt., Royal Artillery. 14th July, 1943. Age 21.

SMART, Pte. WILLIAM ARTHUR, 6147223. 7th Bn. The Green Howards (Yorkshire Regt.). 14th July, 1943. Age 28.

SMITH, Gnr. ROBERT, 224747. 102 (The Northumberland Hussars) Anti-Tank Regt., Royal Artillery. 13th July, 1943. Age 31.

WATKINS, Gnr. FREDRICK CHARLES, 1071265. 98 (The Surrey and Sussex Yeomanry) Field Regt., Royal Artillery. 13th July, 1943.

WESTGATE, Tpr. GORDON ROY, 7897844. 'A' Sqn., 3rd County of London Yeomanry (Sharpshooters), R.A.C. 13th July, 1943. Age 29.

WOOD, Tpr. GEORGE CARR, 4744824. 'A' Sqn., 3rd County of London Yeomanry (Sharpshooters), R.A.C. 13th July, 943. Age 30.

SMITH, Pte. DAVID, 4349825. 5th Bn. The East Yorkshire Regt. 13th July, 1943. Age 36.

WALKER, Pte. JAMES, 4399919. 7th Bn. The Green Howards (Yorkshire Regt.). 14th July, 1943. Age 20.

WAY, Pte. JAMES WALTER, 5337232. 2nd Bn. The Cheshire Regt. 14th July, 1943. Age 27.

WHITTAKER, Cpl. ALFRED, 4347126. 5th Bn. The East Yorkshire Regt. 14th July, 1943. Age 23.

CATANIA WAR CEMETERY

ALCOCK, L. Sjt. GEORGE, 4037197. 9th Bn. The Durham Light Infantry. 16th July, 1943. Age 28.

ARMITAGE, Pte. FRED, 10603338. 6th Bn. The Durham Light Infantry. 17th July, 1943. Age 35.

BACON, Pte. FREDRICK WILLIAM, 6021792. 9th Bn. The Durham Light Infantry. 17th July, 1943. Age 23.

BELL, 2/Lt. WILLIAM ALAN, 287782. 5th Bn. The East Yorkshire Regt. 15th July, 1943. Age 26.

BENTLEY, Pte. JACK HEBERT, 14207157. 10th Bn. The Royal Berkshire Regt. 18th July, 1943. Age 27.

BETLEY, L.Cpl. JACK, 4399889. 5th Bn. The East Yorkshire Regt. 15th July, 1943. Age 20.

BISSETT, Pte. GEORGE DICKIE, 2883077. 1st Bn. The London Scottish, The Gordon Highlanders. 17th July, 1943. Age 20.

BLACKMORE, Sjt. HALLET JOHN, 4749380, M.M. 7th Bn. The Green Howards (Yorkshire Regt.). 18th July, 1943. Age 23.

BRAITHWAITE, Pte. ARTHUR, 4389610. 7th Bn. The Green Howards (Yorkshire Regt.). 16th July, 1943. Age 24.

ANDREWS, Pte. JOHN CHARLES, 4539686. 9th Bn. The Durham Light Infantry. 7th July, 1943. Age 23.

ASTROP, Pte. RICHARD HENRY, 4445009. 9th Bn. The Durham Light Infantry. 17th July, 1943. Age 37.

BARBOUR, L.Cpl. JAMES WILFRED, 7013766. 1st Bn. The London Irish Rifles, The Royal Ulster Rifles. 18th July, 1943. Age 35.

BENNETT, Rfn. ALBERT PHILIP, 7017500. 1st Bn. The London Irish Rifles, The Royal Ulster Rifles. 18th July, 1943. Age 28.

BERRY, L.Cpl. ERNEST, 3656837. 6th Bn. The Durham Light Infantry. 17th July, 1943. Age 25.

BIFFIN, Rfn. FRANCIS LAWRENCE, 7020289. 1st Bn. The London Irish Rifles, The Royal Ulster Rifles. 18th July, 1943. Age 29.

BLACK, L.Cpl. GEORGE CARSTAIRS, 7951109. 'A' Sqn., 44th Royal Tank Regt., R.A.C. 15th July, 1943. Age 20.

BOWEN, Pte PERCY, 4134041. 2nd Bn. The Cheshire Regt. 17th July, 1943. Age 21.

BRANNIGAN, W.O. II (C.S.M.) MATTHEW JOHN, 4449955, M.M. 8th Bn. The Durham Light Infantry. 17th July, 1943. Age 28.

BRITNELL, Pte. TOM, 5347137. 10th Bn. The Royal Berkshire Regt. 17th July, 1943. Age 27.

BROWN, Pte. CYRIL, 4464918. 6th Bn. The Durham Light Infantry. 17th July, 1943.

BRYDEN, Cpl. JOHN ALEXANDER, 6665107. 1st Bn. The London Scottish, The Gordon Highlanders. 18th July, 1943. Age 35.

BURKS, L.Sjt. WILFRED, 4533198. 6th Bn. The Durham Light Infantry. 17th July, 1943.

BUTT, Pte. GORDON ROBERT, 4202204. 8th Bn. The Durham Light Infantry. 18th July, 1943. Age 23.

CARR, Sjt. JOSEPH, 4458586. 8th Bn. The Durham Light Infantry. 17th July, 1943. Age 24.

CARTER, L.Cpl. RICHARD, 4454454. 9th Bn. The Durham Light Infantry. 17th July, 1943. Age 22.

CHADBOURNE, L.Bdr. EDWIN, 1110885. 90 Field Regt., Royal Artillery. 18th July, 1943.

CHURCH, Pte. CHARLES EDWARD, 14200037. 10th Bn. The Royal Berkshire Regt. 18th July, 1943. Age 20.

CLARKE, Lt. FREDERICK, 203388. The Oxfordshire and Buckinghamshire Light Infantry, attd. 8th Bn. The Durham Light Infantry. 17th July, 1943. Age 23.

CLEALL, Rfn. LAWRENCE DUNN, 7016153. 1st Bn. The London Irish Rifles, The Royal Ulster Rifles. 18th July, 1943. Age 25.

COATES, Gnr. WILLIAM NOEL, 942178. 74 Field Regt., Royal Artillery. 17th July, 1943. Age 24.

COLLIN, Dvr. HENRY, 2380725. Royal Corps of Signals, 50th Div. Sigs. 16th/17th July, 1943. Age 30.

COLSELL, Sigmn. ROLAND EDWIN, 2331773. Royal Corps of Signals, 50th Div. Sigs. 16th/17th July, 1943.

COPLESTON, Pte. JOHN HENRY, 4079715. 9th Bn. The Durham Light Infantry. 16th July, 1943. Age 24.

BROOKES, Pte. JACK, 4918722. 7th Bn. The Green Howards (Yorkshire Regt.). 18th July, 1943. Age 25.

BROWN, Pte. THOMAS COLE, 3605934. 9th Bn. The Durham Light Infantry. 17th July, 1943. Age 33.

BURDEN, Cpl. COLIN FREDRICK, 5350280. 10th Bn. The Royal Berkshire Regt. 18th July, 1943. Age 21.

BURNETT, Pte. DAVID HUNTER, 3191129. 8th Bn. The Durham Light Infantry. 17th July, 1943.

CAIN, Pte. ALBERT GEORGE, 10600402. 5th Bn. The East Yorkshire Regt. 15th July, 1943. Age 30.

CARR, 2/Lt. ROBERT KNOTTS, 287853. 9th Bn. The Durham Light Infantry. 17th July, 1943. Age 25.

CANNELL, Pte. GEORGE BENJAMIN, 6022426. 10th Bn. The Royal Berkshire Regt. 18th July, 1943. Age 23.

CATHERALL, L.Cpl. ARTHUR GEORGE, 5338928. 10th Bn. The Royal Berkshire Regt. 18th July, 1943. Age 25.

CLARKE, L.Cpl. ARTHUR, 4618325. 6th Bn. The Durham Light Infantry. 17th July, 1943. Age 23.

CLARKE, Pte. THOMAS, 4462291. 8th Bn. The Durham Light Infantry. 17th July, 1943. Age 28.

CLUTTON, Cpl. HENRY, 4193346. 8th Bn. The Durham Light Infantry. 17th July, 1943. Age 25.

COGHLIN, Lt. THOMAS WILLIAM, 176454. 1st Bn. The London Irish Rifles. 18th July, 1943. Age 37.

COLLINS, Pte. EDWARD, 5889845. 6th Bn. The Durham Light Infantry. 17th July, 1943. Age 30.

CONYERS, L.Cpl. ROBERT ALFRED, 4626936. 8th Bn. The Durham Light Infantry. 18th July, 1943. Age 21.

COSGROVE, Pte. AMBROSE, 3662608. 6th Bn. The Durham Light Infantry. 17th July, 1943. Age 21.

COULTHARD, Pte. BERTRAM, 4451823. 8th Bn. The Durham Light Infantry. 17th July, 1943. Age 28.

CROPP, Pte. REGINALD HENRY CHARLES, 5345419. 10th Bn. The Royal Berkshire Regt. 18th July, 1943.

DANCE, Rfn. KENNETH, 6405530. 1st Bn. The London Irish Rifles, The Royal Ulster Rifles. 18th July, 1943. Age 19.

DEACON, Capt. WILFRED GEORGE, 195189. 9th Bn. The Durham Light Infantry. 17th July, 1943. Age 25.

DEGG, L.Cpl. RAYMOND, 4037245. 9th Bn. The Durham Light Infantry. 16th July, 1943. Age 28.

DENNEHY, Rfn. CHRISTOPHER, 7014448. 1st Bn. The London Irish Rifles, The Royal Ulster Rifles. 18th July, 1943. Age 33.

DIXON, Pte. DAVID, 4460548. 9th Bn. The Durham Light Infantry. 16th July, 1943. Age 26.

DONOVAN, Pte. THOMAS, 4755240. 7th Bn. The Green Howards (Yorkshire Regt.). 18th July, 1943.

ELLIOTT, Pte. JOHN ROBERT, 14229153. 8th Bn. The Durham Light Infantry. 17th July, 1943.

FLEMING, Rfn. PATRICK EDWARD, 7020677. 1st Bn. The London Irish Rifles, The Royal Ulster Rifles. 18th July, 1943. Age 35.

GALLACHER, Cpl. JOHN, 2879620. 1st Bn. The London Scottish, The Gordon Highlanders. 18th July, 1943. Age 28.

GEORGE, Pte. MATTHEW DOUGLAS, 4466751. 6th Bn. The Durham Light Infantry. 17th July, 1943.

GLOVER, Pte. JOHN, 4038895. 6th Bn. The Durham Light Infantry. 17th July, 1943. Age 23.

GORDON, Pte. PETER BURNS, 2884984. 1st Bn. The London Scottish, The Gordon Highlanders. 17th July, 1943. Age 28.

GRACE, Cpl. PATRICK, 7043382. 9th Bn. The Durham Light Infantry. 16th July, 1943.

CRUTCHLEY, Pte. HENRY HARDING, 4469943. 9th Bn. The Durham Light Infantry. 16th July, 1943

CULLUM, Tpr. AUBREY ERNEST, 7949643. 44th Royal Tank Regt., R.A.C. 18th July, 1943. Age 21.

DAWSON, Pte. TURNOUGH, 4467361. 9th Bn. The Durham Light Infantry. 16th July, 1943. Age 23.

DEEPROSE, Rfn. ALBERT JAMES, 14206995. 1st Bn. The London Irish Rifles, The Royal Ulster Rifles. 18th July, 1943. Age 28.

DELL, Pte. FREDERICK JOSEPH, 6016570. 6th Bn. The Durham Light Infantry. 18th July, 1943. Age 22.

DISTON, W.O. II. (C.S.M.) RALPH FOSTER, 4448907, D.C.M. 9th Bn. The Durham Light Infantry. 18th July, 1943. Age 30.

DONALD, Pte. JAMES, 2886415. 1st Bn. The London Scottish, The Gordon Highlanders. 18th July, 1943. Age 28.

DYKE, Pte. FREDERICK, 5672755. 9th Bn. The Durham Light Infantry. 17th July, 1943.

FELGATE, Rfn. FREDERICK ERNEST, 6031828. 1st Bn. The London Irish Rifles, The Royal Ulster Rifles. 18th July, 1943. Age 30.

FROST, Pte. ALFRED, 3390278. 8th Bn. The Durham Light Infantry. 18th July, 1943.

GEDDES, Pte. ANDREW, 2884994. 1st Bn. The London Scottish, The Gordon Highlanders. 18th July, 1943. Age 28.

GIBSON, Cpl. GORDON, 4457267. 9th Bn. The Durham Light Infantry. 16th July, 1943. Age 25.

GOOD, Pte. GEORGE HENRY 13023585. 5th Bn. The East Yorkshire Regt. 14th July, 1943. Age 29.

GORING, Cpl. RICHARD, 4035452. 8th Bn. The Durham Light Infantry. 17th July, 1943.

GREEN, Pte. THOMAS GEORGE, 4037275. 9th Bn. The Durham Light Infantry. 16th July, 1943. Age 28.

GREENFIELD, L.Sjt. FREDERICK JAMES, 5344265. 10th Bn. The Royal Berkshire Regt. 18th July, 1943. Age 28.

GUIDI, Pte. ALELMO, 2159614. 9th Bn. The Durham Light Infantry. 16th July, 1943. Age 20.

HAINES, Pte. WILLIAM REUBEN, 5350448. 10th Bn. The Royal Berkshire Regt. 18th July, 1943. Age 29.

HALL, W.O. II. (C.S.M.) HUBERT JOHN, 7014468. 1st Bn. The London Irish Rifles, The Royal Ulster Rifles. 18th July, 1943. Age 26.

HALL, Pte. JOHN ROBERT DENT, 4469528. 9th Bn. The Durham Light Infantry. 16th July, 1943. Age 28.

HALLSWORTH, Pte. JOHN WILLIAM, 3660865. 8th Bn. The Durham Light Infantry. 17th July, 1943. Age 30.

HAMILTON, Pte. ALEXANDER, 5258616. 9th Bn. The Durham Light Infantry. 17th July, 1943.

HARDMAN, Pte. JOHN ROBERT, 4466148. 9th Bn. The Durham Light Infantry. 17th July, 1943. Age 33.

HARDWICK, Pte. TOM, 4758157. 5th Bn. The East Yorkshire Regt. 14th July, 1943.

HARVEY, Rfn. RAYMOND GEORGE, 6406270. 1st Bn. The London Irish Rifles, The Royal Ulster Rifles. 18th July, 1943. Age 28.

HAY, Capt. IAN THOMAS RUSSELL, 112982, M.C. 7th Bn. The Green Howards (Yorkshire Regt.). 18th July, 1943. Age 22.

HAY, Pte. JAMES HUNTER, 2890741. 1st Bn. The London Scottish, The Gordon Highlanders. 18th July, 1943. Age 35.

HAYES, Pte. DAVID HENRY, 4618110. 5th Bn. The East Yorkshire Regt. 18th July, 1943. Age 23.

HEDGES, L.Cpl. JAMES CHARLES, 5341482. 10th Bn. The Royal Berkshire Regt. 18th July, 1943. Age 25.

HEEPS, Pte. JOHN, 2987632. 6th Bn. The Durham Light Infantry. 17th July, 1943.

HESKETH, Lt. WILLIAM, 219093. The King's Own Royal Regt. (Lancaster), attd. 6th Bn. The Durham Light Infantry. 17th July, 1943. Age 30.

HIGHAM, L.Cpl. CHARLES ROBERT, 4349631. 5th Bn. The East Yorkshire Regt. 14th July, 1943. Age 33.

HOLDEN, Pte. HARRY, 4459092. 9th Bn. The Durham Light Infantry. 17th July, 1943. Age 25.

HOLDEN, Pte. WILLIAM, 3856655. 9th Bn. The Durham Light Infantry. 17th July, 1943. Age 24.

HOLOHAN, Pte. LAWRENCE ANTONY, 2879690. 1st Bn. The London Scottish, The Gordon Highlanders. 18th July, 1943.

HOLT, Pte. FRED, 3718545. 5th Bn. The East Yorkshire Regt. 14th July, 1943. Age 34.

HOOPER, Rfn. FRANK HERBERT SHELTON, 6007057. 1st Bn. The London Irish Rifles, The Royal Ulster Rifles. 18th July, 1943.

HOPKINS, Pte. HERBERT, 4743474. 5th Bn. The East Yorkshire Regt. 14th July, 1943.

HOYTE, Lt. WALTER RAYMOND JULYAN, 164833. The Somerset Light Infantry, attd. 9th Bn. The Durham Light Infantry. 16th July, 943. Age 24.

HUTCHINSON, L.Cpl. JOHN, 4456141. 8th Bn. The Durham Light Infantry. 17th July, 1943.

HUTCHINSON, Pte. ROBERT, 4463604. 9th Bn. The Durham Light Infantry. 15th July, 1943.

IZZARD, Pte. ROY BERNARD, 5350470. 2nd Bn. The Cheshire Regt. 16th July, 1943. Age 21.

JEFFS, Rfn. JAMES RONALD, 5337222. 1st Bn. The London Irish Rifles, The Royal Ulster Rifles. 18th July, 1943.

JENKINS, L.Cpl. EDWARD, 5345158. 6th Bn. The Durham Light Infantry. 18th July, 1943. Age 30.

JOHN, Pte. PHIL, 3910745. 8th Bn. The Durham Light Infantry. 17th July, 1943. Age 25.

JONES, Pte. DAVID, 3970545. 9th Bn. The Durham Light Infantry. 16th July, 1943. Age 29.

JONES, Pte. RICHARD WILLIAM HENRY, 7047070. 1st Bn. The London Scottish, The Gordon Highlanders. 18th July, 1943.

JOYNER, Cpl. ALBERT EDWARD, 3655247. 6th Bn. The Durham Light Infantry. 17th July, 1943.

KAUFMAN, L.Cpl. HENRY PERCIVAL, 5339400. 9th Bn. The Durham Light Infantry. 17th July, 1943. Age 20.

KAY, Pte. SAMUEL, 2884997. 1st Bn. The London Scottish, The Gordon Highlanders. 18th July, 1943. Age 28.

KAYE, Lt. NORMAN, 217431. 10th Bn. The Royal Berkshire Regt. 18th July, 1943.

KEAVNEY, L.Cpl. JOHN, 4128922. 2nd Bn. The Cheshire Regt. 19th July, 1943. Age 23.

KELLY, Cpl. JOHN WILLIAM, 4387348. 7th Bn. The Green Howards (Yorkshire Regt.). 18th July, 1943.

KEMP, Pte. ARTHUR RAYMOND, 454864. 9th Bn. The Durham Light Infantry. 17th July, 1943. Age 32.

KENNEDY, Cpl. DAVID EDWARD, 3656165, M.M. 9th Bn. The Durham Light Infantry. 16th July, 1943.

KERSHAW, Capt. KENNETH OLROYD, 138521. 8th Bn. The Durham Light Infantry. 17th July, 1943. Age 33.

KING, Pte. WILLIAM, 4537802. 9th Bn. The Durham Light Infantry. 18th July, 1943. Age 21.

KINSON, Pte. JAMES CHARLES HENRY ALLEN, 7342084. 9th Bn. The Durham Light Infantry. 17th July, 1943.

LAFFERTY. Rfn. JOHN JOSEPH, 7016150. 1st Bn. The London Irish Rifles. The Royal Ulster Rifles. 18th July, 1943. Age 26.

LALLEY, Rfn. FRANCIS, 6031540. 1st Bn. The London Irish Rifles, The Royal Ulster Rifles. 18th July, 1943. Age 21.

LANGLANDS, Cpt. NINIAN SAMUEL, 134371, D.S.O. 124 Field Regt., Royal Artillery. 14th July, 1943. Age 24.

LATHAM, Cpl. SAMUEL ALFRED, 4123851. 2nd Bn. The Cheshire Regt. 17th July, 1943. Age 20.

LAYBOURN, Pte. ROBERT, 4456483. 6th Bn. The Durham Light Infantry. 17th July, 1943. Age 27.

LEEKE, Pte. FREDERICK CHARLES ARTHUR 4037330. 9th Bn. The Durham Light Infantry. 16th July, 1943. Age 27.

LEWIS, L.Sjt. GEORGE EDMUND, 4466511. 8th Bn. The Durham Light Infantry. 17th July, 1943. Age 33.

LINSKILL, Pte. JAMES, 4466811. 8th Bn. The Durham Light Infantry. 18th July, 1943.

LLOYD, Sjt. IVOR, 3911289. 9th Bn. The Durham Light Infantry. 16th July, 1943. Age 24.

LOHAN, Capt. GERARD HARRIS, 94156. The South Staffordshire Regt., attd. 8th Bn. The Durham Light Infantry. 17th July, 1943. Age 32.

LONG, Lt. GEORGE JAMES, 176214. The Hampshire Regt., attd. 6th Bn. The Durham Light Infantry. 17th July, 1943. Age 27.

LONGDEN, Pte. HORACE, 3859925. 9th Bn. The Durham Light Infantry. 16th July, 1943. Age 26.

LUNNESS, Pte. RICHARD STANLEY, 14200137. 10th Bn. The Royal Berkshire Regt. 18th July, 1943.

LUTY, Pte. ERNEST, 4627326. 6th Bn. The Durham Light Infantry. 17th July, 1943. Age 37.

McLOUGHLIN Lt. GERARD, 176395. 9th Bn. The Durham Light Infantry. 17th July, 1943. Age 27.

McNALLY, Pte. WILLIAM LAURENCE CHRISTOPHER, 2883694. 1st Bn. The London Scottish, The Gordon Highlanders. 18th July, 1943. Age 24.

McSHANE, Pte. ANTHONY, 5344313. 10th Bn. The Royal Berkshire Regt. 18th July, 1943. Age 29.

McTERNAN, Rfn. CHARLES, 7047075. 1st Bn. The London Irish Rifles, The Royal Ulster Rifles. 18th July, 1943. Age 29.

MAGILL, Rfn. JAMES, 7013709. 1st Bn. The London Irish Rifles, The Royal Ulster Rifles. 18th July, 1943.

MARR, Pte. WILLIAM ROSE, 2821412. 1st Bn. The London Scottish, The Gordon Highlanders. 17th July, 1943. Age 22.

MARSHALL, Pte. HENRY VICTOR, 6479843. 7th Bn. The Green Howards (Yorkshire Regt.). 18th July, 1943. Age 23.

MATTON, Pte. CHARLES, 6855596. 2nd Bn. The Cheshire Regt., 17th July, 1943. Age 30.

MEE, Pte. EDWARD, 4039234. 8th Bn. The Durham Light Infantry. 17th July, 1943. Age 28.

MOCKFORD, Pte. DOUGLAS FREDERICK, 2881120. 1st Bn. The London Scottish, The Gordon Highlanders. 18th July, 1943. Age 26.

MORGAN, Pte. EDWARD JOHN, 3606892. 9th Bn. The Durham Light Infantry. 18th July, 1943. Age 20.

MORTON, Pte. LAWRENCE, 4459547. 8th Bn. The Durham Light Infantry. 17th July, 1943. Age 26.

MOUNSEY, Lt. NIGEL DERRICK WALTER, 237910. The Border Regt., attd. 7th Bn. The Green Howards (Yorkshire Regt.). 18th July, 1943.

MUNDY, Pte. JOHN ALFRED, 5350513. 10th Bn. The Royal Berkshire Regt. 18th July, 1943. Age 21.

NICHOLLS, L.Bdr. HENRY, 95904. 124 Field Regt., Royal Artillery. 18th July, 1943. Age 24.

NORTH, Pte. GORDON GLYNNE, 5344939. 10th Bn. The Royal Berkshire Regt. 18th July, 1943. Age 27.

O'DELL, Cpl. EDWIN LEWIS, 594674. Royal Corps of Signals, 50th Div. Sigs. 16th/17th July, 1943. Age 31.

OTHICK, Pte. HARRY, 4544995. 5th Bn. The East Yorkshire Regt. 14th July, 1943. Age 31.

MABLY, Pte. LEONARD, 3912259. 9th Bn. The Durham Light Infantry. 16th July, 1943. Age 29.

MALLETT, Rfn. WALTER JAMES HAROLD, 7017554. 1st Bn. The London Irish Rifles, The Royal Ulster Rifles. 18th July, 1943. Age 26.

MARSDEN, C. Sjt. THOMAS SOULSBY, 4456097. 8th Bn. The Durham Light Infantry. 18th July, 1943. Age 40.

MASON, Pte. WILLIAM HENRY, 5338994. 9th Bn. The Durham Light Infantry. 16th July, 1943. Age 23.

MAY, Pte. GILBERT FRANK, 5510605. 8th Bn. The Durham Light Infantry. 17th July, 1943. Age 36.

MILNER, Pte. JOHN EDWIN, 4470097. 6th Bn. The Durham Light Infantry. 17th July, 1943. Age 22.

MONAGHAN, Sjt. JOHN, 3595640. 6th Bn. The Durham Light Infantry. 17th July, 1943. Age 35.

MORGAN, Rfn. LEWIS THOMAS, 7014601. 1st Bn. The London Irish Rifles, The Royal Ulster Rifles. 18th July, 1943. Age 25.

MOTTRAM, Pte. HARRY, 4463389. 9th Bn. The Durham Light Infantry. 17th July, 1943. Age 31.

MULLEN, Pte. LAWRENCE, 69313, 9th Bn. The Durham Light Infantry. 17th July, 1943. Age 22.

NEWTON, Pte. JOHN GEORGE, 4459576. 9th Bn. The Durham Light Infantry. 16th July, 1943. Age 33.

NORRIS, Pte. ERNEST ARTHUR, 5506558. 5th Bn. The East Yorkshire Regt., 15th July, 1943. Age 28.

OAKES, Pte. GRAHAM LESLIE, 4467009. 9th Bn. The Durham Light Infantry. 17th July, 1943. Age 23.

ORR, Lt. AUSTIN LOUIS FITZGERALD (BUNNY), 156816. 1st Bn. The London Irish Rifles, The Royal Ulster Rifles. 18th July, 1943. Age 29.

OWEN, Capt. JOHN RAMSAY HENRY, 94968. The East Yorkshire Regt., 15th July, 1943. Age 30.

PAGE, Pte. ALBERT LESLIE, 5344943. 10th Bn. The Royal Berkshire Regt. 18th July, 1943. Age 26.

PAGE, Tpr. GERALD, 7957644. 44th Royal Tank Regt., R.A.C. 18th July, 1943. Age 22.

PAGE, Pte. VICTOR, 3966672. 5th Bn. The East Yorkshire Regt., 14th July, 1943. Age 25.

PALLAS, W.O. II (C.S.M.) THOMAS, 4447929, M.M. 6th Bn. The Durham Light Infantry. 17th July, 1943. Age 35.

PALMER, Lt.WILLIAM HENRY, 252336. Mentioned in dispatches. 'C' Sqn. 3rd County of London Yeomanry (Sharpshooters), RAC., 19th July, 1943. Age 25

PARBURY, Maj. PAUL, 56597, M.C. and Bar. 124 Field Regt., Royal Artillery. 14th July, 1943. Age 29.

PARFITT. Pte. FREDERICK GEORGE, 5345736. 10th Bn. The Royal Berkshire Regt. 18th July, 1943. Age 29.

PARKER, Cpl. WILLIAM JOSEPH, 4460661. 9th Bn. The Durham Light Infantry. 16th July, 1943.

PERKINS, Rfn. GEORGE, 7014357. 1st Bn. The London Irish Rifles, The Royal Ulster Rifles. 18th July, 1943.

PETTITT, Pte. ALBERT ERNEST, 5345820. 10th Bn. The Royal Berkshire Regt. 18th July, 1943. Age 30.

PIERCE, Sjt. THOMAS JOHN, 778841. 2nd Bn. The Cheshire Regt. 17th July, 1943. Age 34.

PILKINGTON, Cpl. HARRY, 3858589. 7th Bn. The Green Howards (Yorkshire Regt.). 18th July, 1943. Age 23.

PINDER, L.Cpl. GEORGE WILLIAM, 4393199. 7th Bn. The Green Howards (Yorkshire Regt.). 14th July, 1943. Age 23.

PIPE, Cpl. WALTER, 4461389. 6th Bn. The Durham Light Infantry. 17th July, 1943. Age 28.

PLEAVIN, 2/Lt. LESLEY JOHN, 288946. 9th Bn. The Durham Light Infantry. 16th July, 1943. Age 27.

PRESCOTT, Pte. DAVID, 4196628. 9th Bn. The Durham Light Infantry. 16th July, 1943. Age 24.

PRESCOTT, Pte, JAMES, 3653331. 8th Bn. The Durham Light Infantry. 17th July, 1943.

PRIOR, Cpl. HARRY PERCY, 5884410. 6th Bn. The Durham Light Infantry. 17th July, 1943. Age 25.

PROCTOR, Pte. NORMAN, 4451490. 8th Bn. The Durham Light Infantry. 17th July, 1943. Age 34.

PYRAH, Pte. NORMAN, 4349044. 7th Bn. The Green Howards (Yorkshire Regt.). 18th July, 1943.

RAINE, Pte. THOMAS, 4463763. 9th Bn. The Durham Light Infantry. 16th July, 1943. Age 23.

RAINE, Sjt. WILLIAM, 4457467. 6th Bn. The Durham Light Infantry. 17th July, 1943. Age 24.

RALPH, L.Sjt. JAMES, 3603138. 8th Bn. The Durham Light Infantry. 17th July, 1943. Age 29.

RAWLINGS, Pte. REGINALD HUGH, 5836852. 8th Bn. The Durham Light Infantry. 17th July, 1943. Age 26.

RAWLINS, L.Sjt. LAWRENCE ALBERT, 4346414. 5th Bn. The East Yorkshire Regt. 14th July, 1943. Age 24.

REDHEAD, Sjt. HAROLD, 4448898. 6th Bn. The Durham Light Infantry. 17th July, 1943. Age 35.

ROBERTS, Pte. DAVID, 4463787. 8th Bn. The Durham Light Infantry. 18th July, 1943.

ROBINSON, Pte. CHARLES, 4622207. 9th Bn. The Durham Light Infantry. 16th July, 1943. Age 30.

ROBINSON, Pte. RICHARD, 4450537. 8th Bn. The Durham Light Infantry. 17th July, 1943. Age 28.

ROSIER, Pte. FRANCIS HENRY CHARLES, 5344967. 10th Bn. The Royal Berkshire Regt. 18th July, 1943. Age 30.

ROWLANDS, Pte. THOMAS MORRIS, 4199341. 9th Bn. The Durham Light Infantry. 16th July, 1943. Age 17.

RYLATT, Pte. FRANK, 4626958. 8th Bn. The Durham Light Infantry. 17th July, 1943. Age 20.

SAUNDERS, L.Cpl. JOHN, 5336689. 10th Bn. The Royal Berkshire Regt. 18th July, 1943.

SEDDON, Pte. FRED, 3659065. 6th Bn. The Durham Light Infantry. 17th July, 1943. Age 28.

SEDDON, Pte. WILLIAM, 3603778. 1st Bn. The London Irish Rifles, The Godon Highlanders. 18th July, 1943. Age 21.

SHAW, Pte. HAROLD, 3388119. 6th Bn. The Durham Light Infantry. 17th July, 1943.

SHIMES, L.Cpl. MICHAEL A., 7014605. 1st Bn. The London Irish Rifles, The Royal Ulster Rifles. 18th July, 1943. Age 22.

SMITH, Rfn. ALBERT JOSEPH WILLIAM, 7018364. 1st Bn. The London Irish Rifles, The Royal Ulster Rifles. 18th July, 1943. Age 28.

SMITH, Pte. FRANK, 3910898. 9th Bn. The Durham Light Infantry. 17th July, 1943. Age 25.

SMITH, Capt. FREDERICK, 201135. The West Yorkshire Regt., attd. 7th Bn. The Green Howards (Yorkshire Regt.). 14th July, 1943. Age 39.

SMITH, Pte. HENRY, 4469644. 9th Bn. The Durham Light Infantry. 16th July, 1943.

SNOWDON, Pte. ROBERT, 5957027. 8th Bn. The Durham Light Infantry. 17th July, 1943. Age 27.

SOULSBY, Pte. FREDERICK, 6850602. 8th Bn. The Durham Light Infantry. 18th July, 1943. Age 22.

STANLEY, 2/Lt. DOUGLAS GORDON, 269349. 5th Bn. The East Yorkshire Regt. 15th July, 1943. Age 26.

STEELE, Pte. FRANK, 3660815. 8th Bn. The Durham Light Infantry. 17th July, 1943.

STEPHEN, Rfn. DONALD, 3774000. 1st Bn. The London Irish Rifles, The Royal Ulster Rifles. 18th July, 1943.

STEPHENSON, Pte. JOHN, 4396424. 7th Bn. The Green Howards (Yorkshire Regt.). 18th July, 1943. Age 32.

STOBO, Capt. WALTER OLIVER, 162423. 7th Bn. The Green Howards (Yorkshire Regt.). 14th July, 1943. Age 30.

STODDART, Pte. STANLEY, 4539362. 5th Bn. The East Yorkshire Regt. 14th July, 1943. Age 23.

STURMAN, Pte. WALTER RONALD, 4469927. 8th Bn. The Durham Light Infantry. 17th July, 1943. Age 29.

TAYLOR, Tpr. JOHN JOSEPH, 7931605. 44th Royal Tank Regt., R.A.C. 16th July, 1943. Age 32.

TAYLOR, L.Cpl. JAMES MAYZES, 3708583. 9th Bn. The Durham Light Infantry. 16th July, 1943.

TURNER, Pte. GEORGE WILLIAM, 5117852. 7th Bn. The Green Howards (Yorkshire Regt.). 18th July, 1943. Age 20.

TURNER, Pte. HERBERT FRANK, 5955902. 8th Bn. The Durham Light Infantry. 17th July, 1943. Age 29.

THACKERAY, Pte. FREDERICK, 4346494. 5th Bn. The East Yorkshire Regt. 18th July, 1943.

USHER, 2/Lt. GEOFFREY FREDERICK, 285744, M.M. The Green Howards (Yorkshire Regt.), seconded to 5th Bn. The East Yorkshire Regt. 14th July, 1943. Age 25.

VASEY, Pte. JONATHAN CORBETT, 4466620. 8th Bn. The Durham Light Infantry. 18th July, 1943. Age 33.

WADE, Cpl. BERNARD MAJOR, 7016639. 1st Bn. The London Irish Rifles, The Royal Ulster Rifles. 18th July, 1943. Age 26.

WALTER, Lt. HENRY ANTON, 239413. 10th Bn. The Royal Berkshire Regt. 18th July, 1943. Age 30.

WARD, Sjt. JOSEPH LAWSON, 7887766. 'A' Sqn., 3rd County of London Yeomanry (Sharpshooters), R.A.C. 17th July, 1943.

WATSON, Pte. STEPHEN RICHARD, 4462897. 8th Bn. The Durham Light Infantry. 17th July, 1943. Age 29.

WEIDNER, Gnr. RONALD, 909155. 124 Field Regt., Royal Artillery. 14th July, 1943. Age 23.

WEST, Cpl. TERENCE, 4923388. 9th Bn. The Durham Light Infantry. 15th/16th July, 1943. Age 19.

WHALEY, Sjt. CHARLES SIDNEY, 89984. 98 (The Surrey and Sussex Yeomanry) Field Regt., Royal Artillery. 18th July, 1943. Age 29.

WICKENS, Lt. JOHN RICHARD, 237933. 10th Bn. The Royal Bershire Regt. 18th July, 1943. Age 21.

WILKINSON, Pte. MOSES LESLIE, 4627473. 6th Bn. The Durham Light Infantry. 17th July, 1943. Age 20.

WILLIAMS, Pte. GRANVILLE JOHN, 3910930. 9th Bn. The Durham Light Infantry. 16th July, 1943. Age 25.

WILLIS, L.Col. GEORGE GEOFFREY LIGHTLY, 42264. DSO. 3rd County of London Yeomanry (Sharpshooters), R.A.C. 17th July, 1943.

WILSON, L.Cpl. ARTHUR, 5253386. 7th Bn. The Green Howards (Yorkshire Regt.). 18th July, 1943. Age 23.

WINGROVE, Pte. ERNEST, 4342231. 5th Bn. The East Yorkshire Regt. 18th July, 1943.

WOOLLARD, Pte. WILLIAM GILBERT, 5347073. 10th Bn. The Royal Berkshire Reg. 18th July, 1943. Age 27.

WRIGHT, Rfn. EDWARD, 7017927. 1st Bn. The London Irish Rifles, The Royal Ulster Rifles. 18th July, 1943. Age 29.

WATSON, Pte. THOMAS, 5629154. 8th Bn. The Durham Light Infantry. 17th July, 1943. Age 27.

WELCH, Pte. WALTER DAVID, 5349901. 10th Bn. The Royal Berkshire Regt. 18th July, 1943. Age 21.

WESTON, L.Sjt. RICHARD JOHN, 323119. 9th Bn. The Durham Light Infantry. 16th July, 1943. Age 25.

WHITTINGHAM, Rfn. CHARLES HENRY, 7047650. 1st Bn. The London Irish Rifles, The Royal Ulster Rifles. 18th July, 1943. Age 20.

WILD, L.Cpl. ROBERT HAROLD, 4469377. 9th Bn. The Durham Light Infantry. 17th July, 1943. Age 23.

WILLIAMS, Pte. BERNARD JOHN, 3912346. 9th Bn. The Durham Light Infantry. 17th July, 1943. Age 30.

WILLIAMS, L.Cpl. WILLIAM JOHN, 5346463. 10th Bn. The Royal Berkshire Regt. 18th July, 1943. Age 27.

WILLIS, Pte. HENRY, 3912357. 9th Bn. The Durham Light Infantry. 17th July, 1943. Age 30.

WILSON, Pte. JAMES, 3601694. 6th Bn. The Durham Light Infantry. 17th July, 1943. Age 27.

WITHYCOMBE, Capt. PETER THOMAS GIDLEY, 78361. Mentioned in Despatches. 124 Field Regt., Royal Artillery. 14th July, 1943. Age 26.

WORTHINGTON, Pte. RAYMOND, 5346386. 10th Bn. The Royal Berkshire Regt. 18th July, 1943. Age 29.

CASSINO MEMORIAL TO THE MISSING

AWFORD, Pte. ERNEST, 4037144. 9th Bn. The Durham Light Infantry. 17th July, 1943. Age 29.

BAINBRIDGE, Cpt. JOHN HEYWOOD, 76716. M.C. 74th Fld Regt. Royal Artillery. 13th July, 1943 Age 23.

BAILEY, Pte. EDWARD GEORGE THOMAS, 3913877. 8th Bn. The Durham Light Infantry. 17th July, 1943. Age 33.

BOWNESS, Dvr. JAMES HENRY, 2000213. 233 Fld Coy. Royal Engineers. 13th July, 1943. Age 26.

CLARK, Gnr. LAWRENCE RAYMOND, 887131. 98 Fld Regt. Royal Artillery. (The Surrey and Sussex Yeomanry.). 13th July, 1943. Age 25.

COCHRANE, Lt. DAVID, 259427. 74th Fld Rgt. Royal Artillery. 13th July, 1943.

DAVIES, Cpl. THOMAS GORDON, 7590729. L.A.D. R.E.M.E. attd. 2nd Bn. The Cheshire Regt. 13th July, 1943. Age 31.

EARNSHAW, Tpr. ARTHUR, 319301. 3rd County of London Yeomanry. (Sharpshooters) R.A.C. 17th July, 1943. Age 26.

ELLIOT, Gnr. JAMES WILLIAM, 322489. 102nd (The Northumberland Hussars) Anti Tank Rgt. Royal Artillery. 13th July, 1943. Age 22.

EVANS, Pte. GEORGE, 1488974. 9th Bn. The Durham Light Infantry. 18th July, 1943. Age 34.

FISHER, CRAFTSMAN. HARRY, R.E.M.E. attd. HQ 168th INF BDE. 13th July, 1943. Age 21.

FORSTER, Dvr. EDWARD, 2194310. 233 Fld Coy. Royal Engineers. 13th July, 1943. Age 25.

GILES, Dvr. NORMAN, 2158488. 233 Fld Coy. Royal Engineers. 13th July, 1943. Age 20.

GANT, L/Cpl. FREDERICK RONALD, 7588907. L.A.D. R.E.M.E. attd. 2nd Bn. The Cheshire Regt. 13th July, 1943. Age 31.

GRANTHAM, Gnr. ARTHUR FREDERICK GEORGE, 887473. 90 Fld Rgt. Royal Artillery. 13th July, 1943. Age 22.

GILLIOTT, Pte. CYRIL, 4539628. 9th Bn. The Durham Light Infantry. 16th July, 1943. Age 25.

HARDING, Gnr. WILFRED THOMAS, 987591. 98 (The Surrey and Sussex Yeomanry.). Fld Regt. Royal Artillery. 13th July, 1943. Age 27.

HARMAN, Bdr. WILLIAM, 787246. 74 Fld Rgt. Royal Artillery. 13th July, 1943. Age 30.

HARPER, Dvr. WALTER JAMES, 2000408. 233 Fld Coy. Royal Engineers. 13th July, 1943. Age 25.

HARVEY, Pte. STEPHEN, 5350452. 10th Bn. The Berkshire Regt. 18th July, 1943. Age 21.

HEYES, Pte. WILFRED, 4462179. 9th Bn. The Durham Light Infantry. 13th July, 1943. Age 29.

HOGG, Dvr. GEORGE DOUGLAS, 11265186. Royal Corps of Signals. 50 Div Signals. 13th July, 1943. Age 35.

HOLT, Tpr. FRED, 7151906. 3rd County of London Yeomanry. R.A.C. 17th/18th July, 1943. Age 22.

HOPTON, Tpr. SYDNEY, VERN, 7938208. 'B' SQUADRON. 3rd County of London Yeomanry. R.A.C. 17th July, 1943. Age 36.

HORNER, Gnr. FRANK NORRIS. 25 Lt A.A. Rgt. Royal Artillery. 13th July, 1943. Age 31.

HUDSON, Pte. CLARENCE, 4396350. 7th Bn. The Green Howards (Yorkshire Regt.). 14th July, 1943. Age 31.

JOHNSON, Pte. JOHN THOMAS, 4466492. 9th Bn. The Durham Light Infantry. 16th July, 1943. Age 31.

KENNEDY, Cpl. HENRY JOSEPH, 4460617. 9th Bn. The Durham Light Infantry. 16th July, 1943. Age 27.

KENDRICK, Cpl. ARTHUR JAMES, 6463040. 7th Bn. The Green Howards (Yorkshire Regt.). 17th July, 1943. Age 22.

LAMBORD, CYRIL (served as LAMBERT, Cpl. CYRIL, 5045846.) 151 INF BDE WORKSHOP. R.E.M.E. 13th July, 1943. Age 34.

LOCKETT, Pte. JAMES, 3390907. 9th Bn. The Durham Light Infantry. 16th July, 1943. Age 28.

LUMLEY, Dvr. GEORGE RONALD, 1908036. 233 Fld Coy. Royal Engineers. 13th July, 1943. Age 25.

LYNCH, Gnr. PATRICK, 1112703. 102nd (Northumberland Hussars) Anti Tank Regt. Royal Artillery. 13th July, 1943. Age 31.

McMANUS, Dvr. DOUGLAS, T/62581. R.A.S.C. attd. HQ - 50 Div. 13th July, 1943. Age 23.

MORTON, Dvr. JAMES ARTHUR, 2010160. 235 Fld Park Coy. Royal Engineers. 13th July, 1943. Age 26.

MUNRO, Gnr. HENRY CHARLES, 1117823. 74 Fld. Rgt. Royal Artillery. 13th July, 1943. Age 32.

NORTH, Gnr. THOMAS ALWYN, 1083726. 90 Fld Rgt. Royal Artillery. 13th July, 1943. Age 33.

PIMPERTON, Gnr. FRANK, 1569514. 82 Bty. 25 Lt A.A. Rgt. Royal Artillery. 13th July, 1943. Age 23.

POLLARD, CRAFTSMAN, WILLIAM, 10546735. 151 INF BDE WORKSHOP. R.E.M.E. 13th July, 1943. Age 32.

REID. L/Cpl. WILLIAM WALKER, 2067643. 233 Fld Coy. Royal Engineers. 14th July, 1943. Age 23.

SALLOWS, Craftsman, ALEXANDER, 10575169. 151 Inf. BDE WORKSHOP. REME. 13th July, 1943. Age 22.

SHORT, Gnr. JOHN, 1525600. 102nd (Northumberland Hussars) Anti Tank Rgt. Royal Artillery. 13th July, 1943. Age 27.

SMITH, Gnr. GEORGE RICHARD, 1120473. 74th Fld Rgt. Royal Artillery. 13th July, 1943. Age 22.

UPCOTT, Pte. ARTHUR EDWARD, 5346131. 9th Bn. The Durham Light Infantry. 16th July, 1943. Age 23.

WRIGHT, Dvr. RAYMOND, 2580769. Royal Corps of Signals. 50 Div Signals. 13th July, 1943. Age 24.

MORRIS, Gnr. RONALD HENRY, 978358. 98 (The Surrey and Sussex Yeomanry.). Fld Rgt. Royal Artillery. 13th July, 1943. Age 26.

MOONEY, Gnr. ROBERT, 317914. 74 Fld Rgt. Royal Artillery. 13th July, 1943. Age 27.

OAKLEY, L/Bdr. DENIS HERBERT, 1082830. 74th Fld Rgt. Royal Artillery. 13th July, 1943. Age 28.

POOK, Bdr. HENRY RICHARD, 785827. 74th Fld Rgt. Royal Artillery. 13th July, 1943. Age 36.

REES, Spr. WILLIAM HARRY, 2070555. 235 Fld Park Coy. Royal Engineers. 13th July, 1943. Age 28.

RICHARDSON, Dvr. DONOVAN, 2000380. 233 Fld Coy. Royal Engineers. 14th July, 1943. Age 26.

SCOTT, Pte. KENNETH, 3957904. 9th Bn. The Durham Light Infantry. 14th July, 1943. Age 32.

SIMPSON, Gnr. EDWARD, 1134887. 102nd (Northumberland Hussars) Anti Tank Regt. Royal Artillery. 13th July, 1943. Age 21.

SMITH, Sgt. LESLEY GUY, 4037393. 9th Bn. The Durham Light Infantry. 16th July, 1943. Age 28.

WOOD, Pte. CHARLES, 5047607. 9th Bn. The Durham Light Infantry. 18th July, 1943. Age 31.

APPENDIX 'C'

ORDER OF BATTLE: JULY 1943

50TH NORTHUMBRIAN DIVISION
Commanding Officer:
Major General S. C. Kirkman. CBE. MC.

ROYAL ARTILLERY
Commanding Officer:
Brigadier C. H. Norton. DSO. OBE.

74th Fld Rgt: Lt. Colonel G. Marnham
90th Fld Rgt: Lt. Colonel I. G. G. S. Hardie
124th Fld Rgt: Lt. Colonel C. F. Tod
102nd (Northumberland Hussars) Anti-tank Rgt:
Lt. Colonel A. K. Mathews
25th Lt Anti-aircraft Rgt: Lt. Colonel G. G. O. Lyons. MBE.

ROYAL ENGINEERS

Cre: Lt. Colonel E. N. Bickford

505th Fld Coy.
233nd Fld Coy.
235th Fld Park Coy.

50TH DIV SIGNALS
Commanding Officer:
Lt. Colonel G. B. Stevenson

MACHINE-GUN BATTALION
2nd B'n The Cheshire Rgt.
C/O: Lt. Colonel S. V. Keeling. DSO.

69TH INFANTRY BRIGADE

Commanding Officer:
Brigadier E. C. Cooke-Collis. DSO.

5th B'n The East Yorkshire Rgt.
C/O: Lt. Colonel R. B. James. DSO and TWO BARS
(killed 1944)

6th B'n The Green Howards
C/O: Lt. Colonel D. J. M. Smith
(wounded 13th July 1943)

7th B'n The Green Howards
C/O: Lt. Colonel D. G. Jebb. DSO.

151ST INFANTRY BRIGADE

Commanding Officer:
Brigadier R. H. Senior. DSO. Td.

6th B'n The Durham Light Infantry
C/O: Lt. Colonel W. I. Watson.

8th B'n The Durham Light Infantry
C/O: Lt. Colonel R. B. Lidwell. DSO.

9th B'n The Durham Light Infantry
C/O Lt. Colonel. A. B. S. Clarke. DSO.
(killed 23rd July, 1943)

168TH INFANTRY BRIGADE

Commanding Officer:
Brigadier K. C. Davidson. MC.

10th B'n The Royal Berkshire Rgt.
C/O: Lt. Colonel I. R. Baird. MC.

1st B'n The London Scottish:
The Gordon Highlanders
C/O: Lt. Colonel H. J. Wilson. OBE.

1st B'n London Irish The Royal Ulster Rifles
C/O: Lt. Col. I. H. Good

Attached Units

44th Royal Tank Regiment

3rd County Of London Yeomanry

'A' Squadron The Royals

98th Army Fld Rgt. RA:
Lt. Colonel. Hon. C. G. Cubitt. DSO.

No. 34 (Beach) Brick:
Colonel J. T. Gibson

APPENDIX 'D'

GERMAN PARATROOPS IN ACTION AT PRIMOSOLE BRIDGE

1st Parachute Division: Commanded by Lt. Gen. Richard Heidrich: Stationed in France; July 1943. Elements of this division landed at various times and were not all in the action at Primosole Bridge.

FJR ¹ 1st Parachute Regiment: Commanded by Major Rudolph Bohmler, this unit was sent to Salerno and its supply units to Rome: Did not see service in Sicily.

FJR ³ 3rd Parachute Regiment: Commanded by Lt. Col. Heilman, this unit air dropped into Sicily on the evening of July 12th and fought with Group Smalz around Lentini and Carlentini to hold up the advance of the 50th and 5 Divisions until cut off by the British advance, Heilman led his men out of this trap and did not join the action again until 17th/18th July.

FJR ⁴ 4th Parachute Regiment: Commanded by Lt. Col. Walther, this unit air dropped into Sicily on the evening of July 17th and went straight into the line.

1st Parachute Pioneer Battalion (Engineers): Commanded by Captain Paul Adolph: who was acting commander since the regular CO was on a course in Paris. This unit air dropped into Sicily on the evening of July 14th and took up positions around Highway 114 at the northern end of Primosole Bridge. Captain Adolph was killed at Primosole and posthumously promoted Major and awarded the coveted Ritterkreuz for his courage in action.

1st Parachute Machine Gun Battalion: Commanded by Major Schmidt. Air landed on the morning of 13th July. Fought around the Johnny positions 13th July and throughout the Primosole action.

1st Parachute Signals Company: Commanded by Captain Eric Fassl. This unit counter attacked at Primosole on July 14th and re-took the bridge from the British Paras. This counter attack was organised by Captain Franz Strangenberg who, seeing the dire situation at Primosole, recruited clerks, drivers, HQ staff, cooks and mechanics from Catania (200 in all) and transported them with Fassl's Signals Company to the bridge area. This ad-hoc force took part in the counter attack on the 14th. Once the bridge was taken the Machine Gun Battalion and the Pioneer Battalion relieved their victorious comrades on the night of the 14th July and Strangenberg and Fassl took their troops back to Catania. Fassl's Signal Company returned to the battle on 15th July.

N.W. EUROPE: 1944

FOOTNOTES

The following abbreviations apply regarding these first hand accounts.

Iwm: Imperial War Museum
Tiwa: Taped Interview With Author
Msta: Manuscript Sent To Author

1. Sgt. Max Hearst. 5th B'n East York's Regt'. (Tiwa) 1991
2. Pte. J. Forster. 6th DLI (Msta) 1995
3. Pte. G. Worthington. MM. 6th DLI (Tiwa) 1994
4. Csm. G. Warters. 7th B'n Green Howards (Msta) 1992
5. Pte. Tateson. 7th B'n Green Howards (Iwm)
6. Pte. Peter Cuerdon. 1st Hampshire's. (Tiwa) 1994
7. Pte. Stanley Dwyer. 50 Div' Signals. (Msta) 1992
8. Pte. Tateson
9. Ibid
10. Pte. S. Dwyer
11. L/Sgt Ken Rutherford. 5th B'n East York's Regt'. (Tiwa) 1992
12. Sgt. W. E. Wills. 2nd B'n Devon Regt'. (Msta) 1994
13. Bdr. Jack Styan. Royal Artillery. (Tiwa) 1991
14. Pte. D. Bowen. 5th B'n East York's Regt'. (Msta) 1994
15. Brigadier D. Warren 2 I/C. 1st Hamp's Regt'. (Msta) 1993
16. Major Clayton. MC. Officer Commanding 280th Fld Coy - RE. (Msta By Mr J. N. Rhodes, Curator R E Museum, Chatham.)
17. Lt. Peard. Mc. 280th Fld Coy - RE. (Msta By Mr J. N. Rhodes, Curator R E Museum, Chatham.)
18. Sgt. M. Hearst
19. Csm. Laurie Whittle. 5th B'n East York's Regt'. (Tiwa) 1994
20. Pte. Roy Walker. 5th B'n East York's Regt'. (Tiwa) 1992
21. Cpl. P. Goodman-Tyson. 5th B'n East York's Regt'. (Iwm)
22. Pte. K. Chapman. 5th B'n East York's Regt'. (Msta) 1995
23. Pte. Francis William Vickers. MM. 6th B'n Green Howards. (Msta) 1994
24. Csm. Stanley E. Hollis. VC. Interview: 1957
25. Ibid
26. Ibid
27. Ibid
28. Major Jackson. 6th B'n Green Howards. (Msta) 1994
29. Csm. Jack Verity. 7th B'n Green Howards. (Tiwa) 1993
30. Csm. G. Warters
31. Pte. Tateson
32. Pte. F. Wiltshire. 1st B'n Dorsetshire Regt'. (Msta) 1994
33. Pte. J. Minogue. 7th Arm' Division. (Msta) 1994
34. Tpr. E. Lawrenson. Westminster Dragoons. (Msta) 1993
35. Pte. Peter Cuerdon. 1st B'n Hampshire Regt'. (Tiwa) 1992
36. Pte. I. G. Holley. 1st B'n Hampshire Regt'. (Msta) 1992
37. Lt. M. Barraclough. 22nd Dragoons. (Msta) 1991
38. L/Cpl. N. Travett. 2nd B'n Devonshire Regt' (Msta) 1993
39. Tpr. C. Wilson. Royal Artillery. Essex Yeomanry Journal. 1969
40. Colonel. D. J. Fenner. 6th B'n DLI (Msta) 1995
41. Lt. W. Jalland. 8th B'n DLI (Msta) 1993

42. Cpt. E. Hooper. 9th B'n DLI (Msta) 1994
43. Pte. P Kendrick. MM. 47 Royal Marine Commando. (Msta) 1994
44. Pte. Tateson
45. Colonel D. J. Fenner
46. Lt. Col. Bredin. DSO. MC. 'Three Assault Landings.' P-58
47. Cpl. F. Spencer. 8th B'n Dli. (Msta) 1994
48. Tpr. Fred Ebb 61st Recce' Regt'. (Tiwa) 1991
49. Sgt. R. Branwell. MM. 4th County Of London Yeomanry. (Msta) 1994
50. Dvr. T. D. Hawken. MM. 4th County Of London Yeomanry. (Msta) 1996
51. Pte Tateson
52. Pte. J. H. Clarke. 8th DLI (Tiwa) 1991
53. Pte Mawson. 86th Field Rgt: RA (Msta) 1992
54. Pte Tateson
55. Sgt Max Hearst
56. Pte. Mountford. 7th Green Howards. (Msta) 1994
57. Pte. Tateson
58. Tpr. D. Dewar. Nott's Yeomanry - RAC. (Msta) 1994
59. B'dr Jack Styan. Battle-Axe Coy: RA. (Tiwa) 1992
60. Lt. Blackmore. 1st Hampshire's. (Msta) 1989
61. Pte. Peter Cuerdon. 1st Hampshire's. (Tiwa) 1992
62. Lt. Blackmore.
63. Pte. Albert Carman. 6th DLI. (Tiwa) 1992
64. Lt. Col. Hastings. 6th Green Howards. (Msta) 1991
65. Pte. W. M. Hewitt. 6th DLI (Tiwa) 1993
66. Pte. Reg Pope. 2nd Cheshire Regt'. (Tiwa) 1992
67. Pte. Jim Betts. 5th B'n East York's Regt' (Tiwa) 1993
68. Bd'r Jack Styan
69. Pte. Norman Hardy. 5th B'n East York's Regt' (Tiwa) 1991
70. Sgt. Ken Rutherford
71. Pte. Reg Pope
72. Csm William Brown. 8th DLI. (Msta) 1995
73. Pte. W. M. Hewitt
74. Pte. Albert Carman
75. Sgt. Max Hearst
76. Major. W. J. R. Scott. 9th DLI (Msta) 1991
77. Pte. J. H. Clarke. 8th DLI (Msta) 1994
78. Sgt. Max Hearst
79. Ibid
80. Pte. Roy Walker
81. Sgt. Max Hearst
82. Cpt. Gus Mason. 7th Green Howards. (Msta) 1992
83. Pte. Reg Pope
84. Sgt. Max Hearst
85. Pte. Jim Betts. 5th B'n East York's Regt' (Tiwa) 1992
86. Pte. Roy Walker
87. Pte. Jim Betts
88. Pte. Harry Forth. 5th B'n East York's Regt' (Tiwa) 1994
89. Pte. George Worthington. MM. 6th DLI (Tiwa) 1993
90. Sgt Bob Gibson. MM. 151 B'de Provost Coy. (Tiwa) 1992
91. Sgt. Max Hearst
92. Major Peter Martin. (Msta) 1995

BIBLIOGRAPHY

Bredin. A. E. C. Lt Colonel.	'Three Assault Landings: 1st Bn The Dorsetshire Rgt'. Gale And Polden. 1946
Chicken. S.	'The Overlord Coast-line'. Spellmount Ltd. 1993
Clay. E. W. Major.	'The Path Of The 50th'. Gale And Polden. 1950
Cooper. M.	'The German Army: 1933 To 1945'. Cooper And Lucas. 1978
Crookenden. A.	'The Cheshire Reg't In The Second World War'. W. H. Evans. 1949.
Daniell. D. S.	'Cap Of Honour. The Gloucestershire Rgt. 1694 To 1950'. Harrap. 1951
Daniell. D. S	'The Royal Hampshire Rgt. Vol 3. 1918 To 1954'. Gale And Polden. 1955.
Ellis. J.	'Brute Force'. Andre Deutsch. 1990
Ellis. L. F. Major.	'Victory In The West: The Battle For Normandy'. HMSO. 1962
Hastings. M.	'Overlord'. Michael Joseph. 1984
Hamilton. N.	'Monty, 1942 To 1944'. Hamish Hamilton. 1983
Keegan. J.	'Six Armies In Normandy'. Penguin. 1988
Liddel-Hart. B.	'History Of The Second World War'. Papermac. 1992
Lewis. P. J. Major. MC. and English. I. R. Major. MC.	'Into Battle With The Durhams'. 1949
Miller. R.	'Nothing Less Than Victory'. Michael Joseph. 1993
Maule. H.	'Caen'. David And Charles. 1988
Martin. T. A. Colonel.	'The Essex Rgt: 1929 To 1945'. Essex Rgt. 1952
Mitcham. S. W.	'Hitler's Legions'. Leo Cooper. 1985
Neillands. R. and De Normann. R.	'D-day 1944'. Orion. 1994

Nightingale. P. R.   'A History Of The East Yorkshire Rgt. 1939 To 1945'. W. Sessions. 1952

Rissik. D. Major.   'The DLI At War. 1939 To 1945'. DLI Depot. 1953

Synge. W. A. T. Captain.   'The Story Of The Green Howards. 1939 To 1945'. Richmond, Yorks. 1952

Thompson. J.   'Victory In Europe: Imperial War Museum'. Sigwick And Jackson. 1994

Taylor. J.   'The Devonshire Rgt. 1685 To 1945'. White Swan Press. 1951

Warner. P.   'The D-day Landings'. Mandarin. 1990

APPENDIX 'A'

50th Northumbrian Division

Honours And Awards: 6th To 12th June, 1944.

Abbreviations Used In The Text:

DSO: Distinguished Service Order
DCM: Distinguished Conduct Medal
MC: Military Cross
BEM: British Empire Medal
MM: Military Medal
MID: Mentioned In Dispatches

BAR: If a bar was awarded it means the individual has been awarded the same gallantry medal for the second time. This was worn on the ribbon of the original award.

The following list has been taken from the original recommendations. There are bound to be ommisions as these were written some fifty three years ago and things get lost along the way - for this I apologise, however the bulk of awards are contained here.

69TH BRIGADE

NAME	AWARD	DATE OF ACTION	DATE GAZETTED	UNIT
BDR. F. Y. C. KNOX. DSO.	BAR TO DSO	6th JUNE	31/8/44	OC: 69th BRIGADE
PTE. T. ADDIS	MM	6th JUNE	31/8/44	6th GREEN HOWARDS
PTE. G. BACKHOUSE	MM	6th JUNE	31/8/44	6th GREEN HOWARDS

69TH BRIGADE
(Continued)

NAME	AWARD	DATE OF ACTION	DATE GAZETTED	UNIT
LT. P. C. BANCOMBE	MC	11th JUNE	31/8/44	6TH GREEN HOWARDS
CSM G. CALVERT	DCM	11th JUNE	31/8/44	6th GREEN HOWARDS
PTE. A. E. V. CLARKE	MM	11th JUNE	31/8/44	6th GREEN HOWARD
LT. COL. R.H.W S. HASTINGS. MC.	DSO	6th JUNE	31/8/44	6th GREEN HOWARDS
CSM S. E. HOLLIS	VC	6th JUNE	17/8/44	6th GREEN HOWARDS
PTE. J. M. HENSON	MM	11th JUNE	31/8/44	6th GREEN HOWARDS
MAJOR F. H. HONEYMAN	MC	6th JUNE	31/8/44	6th GREEN HOWARDS
L/CPL. A. JOYCE	MM	6th JUNE	31/8/44	6th GREEN HOWARDS
PTE. J. LEARY	MM	11th JUNE	31/8/44	6th GREEN HOWARDS
L/SGT. H. PRENTY	MM	6th JUNE	31/8/44	6th GREEN HOWARDS
PTE. J. T. THOMPSON	MM	6th JUNE	31/8/44	6th GREEN HOWARDS
MAJOR G. M. YOUNG	MC	11th JUNE	31/8/44	6th GREEN HOWARDS
MAJOR R. LOFTHOUSE	MC	6th JUNE	31/8/44	6th GREEN HOWARDS
PTE. R. CLARE	MM	6th JUNE		5th EAST YORKS REGT
CSM. W. E. MCDOUGALL	MM	6th JUNE	31/8/44	5th EAST YORKS REGT
L/CPL. T. MILLS	MM	6th JUNE	31/8/44	5th EAST YORKS REGT
MAJOR A. N. M. RICE	MC	6th JUNE	31/8/44	5th EAST YORKS REGT
SGT. F. WEBBER	MM	6th JUNE	31/8/44	5th EAST YORKS REGT
PTE. S. BALDWIN	MM	7th JUNE	31/8/44	7th GREEN HOWARDS
PTE. G. GODDARD	MM	11/12th JUNE	31/8/44	7th GREEN HOWARDS
SGT. W. POTTERTON	MM	7th JUNE	31/8/44	7th GREEN HOWARDS
CPT. W. R. LAMB	MC	6th JUNE	NOT FOUND	RAMC: ATTACHED TO 5th EAST YORKSHIRES
DVR. G. S. KERR	MM	11th JUNE	19/10/44	RASC: 69 BDE.
LT. P. R. PHILIPS	MC	11th JUNE	19/10/44	2nd CHESHIRES
DVR. C. J. COLES	MM	11th JUNE	19/10/44	186 FLD AMB'

NAME	AWARD	DATE OF ACTION	DATE GAZETTED	UNIT
CPT. W. W. MARSDEN	MC	6th JUNE	19/10/44	186 FLD AMB'
CPL. R. H. SHOWERING	MM	6th JUNE	19/10/44	186 FLD AMB'
MAJOR D. R. SANDISON	MC	11th JUNE	19/10/44	186 FLD AMB'
L/CPL. J. WHITE	MM	6th JUNE	19/10/44	186 FLD AMB'
SPR. R. DAVIS	MM	6th JUNE	19/10/44	233 FLD COY: RE
L/SGT. W. A. HARRISON	MM	6th JUNE	19/10/44	233 FLD COY: RE
SPR. LIVINGSTONE	MM	6th JUNE	19/10/44	233 FLD COY: RE
SPR. T. M. WALLACE	MM	6th JUNE	19/10/44	233 FLD COY: RE
SPR. J. WATSON	MM	6th JUNE	19/10/44	233 FLD COY: RE

231ST BRIGADE

NAME	AWARD	DATE OF ACTION	DATE GAZETTED	UNIT
CPL. V. E. CARTER	MM	6th JUNE	31/8/44	1st DORSETS
PTE. R. GODDARD	MM	11th JUNE	31/8/44	1st DORSETS
CPL. W. HAWKINS	MM	6th JUNE	31/8/44	1st DORSETS
MAJOR W. N. HAYES	MC	6th JUNE	31/8/44	1st DORSETS
CPL. G. HUCKLEY	MM	11th JUNE	31/8/44	1st DORSETS
L/CPL. J. MILLER	MM	6th JUNE	31/8/44	1st DORSETS
MAJOR R. M. NICOL	MC	6th JUNE	31/8/44	1st DORSETS
LT. COL. E. A. M. NORIE	DSO	6th JUNE	31/8/44	1st DORSETS
CPL. J. REDPATH	MM	9th JUNE	31/8/44	1st DORSETS
SGT. A. W. TALBOT	MM	6th JUNE	31/8/44	1st DORSETS
CPL. S. THOMPSON. MM	DCM	6th JUNE	31/8/44	1st DORSETS
CPT. C. R. WHITTINGTON	MC	6th JUNE	31/8/44	1st DORSETS
SGT. C. BISON	MM	6th JUNE	31/8/44	1st HAMPSHIRES
LT. J. N. BOYS	MC	6th JUNE	31/8/44	1st HAMPSHIRES
PTE. W. R. BUTT	MM	6th JUNE	31/8/44	1st HAMPSHIRES

231ST BRIGADE
(Continued)

NAME	AWARD	DATE OF ACTION	DATE GAZETTED	UNIT
LT. A. L. KING	MC	6th JUNE	31/8/44	1st HAMPSHIRES
MAJOR J. L. G. LITTLEJOHNS	MC	6th JUNE	31/8/44	1st HAMPSHIRES
PTE. R. PLAYFORD	MM	12th JUNE	31/8/44	1st HAMPSHIRES
L/SGT. A. E. C. SIPPETTS	MM	6th JUNE	31/8/44	1st HAMPSHIRES
CPL. G. SLADE	MM	6th JUNE	31/8/44	1st HAMPSHIRES
L/CPL. V. WALLER	MM	6th JUNE	31/8/44	1st HAMPSHIRES
MAJOR D. J. WARREN. MC.	DSO	6th JUNE	31/8/44	1st HAMPSHIRES
L/CPL. L. WEBB	MM	6th JUNE	28/9/44	1st HAMPSHIRES
CPT. J. M. C. WICKS	MC	6th JUNE	28/9/44	1st HAMPSHIRES
LT. M. HOLDSWORTH	MC	11th JUNE	31/8/44	2nd DEVONS
PTE. A. KEENOR	MM	6th JUNE	31/8/44	2nd DEVONS
LT. COL. C. A. R. NEVILL	DSO	6th JUNE	31/8/44	2nd DEVONS
PTE. C. OLDRIDGE	MM	6th JUNE	28/9/44	2nd DEVONS
L/CPL. A. PERKINS	MM	9th JUNE	31/8/44	2nd DEVONS
L/SGT. F. ROTHERHAM	MM	8th JUNE	31/8/44	2nd DEVONS
MAJOR F. D. SADLER. MBE.	MC	6th JUNE	31/8/44	2nd DEVONS
SGT. J. SEAR	MM	7th JUNE	31/8/44	2nd DEVONS
SGT. S. WILLIAMS	MM	11th JUNE	31/8/44	2nd DEVONS
LT. J. N. AUSTIN	MC	6th JUNE	19/10/44	295 FLD COY: RE
L/SGT. F. B. BRADSHAW	MM	6th JUNE	19/10/44	295 FLD COY: RE
CPL. R. W. BURNS	MM	6th JUNE	19/10/44	295 FLD COY: RE
SPR. N. WINT	MM	6th JUNE	19/10/44	295 FLD COY: RE
LT. F. S. COOPER	MC	7th JUNE	19/10/44	200 FLD AMB
CPL. G. E. DYER	MM	7th JUNE	19/10/44	200 FLD AMB
L/CPL. C. W. FARROW	MM	7th JUNE	19/10/44	200 FLD AMB
CPL. L. E. RICHARDS	MM	12th JUNE	31/8/44	231 BDE SIGNALS

NAME	AWARD	DATE OF ACTION	DATE GAZETTED	UNIT
SGMN. L. GRIMSHAW	MM	11th JUNE	31/8/44	231 BDE SIGNALS
SGT. D. S. McKENZIE	MM	6th JUNE	31/8/44	R.E.M.E. ATT 231 BDE HQ
L/CPL. R. KINGSWELL	MM	6th JUNE	31/8/44	DEF PLN: 231 BDE HQ
SGT. W. J. TAMS	MM	11th JUNE	31/8/44	522 COY: RASC SUPPLYING 1st DEVONS
SGT. T. BURT	MM	8th JUNE	31/8/44	522 COY: RASC SUPPLYING 47 ROYAL MARINE COMMANDO
CPT. B. W. M. LINDON	MC	7th JUNE	31/8/44	522 COY: SUPPLYING 47 ROYAL MARINE COMMANDO

56TH BRIGADE

NAME	AWARD	DATE OF ACTION	DATE GAZETTED	UNIT
SGT. G. BRAIN	MM	11th JUNE	19/10/44	2nd GLOS' REGT
LT. COL. D. W. BIDDLE	DSO	11th JUNE	19/10/44	2nd GLOS' REGT
SGT. D. G. OVER	MM	11th JUNE	19/10/44	2nd GLOS' REGT
CPL. F. RHODES	MM	10th JUNE	31/8/44	2nd GLOS' REGT
MAJOR J. K. LANCE	MC	6th JUNE	31/8/44	2nd GLOS' REGT
SGT. A. BOOCOCK	MM	8th JUNE	31/8/44	2nd SWB'S
LT. COL. R. CRADDOCK	DSO	8th JUNE	31/8/44	2nd SWB'S
CPT. G. R. CLARK	MC	8th JUNE	31/8/44	RAMC. ATT'D TO 2nd SWB'S
MAJOR G. DAUNCEY	MC	8th JUNE	31/8/44	2nd SWB'S
L/CPL. R. C. KENWOOD	MM	8th JUNE	31/8/44	2nd SWB'S
CPL. J. LOCKHART	MM	8th JUNE	31/8/44	2nd SWB'S
PTE. M. MURGATROYD	MM	8th JUNE	31/8/44	2nd SWB'S
LT. D. M. E. RANDELL	MC	8th JUNE	31/8/44	2nd SWB'S
PTE. L. THOMAS (LEONARD)	MM	8th JUNE	31/8/44	2nd SWB'S
PTE. L. THOMAS (LESLIE)	MM	8th JUNE	31/8/44	2nd SWB'S

56TH BRIGADE
(Continued)

NAME	AWARD	DATE OF ACTION	DATE GAZETTED	UNIT
CPL. W. J. THOMAS	MM	7th JUNE	31/8/44	2nd SWB'S
CPT. A. F. THOMPSON	MC	8th JUNE	NOT FOUND	2nd SWB'S
REV. W. R. THOMAS	MC	11/12th JUNE	31/8/44	2nd ESSEX REGT

151ST BRIGADE

NAME	AWARD	DATE OF ACTION	DATE GAZETTED	UNIT
MAJOR G. R. ATKINSON. MC.	BAR TO MC	10th JUNE	31/8/44	6th BN DLI
SGT. W. BOTTERMAN	MM	8th JUNE	31/8/44	6th BN DLI
CPT. I. A. DAW	MC	7th JUNE	31/8/44	6th BN DLI
CPL. W. RICHARDSON	MID	8th JUNE	UNKNOWN	6th BN DLI
LT. T. M. KIRK	MC	6th JUNE	31/8/44	6th BN DLI
MAJOR G. WOOD. MC AND BAR	DSO	10th JUNE	31/8/44	6th BN DLI
L/CPL. J. WEAR	MM	10th JUNE	31/8/44	6th BN DLI
CPL. S. L. BRYGES	MM	9/13th JUNE	31/8/44	8th BN DLI
PTE. J. CAWLEY	MM	11th JUNE		8th BN DLI
CPL. W. HIGGINSON. MM	BAR TO MM	9th JUNE	31/8/44	8th BN DLI
LT. P. M. LAWS	MC	10th JUNE	31/8/44	8th BN DLI
CPL. D. MICHAEL	MM	11th JUNE	31/8/44	8th BN DLI
PTE. F. PROTANO	MM	10th JUNE	31/8/44	8th BN DLI
L/SGT. R. RICHMOND	MM	9th JUNE	31/8/44	8th BN DLI
CPL. B. THOMAS	MM	12th JUNE	31/8/44	8th BN DLI
L/SGT. S. P. WALLBANKS	MM	10th JUNE	31/8/44	8th BN DLI
SGT. A. PICKIN	MM	9th JUNE	31/8/44	2nd CHESHIRE REGT
SGT. W. D. CHIPCHASE	MM	6/7th JUNE	19/10/44	149 FLD AMB
SGT. T. W. GALLAGHER	MM	6th JUNE	19/10/44	149 FLD AMB

ROYAL ARTILLERY

NAME	AWARD	DATE OF ACTION	DATE GAZETTED	UNIT
MAJOR R. A. BARNETT	MC	9th JUNE	31/8/44	102nd (NORTHUMBER-LAND HUSSARS) ANTI TANK REGT
LT. R. N. BAYLISS	MC	9th JUNE	31/8/44	102nd (NORTHUMBER-LAND HUSSARS) ANTI TANK REGT
GNR. C. F. BERESFORD	MM	9/10th JUNE	31/8/44	102nd (NORTHUMBER-LAND HUSSARS) ANTI TANK REGT
LT. W. S. BRAMELD	DSO	6/9th JUNE	31/8/44	102nd (NORTHUMBER-LAND HUSSARS) ANTI TANK REGT
SGT. F. BAYLEY	MM	9th JUNE	31/8/44	102nd (NORTHUMBER-LAND HUSSARS) ANTI TANK REGT
SGT. A. DOWN	DCM	6/9th JUNE	31/8/44	102nd (NORTHUMBER-LAND HUSSARS) ANTI TANK REGT
BDR. G. H. GILMOUR	MM	9th JUNE	31/8/44	102nd (NORTHUMBER-LAND HUSSARS) ANTI TANK REGT
BDR. E. C. HINDER	MM	9/10th JUNE	31/8/44	102nd (NORTHUMBER-LAND HUSSARS) ANTI TANK REGT
LT. COL. A. K. MATHEWS	DSO	6/9th JUNE	31/8/44	OC 102nd (NORTHUMBER-LAND HUSSARS) ANTI TANK REGT
SGT. G. H. SEATON	MM	10th JUNE	31/8/44	102nd (NORTHUMBER-LAND HUSSARS) ANTI TANK REGT
SGT. W. D. THOMPSON	MM	6/8th JUNE	31/8/44	102nd (NORTHUMBER-LAND HUSSARS) ANTI TANK REGT
LT. G. D. GREIG	MC	11th JUNE	31/8/44	124 FLD REG: ATTACHED TO 86 (HERTS YEO.) FLD REGT
L/BDR. S. M. MITCHLEY	MM	6/14th JUNE	31/8/44	124 FLD REG: ATTACHED TO 86 (HERTS YEO.) FLD REGT

ROYAL ARTILLERY
(Continued)

NAME	AWARD	DATE OF ACTION	DATE GAZETTED	UNIT
MAJOR J. B. M. SMITH	DSO	6th JUNE	31/8/44	86 (HERTS YEO) FLD REGT
CPT. N. J. D. BISHOP	MC	7th JUNE	31/8/44	90th FLD REGT
L/CPL. D. BOWSTEAD	MM	6th JUNE	31/8/44	'E' SECTION: NO2 COY. SIGNALS ATTACHED TO 90th FLD REGT
CPT. P. A. HAMILTON	MC	9th JUNE	31/8/44	74 FLD REGT: ATTACHED TO 90th FLD REGT
CPT. E. C. B. EDWARDS	MC	6th JUNE	31/8/44	147th FLD REGT
LT. K. MUNRO	MC	6/7th JUNE	31/8/44	147th FLD REGT
SGT. R. E. PALMER	MM	6th JUNE	31/8/44	147th FLD REGT
LT. COL. R. A. PHAYRE	DSO	6/11th JUNE	31/8/44	147th FLD REGT
MAJOR C. J. SIDGWICK	MC	6th JUNE	31/8/44	147th FLD REGT
CPT. D. B. TAYLOR	MC	6th JUNE	31/8/44	147th FLD REGT

ROYAL ENGINEERS BEACH CLEARANCE PARTY

NAME	AWARD	DATE OF ACTION	DATE GAZETTED	UNIT
LT. A. G. B. BUCKLEY	MC	6th JUNE	19/10/44	73rd FLD COY: RE
SAPPER A. CLOSE	MM	6th JUNE	19/10/44	73rd FLD COY: RE
L/CPL. J. M. FITZGERALD	MM	6th JUNE	19/10/44	73rd FLD COY: RE
LT. I. T. C. WILSON	MC	6th JUNE	19/10/44	73rd FLD COY: RE
MAJOR L. E. WYATT	MC	6th JUNE	19/10/44	73rd FLD COY: RE
LT. PEARD	MC	6th JUNE	NOT KNOWN	280th FLD COY: RE

8TH ARMOURED BRIGADE

NAME	AWARD	DATE OF ACTION	DATE GAZETTED	UNIT
LT. T. E. ABBS	MC	11th JUNE	31/8/44	4/7 DRAGOON GUARDS
SGT. W. BRACEGIRDLE	MM	6th JUNE	31/8/44	SHERWOOD RANGERS YEO

NAME	AWARD	DATE OF ACTION	DATE GAZETTED	UNIT
BRIG. H. J. B. CRACROFT	DSO	6th JUNE	31/8/44	C.O. 8TH ARMR'D BDE
MAJOR J. A. D'AIGDOR-GOLDSMITH	MC	13th JUNE	31/8/44	4/7 DRAGOON GUARDS
MAJOR E. M. FRENCH	MC	13th JUNE	31/8/44	1/7 QUEEN'S R.R.
MAJOR R. M. JENKINS	MC	11th JUNE	31/8/44	4/7 DRAGOON GUARDS
LT. N. S. WIDE	MC	12th JUNE	31/8/44	4/7 DRAGOON GUARDS

PROVOST AND SIGNALS

NAME	AWARD	DATE OF ACTION	DATE GAZETTED	UNIT
L/CPL. R. W. BENNET. MM.	BAR TO MM	6th JUNE	31/8/44	30 CORPS: HQ SIGNALS
SGT. J. FORD	MM	6th JUNE	31/8/44	50 DIV PROVOST COY ATT' 69 BDE.
SGT. R. JACKLIN	MM	6th JUNE	31/8/44	50 DIV PROVOST COY

'47 R.M. COMMANDO'

NAME	AWARD	DATE OF ACTION	DATE GAZETTED	UNIT
LT. W. T. B. JAMES	MC	8th JUNE	31/5/44	47 R.M. COMMANDO
L/SGT. W. E. ELLIS	MM	8th JUNE	12/9/44	47 R.M. COMMANDO
MARINE R. EMSLEY	MM	7th JUNE	12/9/44	47 R.M. COMMANDO
MARINE D. R. GADSDEN	MM	7th JUNE	12/9/44	47 R.M. COMMANDO
SGT. D. H. G. GARDNER	MM	7th JUNE	12/9/44	47 R.M. COMMANDO
MARINE J. A. GRIFFIN	MM	7th JUNE	12/9/44	47 R.M. COMMANDO
L/CPL. P. G. KENDRICK	MM	7th JUNE	19/10/44	47 R.M. COMMANDO
MARINE W. MACDONALD	MM	7th JUNE	12/9/44	47 R.M. COMMANDO
LT/COL. P. M. DONNELL Mentioned in Despatches	CROIX DE GUERRE WITH VERMILION STAR	6th JUNE	Not Gazetted	47 R.M. COMMANDO

APPENDIX 'B'

'THE FALLEN': 50TH NORTHUMBRIAN DIVISION

Normandy: 6th, 7th And 8th June, 1944

BAYEUX WAR CEMETERY

ABELL, L. Sjt. ERIC EVAN, 6016672. 1st Bn. The Dorsetshire Regt. 6th June, 1944. Age 25.

ALLAN, L. Cpl. THOMAS ALFRED, 2038939. A Sqn. 4th/7th Royal Dragoon Guards, R.A.C. 6th June, 1944. Age 24.

ALLEN, Pte. ROBERT, 14337600. 9th Bn. The Durham Light Infantry. 8th June, 1944. Age 35.

APPLETON, Lt. ROY, 296983. 5th Bn. The East Yorkshire Regt. 6th June, 1944. Age 22.

ARCHER, Pte. LEONARD THOMAS, 13070153. 1st Bn The Hampshire Regt. 6th June, 1944. Age 32.

ARMSTRONG. Pte. WILLIAM, 7369977. 200 Field Amb., R.A.M.C. 6th June, 1944. Age 25.

ASHCROFT, Pte. TREVOR EDWARD, 3907811. 2nd Bn. The South Wales Borderers. 8th June, 1944. Age 31.

AYRES, Pte. WILFRED JOHN, 14224634. 1st Bn. The Hampshire Regt. 6th June, 1944. Age 20.

BAINBRIDGE, Marine CYRIL, PLY/X. 103334. Royal Marines. No. 47 R.M. Commando. 6th June, 1944. Age 23.

BAINES, Maj. RICHARD GOUGH TALBOT, 62620. 1st Bn. The Hampshire Regt. 6th June, 1944. Age 30.

BAKER, Pte. THOMAS HENRY, 3910118. 5th Bn. The East Yorkshire Regt. 6th June, 1944. Age 26.

BALL, Pte. JOHN REGINALD, 14687995. 2nd Bn. The Devonshire Regt. 6th June, 1944. Age 22.

BARNES. Pte. HARRY LESLIE DELL, 5954730. 1st Bn. The Hampshire Regt. 6th June, 1944. Age 29.

BARTLETT, Sjt. ERNEST HARRY EDWIN, 5505038. 1st Bn. The Hampshire Regt. 6th June, 1944. Age 24.

BOND, Pte. THOMAS ALEXANDER, 14387161. 2nd Bn. The South Wales Borderers. 8th June, 1944. Age 19.

BARTON, Pte. FREDERICK ARTHUR, 4343005. 5th Bn. The East Yorkshire Regt. 6th June, 1944. Age 28.

BAWDEN, Lt. LIONEL ARTHUR, 288933. 1st Bn. The Hampshire Regt. 6th June, 1944. Age 27.

BAXTER, Marine GEORGE HENRY, CH/X. 104134. Royal Marines. No. 47 R.M. Commando. 7th June, 1944. Age 21.

BEACH, Pte. FREDERICK CHARLES HENRY WALTER, 6848398. 1st Bn. The Hampshire Regt. 6th June, 1944. Age 26.

BEARD, Pte. CHARLES ALFRED, 14356651. 1st Bn. The Dorsetshire Regt. 6th June, 1944. Age 36.

BEDWORTH, Marine HORACE WILLIAM, PO/X. 106733. Royal Marines. No. 47 R.M. Commando. 6th June, 1944. Age 23.

BEE, Sgt. ERIC ERNEST, PO/X. 100001. Royal Marines. No. 47 R.M. Commando. 6th June, 1944. Age 24.

BEER, Pte. HAROLD EDWIN, 5625061. 2nd Bn. The Devonshire Regt. 6th June, 1944. Age 28.

BELL, Pte. WILLIAM HERBERT, 14348116. 1st Bn. The Hampshire Regt. 6th June, 1944. Age 30.

BELLOT, Pte. ARTHUR GEORGE, 5442707. 6th Bn. The Green Howards (Yorkshire Regt.). 6th June, 1944. Age 32.

BISHOP, Pte. MONTAGUE, 5505944. 1st Bn. The Hampshire Regt. 6th June, 1944. Age 30.

BLACK, Cpl. ROBERT, 1500623. 'B' Sqn., 61st Regt., Reconnaissance Corps, R.A.C. 7th June, 1944. Age 26.

BLACKETT, Pte. WALTER EDWARD, 14558272. 2nd Bn. The South Wales Borderers. 8th June, 1944. Age 19.

BLANCHARD, L. Bdr. KENNETH WILLIAM, 912132. 90 Field Regt., Royal Artillery. 6th June, 1944. Age 35.

BOTTOMS, Bdr. NORMAN HARRY, 914849. 147 (The Essex Yeomanry) Field Regt., Royal Artillery. 6th June, 1944. Age 23.

BLERKOM, Pte. ARTHUR, 4620864. 5th Bn. The East Yorkshire Regt. 6th June, 1944. Age 28.

BRADBURY, Lt. JOSEPH, 287835. The Hampshire Regt., attd. 1st Bn. The Dorsetshire Regt. 6th June, 1944. Age 26.

BRADLEY, Sgt. ARTHUR JOHN, PO/X. 4118. Mentioned in Despatches. Royal Marines. No. 47 R.M. Commando. 7th June, 1944. Age 25.

BREACH, Marine ERNEST THOMAS LLOYD, PO/X 113949. Royal Marines. No. 47 R.M. Commando. 7th June, 1944. Age 20.

BREDEN, Pte. EDWARD THOMAS, 14650055. 1st Bn. The Dorsetshire Regt. 6th June, 1944. Age 20.

BRICE, Pte. LESLIE RONALD, 6353843. 1st Bn. The Dorsetshire Regt. 6th June, 1944. Age 23.

BRISTOW, Pte. PETER JOHN, 14430379. 1st Bn. The Hampshire Regt. 6th June, 1944. Age 20.

BRITTON, Pte. FREDERICK, 4978164. 1st Bn. The Hampshire Regt. 6th June, 1944. Age 25.

BROOKS, Pte. ALBERT EDWARD, 14649399. 1st Bn. The Hampshire Regt. 6th June, 1944. Age 23.

BROWN, L/Cpl. DIXON, 2091163. 233 Field Coy., Royal Engineers. 6th June, 1944. Age 24.

BULPITT, Pte. REGINALD GEORGE, 5502564. 1st Bn. The Hampshire Regt. 6th June, 1944. Age 25.

BUNN, Pte. ERNEST WILLIAM,5511910. 1st Bn. The Hampshire Regt. 6th June, 1944. Age 19.

BUNNING, L/Sgt. LEONARD WILLIAM, 5728866. MM. 1st Bn. The Dorsetshire Regt. 6th June, 1944. Age 27.

BUNYAN, Marine KENNETH CHARLES, CH/X. 103608. Royal Marines. No. 47 R.M. Commando. 6th June, 1944. Age 23.

BURN, Cpl. EDMUND WILLIAM, 7881703. 4th/7th Royal Dragoon Guards, R.A.C. 6th June, 1944. Age 33.

BURNETT, Pte. ARTHUR FRANK, 14406233. 1st Bn. The Hampshire Regt. 6th June, 1944. Age 20.

BURR, Spr. PERCY JOHN. 6355469. 280 Field Coy. Royal Engineers. 6th June, 1944. Age 21.

BUTT, Pte. RONALD ALFRED, 1468127. 1st Bn. The Hampshire Regt. 6th June, 1944. Age 21.

CALKIN, Lt. NIGEL DAVID RIVIERE, 229051. 90 Field Regt., Royal Artillery. 6th June, 1944. Age 22.

CALLAGHAN, Pte. JOHN DAVID, 53397310. 1st Bn. The Hampshire Regt. 6th June, 1944. Age 25.

CAMPBELL, Spr. ROBERT, 2129982. 295 Army Field Coy., Royal Engineers. 6th June, 944. Age 35.

CANNING, Pte. GEORGE JAMES, 14679122. 1st Bn. The Dorsetshire Regt. 6th June, 1944. Age 18.

CARPENTER, Pte. LESLIE, 5735714. 1st Bn. The Dorsetshire Regt. 6th June, 1944. Age 20.

CARTER, Marine ARTHUR, PO/X. 2367. Royal Marines. No. 47 R.M. Commando. 7th June, 1944. Age 24.

CARTER, Pte. JOHN EDWIN, 5350162. 1st Bn. The Dorsetshire Regt. 6th June, 1944. Age 21.

CARTER, Cpl. PERCY, 6099074. 1st Bn. The Dorsetshire Regt. 6th June, 1944. Age 32.

CARTWRIGHT, L/Cpl. FRANCIS RICHARD, 4391434. 6th Bn. The Green Howards (Yorkshire Regt.). 6th June, 1944. Age 29.

CHAPMAN, Sgt. GEORGE SAMUEL, 5826367. Royal Armoured Corps, attd. 8th Armd. Bde. 7th June, 1944. Age 28.

CHATFIELD, L/Cpl. ALFRED JAMES, 7346931. R.A.M.C., attd. No. 47 R.M. Commando. 6th/7th June, 1944. Age 22.

CHRISTOPHER, Pte. ALBERT EDMUMD, 6351679. 1st Bn. The Hampshire Regt. 6th June, 1944. Age 32.

CLARK, Marine DOUGLAS JAMES, PO/X. 105862. Royal Marines. No. 47 R.M. Commando. 7th June, 1944. Age 22.

CLARK, Pte. GEORGE LEONARD, 4756579. 5th Bn. The East Yorkshire Regt. 6th June, 1944. Age 29.

CLARKE, Pte. FREDERICK WILLIAM, 6411162. 1st Bn. The Hampshire Regt. 6th June, 1944. Age 24.

CLEFT, L/Cpl. IRVINE DONALD, 5505035. 1st Bn. The Hampshire Regt. 6th June, 1944. Age 29.

CLIFFORD, Pte. ALFRED CHARLES, 14311504. 1st Bn. The Hampshire Regt. 6th June, 1944. Age 20.

COCKERILL, L/Sgt. ADDISON, 1891634. 233 Field Coy., Royal Engineers. 6th June, 1944. Age 25.

COLLINS, Pte. CHARLES WILLIAM, 4396231. 1st Bn. The Hampshire Regt. 6th June, 1944. Age 30.

COLLINS, Marine JAMES WASHINGTON, P/JX. 111269. Royal Marines. No. 47 R.M. Commando. 7th June, 194. Age 21.

COSSOM, Pte. ERNEST EDWARD ALAN, 5383976. 9th Bn. The Durham Light Infantry. 7th June, 1944. Age 31.

COSTEN, Pte. PERCY RICHARD, 5509914. 1st Bn. The Hampshire Regt. 6th June, 1944. Age 33.

COTTON, L/Sgt. HARRY, 5616314. 2nd Bn. The Devonshire Regt. 6th June, 1944. Age 33.

COUSINS. Capt. TERENCE FREDERICK. Mentioned in Despatches. Royal Marines. No. 47 R.M. Commando. 7th June, 1944. Age 22.

COWDREY, L/Sgt. CECIL IVOR, 5497092. 1st Bn. The Hampshire Regt. 6th June, 1944. Age 28.

COX, Cpl. RONALD, 320500. 'A' Sqn., 4th/7th Royal Dragoon Guards, R.A.C. 6th June, 1944. Age 21.

CRONIN, Pte. WALTER FREDERICK AUGUSTUS, 5442202. 9th Bn. The Durham Light Infantry. 6th June, 1944. Age 31.

CROOKE. L, Tpr. WILLIAM ERIC, 7949575. 'A' Sqn., 4th/7th Royal Dragoon Guards, R.A.C. 6th June, 1944. Age 20.

CROSSWELL, Pte. HORACE REGINALD, 5259830. 2nd Bn. The Gloucestershire Regt. 6th June, 1944. Age 35.

CURTIS, Pte, RONALD LEONARD, 5504934. 1st Bn. The Hampshire Regt. 6th June, 1944. Age 27.

CURTIS, Pte. STANLEY RONALD, 5726315. 1st Bn. The Dorsetshire Regt. 6th June, 1944. Age 23.

DAGLISH, Spr. EDWARD GRAHAM, 2074490. 233 Field Coy., Royal Engineers. 6th June, 1944. Age 23.

DANSIE, Spr. KENNETH WILLIAM. 6355483. 280 Field Coy. Royal Engineers. 6th June, 1944. Age 22.

DAVID, L/Cpl. EDWARD NEVILLE, PLY/X. 111698. Royal Marines. No. 47 R.M. Commando. 7th June, 1944. Age 19.

DAVIES, W.O.III. (T.S.M.) SYDNEY H., 406639. 'A' Sqn., 4th/7th Royal Dragoon Guards, R.A.C. 6th June, 1944. Age 28.

DAWKINS, Pte. JOHN, 4388281. 6th Bn. The Green Howards (Yorkshire Regt.). 6th June, 1944. Age 30.

DEERE, Pte. THOMAS JAMES, 14655518. 5th Bn. The East Yorkshire Regt. 6th June, 1944. Age 19.

DEMPSEY, Pte. JAMES, 5616397. 2nd Bn. The Devonshire Regt. 6th June, 1944. Age 34.

DIGBY, Cpl. WILLIAM, 323418. The Nottinghamshire Yeomanry. RAC. 8th June, 1944. Age 22.

DIXON, Pte. MATTHEW GEORGE, 1590685. 1st Bn. The Dorsetshire Regt. 6th June, 1944. Age 31.

DENNING, Pte. JOHN FREDERICK, 5725714. 1st Bn. The Dorsetshire Regt. 6th June, 1944. Age 22.

DONOHUE, Pte. JACK, 14666034. 6th Bn. The Green Howards (Yorkshire Regt.). 6th June, 1944. Age 18.

DOSSOR, Pte. CECIL, 4398823. 1st Bn. The Hampshire Regt. 6th June, 1944. Age 35.

DOUBLE, L/Cpl. ROWLAND WILLIAM, 5951893. 2nd Bn. The Devonshire Regt. 6th June, 1944. Age 27.

DUKE, L. Bdr. ALFRED EWARD, 955364. 90 Field Regt., Royal Artillery. 8th June, 1944. Age 26.

DUKE, Maj. HUGH VICTOR, 85611, MC and Bar. Mentioned in Despatches. 2nd Bn. The Devonshire Regt., 6th June, 1944. Age 25.

DUTTON, Marine CYRIL, PO/X. 106964. Royal Marines. No. 47 R.M. Commando. 7th June, 1944. Age 34.

EDWARDS, Tpr. WILLIAM, 7882656. 'C' Sqn., 4th/7th Royal Dragoon Guards, R.A.C. 6th June, 1944. Age 31.

ELPHINSTONE, MAJOR. HAROLD GEORGE ALMOND, 44867. Royal Engineers. 6TH June, 1944. Age 34.

ENGLISH, Sgt. ANTHONY ERNEST, 5830358. 5th Bn. The East Yorkshire Regt. 6th June, 1944. Age 25.

EMMERSON, L/Sgt. JOHN, 4389443. 6th Bn. The Green Howards (Yorkshire Regt.). 6th June, 1944. Age 25.

EVANS, Marine JOHN EDWARD MORGAN, PLY/X. 108771. Royal Marines. No. 47 R.M. Commando. 7th June, 1944.

EVANS, Sgt. WILLIAM JOHN, 3907199, MM and Bar. 1st Bn. The Dorsetshire Regt. 6th June, 1944. Age 34.

FARRER, Pte. ARTHUR, 4617550. 1st Bn. The Hampshire Regt. 6th June, 1944. Age 25.

FEACEY, Maj. JAMES RICHARD. Royal Marines. No. 47 R.M. Commando. 6th June, 1944.

FELLOWS, Marine PETER BREARLEY, PLY/X. 106565. Royal Marines. No. 47 R.M. Commando. 6th June, 1944. Age 19.

FLAHERTY, Marine JOHN, CH/X.103631. Royal Marines. No. 47 R.M. Commando. 6th June, 1944.

FLEET, Marine ARTHUR, EX/1895. Royal Marines. No. 47 R.M. Commando. 7th June, 1944.

FLETCHER, Sgt. TEDDY PEARCE, PO/X.4497. Royal Marines. No. 47 R.M. Commando. 7th June, 1944. Age 22.

FOX, L/Cpl. GEORGE, 4755004. 5th Bn. The East Yorkshire Regt. 6th June, 1944. Age 29.

FRANCIS, Pte. JOSEPH HAYDN, 3909836. 2nd Bn. The South Wales Borderers. 8th June, 1944. Age 25.

FURZE, Pte. JOHN HENRY, 14622430. 2nd Bn. The Devonshire Regt. 6th June, 1944. Age 22.

FUTTER, Pte. LEONARD JOHN, 6013402. 1st Bn. The Hampshire Regt. 6th June, 1944. Age 22.

GALLANT, Pte. STANLEY FREDERICK, 6029379 1st Bn. The Dorsetshire Regt. 6th June, 1944. Age 20.

GANNON, Cpl. REGINALD GEORGE GROSE, 6012440. 2nd Bn. The Devonshire Regt. 6th June, 1944. Age 24.

GATES, Bdr. LEONARD FREDERICK JOHN, 935233. 90 Field Regt., Royal Artillery. 6th June, 1944. Age 26.

GEEN, Tpr. WILLIAM GEORGE, 14527539. The Nottinghamshire Yeomanry. RAC. 6th June, 1944. Age 19.

GEORGE, L/Sgt. ELI. 1872529. 82nd Assault Squadron. Royal Engineers. 6th June, 1944. Age 26.

GOSLING, L/Cpl. GEORGE, 4395893. 5th Bn. The East Yorkshire Regt. 6th June, 1944. Age 26.

GOUDE, Marine MICHAEL HERBERT, PO/X. 118564. Royal Marine. No. 47 R.M. Commando. 7th June, 1944. Age 20.

GOUGH, Pte. CHARLES FREDERICK BENDELL, 5505055. 1st Bn. The Hampshire Regt. 6th June, 1944. Age 24.

GRANT, Spr. WILLIAM, 2074403. 295 Army Field Coy., Royal Engineers. 6th June, 1944. Age 22.

GRATTAN, Pte. FREDERICK THOMAS HENRY, 14356997. 5th Bn. The East Yorkshire Regt. 6th June, 1944. Age 28.

GRIFFITHS, Pte. CHARLES WILLIAM, 14370046. 9th Bn. The Durham Light Infantry. 7th June, 1944. Age 33.

GUMMERSON, Pte. YANNIK GEORGE, 14299617. 1st Bn. The Dorsetshire Regt. 6th June, 1944. Age 20.

HALL, Pte. WALTER RICHARD, 14599635. 2nd Bn. The Devonshire Regt. 6th June, 1944. Age 34.

HALLETT, Sgt. WILLIAM HENRY, 6468366. 2nd Bn. The Devonshire Regt. 6th June, 1944. Age 26.

HAMBLIN, Pte. HILBURN JAMES, 14405157. 1st Bn. The Dorsetshire Regt. 6th June, 1944. Age 19.

HARMER, Pte. HAROLD, 14378571. 9th Bn. The Durham Light Infantry. 7th June, 1944. Age 34.

HARRIS, L/Cpl. JOHN ARTHUR, 14425249. 2nd Bn. The South Wales Borderers. 8th June, 1944. Age 18.

HARTILL, Pte. WILLIAM FREDERICK, 5048190. 9th Bn. The Durham Light Infantry. 6th June, 1944. Age 29.

HASSETT, Pte. JOHN PATRICK, 5499327. 1st Bn. The Hampshire Regt. 6th June, 1944. Age 23.

HATFIELD, Pte. LUTHER, 13061854. 1st Bn. The Hampshire Regt. 6th June, 1944. Age 29.

HEWETT, L/Cpl. FREDERICK CHARLES, 811400. 1st Bn. The Dorsetshire Regt. 6th June, 1944. Age 32.

HEWLETT, Tpr. WILLIAM JOHN. 403450. The Nottinghamshire Yeomanry. RAC. 6th June, 1944. Age 31.

HERRIDGE, Pte. HARRY, 3910630. 2nd Bn. The South Wales Borderers. 8th June, 1944. Age 24.

HILL, L/Sgt. WILLIAM ALLAN, 4389766. 6th Bn. The Green Howards (Yorkshire Regt.). 6th June, 1944. Age 22.

HINKS, Pte. ARTHUR ROY JOHN, 1694742. 5th Bn. The East Yorkshire Regt. 6th June, 1944. Age 23.

HIRST, Spr. JOHN HENRY COX, 1906490. 233 Field Coy., Royal Engineers. 6th June, 1944. Age 24.

HOBBY, Pte. VICTOR REGINALD, 5494206. 1st Bn. The Hampshire Regt. 6th June, 1944. Age 37.

HOMER, Pte. THOMAS PERCY, 321716. 1st Bn. The Dorsetshire Regt. 6th June, 1944. Age 25.

HORLICK, Sgt. ARTHUR, 5724419. 1st Bn. The Dorsetshire Regt. 6th June, 1944. Age 29.

HUGHES, Sgt. DENIS, EX/1222. Royal Marines. No. 47 R.M. Commando. 6th June, 1944. Age 24.

ILES, L/Cpl. ERNEST, 14610273. 2nd Bn. The Devonshire Regt. 6th June, 1944. Age 33.

IRELAND, Pte. FRANK, 6107796. 1st Bn. The Dorsetshire Regt. 6th June, 1944. Age 20.

JACKSON, Tpr. ALFRED, 5053468. The Nottinghamshire Yeomanry. RAC. 6th June, 1944. Age 29.

JEFFRESS, L/Sgt. REGINALD, 4395936. 7th Bn. The Green Howards (Yorkshire Regt.). 6th June, 1944. Age 24.

JENKINS, Cpl. ALEC ARTHUR, PLY/X. 101844. Royal Marines No. 47 R.M. Commando. 7th June, 1944. Age 30.

JENNINGS, Pte. WILFRED ERNEST, 5729122. 2nd Bn. The Devonshire Regt. 6th June, 1944. Age 27.

JENSON, Sgt. JAMES THOMAS, 4534313. 1st Bn. The Hampshire Regt. 6th June, 1944. Age 32.

JEVONS, Pte. WILFRED FRANCIS, 14435007. 2nd Bn. The Devonshire Regt. 6th June, 1944. Age 18.

JOHNSON, Pte. ERIC, 4344551. 5th Bn. The East Yorkshire Regt. 6th June, 1944. Age 23.

JOHNSON, Pte. WALTER LESLIE, 14392169. 1st Bn. The Dorsetshire Regt. 6th June, 1944. Age 23.

JONES, Cpl. NOEL, PO/X.105351. Royal Marines No. 47 R.M. Commando. 7th June, 1944. Age 23.

JONES, Pte. WILLIAM GEORGE, 14513628. 2nd Bn. The South Wales Borderers. 7th June, 1944. Age 19.

KAYE, Pte. NORMAN, 14394195. 5th Bn. The East Yorkshire Regt. 6th June, 1944. Age 30.

KING, Pte. ERNEST, 14567603. 2nd Bn. The Devonshire Regt. 8th June, 1944. Age 24.

KING, Cpl. LESLIE JOHN, 6023396. 6th Bn. The Durham Light Infantry. 7th June, 1944. Age 24.

KINLOCH, Marine WILLIAM CHARLES DOYLE, PLY/X. 102749. Royal Marines No. 47 R.M. Commando. 6th June, 1944.

KIRKPATRICK, Lt. JOHN ANDERSON, 285501. 6th Bn. The Green Howards (Yorkshire Regt.). 6th June, 1944. Age 28.

LAMBETH, Pte. WILLIAM ERNEST, 6474744. 6th Bn. The Green Howards (Yorkshire Regt.). 6th June, 1944. Age 30.

LANCASTER, Pte. SYDNEY, 3909952. 2nd Bn. The South Wales Borderers. 8th June, 1944. Age 25.

LANCASTER, Lt. TURLOCK JOHN, 212762. The Dorsetshire Regt. 6th June, 1944.

LANNING, Pte. HORACE JOHN, 14414983. 1st Bn. The Hampshire Regt. 6th June, 1944. Age 19.

LARBY, Pte. CHARLES EDWIN JAMES, 5504995. 1st Bn. The Hampshire Regt. 6th June, 1944. Age 27.

LAWSON, Pte. HAROLD, 4539952. 1st Bn. The Dorsetshire Regt. 6th June, 1944. Age 25.

LEOPOLD, Gnr. FREDERICK HENRY, 943201. 90 Field Regt. Royal Artillery. 6th June, 1944. Age 24.

LEWIS, Lt. WILLIAM MONTFORD AYLMER, 256530. 4/7th Royal Dragoon Gurards. RAC. 6th June, 1944. Age 29.

LINN, Capt. JOHN CHARLES, 91105. 6th Bn. The Green Howards (Yorkshire Regt.). 6th June, 1944. Age 27.

LISTER, Sgt. HENRY, 4340471, MM. 5th Bn. The East Yorkshire Regt. 6th June, 1944. Age 35.

LOCKWOOD, Pte. ARTHUR CARDEN, 14289853. 6th Bn. The Durham Light Infantry. 7th June, 1944. Age 21.

LOWE, Tpr. JOHN THOMAS. 3458625. The Nottinghamshire Yeomanry. RAC. 6th June, 1944. Age 29.

LOWE, Lt. THOMAS FREDERICK, 164778, MC. The Suffolk Regt., seconded to 5th Bn. The East Yorkshire Regt. 7th June, 1944. Age 25.

LUMSDEN, Marine JOHN, 117207. Royal Marines. No. 47 R.M. Commando. 6th June, 1944. Age 19.

McCAFFERTY, Pte. HENRY CULLEY, 14504068. The East Yorkshire Regt. 6th June, 1944. Age 34.

McDERMID, Spr. SAMUEL MARSHALL, 14213636. 73 Field Coy., Royal Engineers. 6th June, 1944. Age 28.

McDONALD, Pte. JOHN EDWARD, 5623626. 2nd Bn. The Devonshire Regt. 6th June, 1944. Age 27.

McILROY, Lt. WILLIAM HERBERT JAMES, 261956. 5th Bn. The East Yorkshire Regt. 6th June, 1944. Age 22.

MAHONEY, Pte. BRENDAN, 14680770. 7th Bn. The Green Howards (Yorkshire Regt.). 7th June, 1944. Age 18.

MARCH, Pte. WILLIAM, 14433597. 1st Bn. The Dorsetshire Regt. 8th June, 1944. Age 20.

MARSH, Pte. SIDNEY GEORGE, 6407940. 1st Bn. The Hampshire Regt. 6th June, 1944. Age 28.

MARSH, Sgt. VICTOR BERTRAM, 5725390. 1st Bn. The Dorsetshire Regt. 8th June, 1944. Age 28.

MARSHALL, L/Sgt. WILLIAM HENRY, 5497656. 1st Bn. The Hampshire Regt. 6th June, 1944. Age 28.

MARTIN, Pte. ERNEST FREDERICK CHARLES, 6098618. 1st Bn. The Dorsetshire Regt. 6th June, 1944. Age 30.

MASSEY, Pte. ALBERT EDWARD, 4194378. 2nd Bn. The South Wales Borderers. 6th June, 1944. Age 34.

MASSEY, Pte. FREEMAN, 1425598. 5th Bn. The East Yorkshire Regt. 6th June, 1944. Age 18.

MATHEWS, Tpr. ALBERT WILLIAM JAMES, 14260423. 4/7th Royal Dragoon Guards. RAC. 6th June, 1944. Age 20.

MATTHEWS, Pte. MARTIN WILLIAM, 5623651. 2nd Bn. The Devonshire Regt. 6th June, 1944. Age 24.

MERRIKIN, Pte. HARRY, 4350053. 5th Bn. The East Yorkshire Regt. 6th June, 1944. Age 33.

MIDDLETON, Pte. JOHN EDWARD EMPSON, 14450028. 5th Bn. The East Yorkshire Regt. 6th June, 1944. Age 19.

MILLS, Marine GEORGE WILLIAM FRANK, PO/X.110891. Royal Marines. No. 47 R.M. Commando. 7th June, 1944. Age 21.

MOLLETT, Pte. JOHN ALVERT, 13097760. 7th Bn. The Green Howards (Yorkshire Regt.). 6th June, 1944. Age 23.

MOLYNEUX, Dvr. RALPH, 1949117. 90 Field Coy., Royal Enginers. 6th June, 1944. Age 30.

MOORTON, Pte. WILLIAM HENRY CHARLES, 6406570. 1st Bn. The Hampshire Regt. 6th June, 1944. Age 28.

MORRIS, Pte. ALFRED JOHN, 5831843. 1st Bn. The Dorsetshire Regt. 6th June, 1944. Age 30.

MORRIS, Pte. JOHN VICTOR, 4035642. 6th Bn. The Green Howards (Yorkshire Regt.). 6th June, 1944. Age 25.

MOUNSEY, Spr. HORACE FREDERICK. 4042753. 280 Field Coy. Royal Engineers. 6th June, 1944. Age 21.

MOSS, Sgt. WILLIAM RICHARD, 5385691. 61st Regt, Reconnaissance Corps, R.A.C. 6th June, 1944. Age 24.

MULLALLY, Pte. JOSEPH, 14438660. The Green Howards (Yorkshire Regt.). 6th June, 1944. Age 28.

NENO, Cpl. LEONARD, 5616950. 2nd Bn. The Devonshire Regt. 6th June, 1944. Age 32.

NEWELL, Tpr. ARTHUR HARRY, 6352355. 61st Regt., Reconnaissance Corps, R.A.C. 6th June, 1944. Age 31.

NICHOLSON, L/Cpl. STANLEY, 6028290. 5th Bn. The East Yorkshire Regt. 6th June, 1944. Age 31.

NUGENT, Pte. PERCY, 5889337. 1st Bn. The Dorsetshire Regt. 6th June, 1944. Age 24.

NORIE, Marine GEORGE, CH/X. 106948. Royal Marines. No. 47 R.M. Commando. 6th June, 1944. Age 27.

OATES, Marine BRIAN, PLY/X. 109015. Royal Marines. No. 47 R.M. Commando. 7th June, 1944. Age 20.

OLDFIELD, Pte. HARRY LESLIE, 4755075. 5th Bn. The East Yorkshire Regt. 6th June, 1944. Age 30.

OLDRIDGE, Pte. CYRIL JOHN EDWARD, 14656022, MM. 2nd Bn. The Devonshire Regt. 8th June, 1944. Age 19.

OLIVER, Pte. SYDNEY CHARLES, 2571359. 2nd Bn. The Devonshire Regt. 8th June, 1944. Age 23.

OWENS, Sgt. FRANK, 4387708. 1st Bn. The Hampshire Regt. 6th June, 1944. Age 28.

PEART, L/Cpl. FREDERICK GEORGE, 14630721. 2nd Bn. The Devonshire Regt. 6th June, 1944. Age 19.

PIDDOCK, Pte. WILLIAM GEORGE, 6408787. 1st Bn. The Dorsetshire Regt. 6th June, 1944. Age 22.

PIERCE, Pte. GEORGE ALBERT, 1576221. 1st Bn. The Dorsetshire Regt. 6th June, 1944. Age 27.

PIKE, Pte. TREVOR, 14200927. 2nd Bn. The South Wales Borderers. 8th June, 1944. Age 21.

PILLMAN, Lt. CHARLES HASTINGS, 214492. 4th/7th Royal Dragoon Guards, R.A.C. 6th June, 1944. Age 23.

PLOWRIGHT, Spr. THOMAS JAMES, 2020747. 233 Field Coy., Royal Engineers. 6th June, 1944. Age 24.

POSTGATE, L/Cpl. GEORGE, 4390270. 6th Bn. The Green Howards (Yorkshire Regt.). 6th June, 1944. Age 23.

POWIS, Tpr. HARVEY WILLIAM. 14363470. The Nottinghamshire Yeomanry. RAC. 6th June, 1944. Age 20.

POWNALL, Tpr. SIDNEY. 14376364. The Nottinghamshire Yeomanry. RAC. 6th June, 1944. Age 22.

PRESTON, Spr. HORACE RONALD, 1876923. 295 Field Coy., Royal Engineers. 6th June, 1944. Age 29.

PRICE, Pte. MORGAN REES, 14205199. 2nd Bn. The South Wales Borderers. 6th June, 1944. Age 21.

PRINCE, Bdr. STEPHEN ROPER, 913871. 90 Field Regt., Royal Artillery. 6th June, 1944. Age 24.

PROUD, L/Cpl. JOSEPH, 4460795. 5th Bn. The East Yorkshire Regt. 6th June, 1944. Age 24.

PULLEN, Pte. GEORGE RICHARD, 5506783. 1st Bn. The Hampshire Regt. 6th June 1944. Age 30.

RAINFORD, Tpr. RICHARD HENRY, 14546131. 61st Regt., Reconnaissance Corps. R.A.C. 6th June, 1944. Age 19.

RANDALL, L/Cpl. EDWARD STEPHEN CHARLES, 6014741. 2nd Bn. The Essex Regt. 8th June, 1944. Age 23.

RAWLINGS, Sgt. FREDERICK SAMUEL, 4344491. 5th Bn. The East Yorkshire Regt. 6th June, 1944. Age 25.

READ, Pte. BENJAMIN HENRY, 5627017. 2nd Bn. The Devonshire Regt. 6th June, 1944. Age 30.

REDDING, Pte. HENRY, 4399878. 7th Bn. The Green Howards (Yorkshire Regt.). 6th June, 1944. Age 21.

REDHEAD, Pte. ALBERT EDWARD, 421339. 1st Bn. The Hampshire Regt. 6th June, 1944. Age 24.

REDMAN, Pte. WALTER ALEXANDER, 5345894. 1st Bn. The Hampshire Regt. 6th June, 1944. Age 29.

REDMAN, Marine WILLIAM, CH/X. 107831. Royal Marines. No. 47 R.M. Commando. 6th June, 1944. Age 24.

REEVES, Pte. ALBERT JESSE, 5625828. 2nd Bn. The Devonshire Regt. 6th une, 944. Age 28.

REYNOLDS, Sgt. EDWARD ELI, 3907378. 2nd Bn. The South Wales Borderers. 6th June, 1944. Age 33.

RILEY, Pte. FRANK, 4697627. 5th Bn. The East Yorkshire Regt. 6th June, 1944. Age 32.

ROBERTS, Pte. JOHN, 1133675. 5th Bn. The East Yorkshire Regt. 6th June, 1944. Age 25.

ROBERTS, L/Cpl. JOHN RICHARD, 4197815. 1st Bn. The Dorsetshire Regt. 6th June, 1944. Age 25.

ROBINSON, Pte. ARTHUR RAYMOND, 4396874. 7th Bn. The Green Howards (Yorkshire Regt.). 6th June, 1944.

ROLF, Pte. ROBERT FREDERICK, 6402825. 2nd Bn. The Devonshire Regt. 8th June, 1944. Age 24.

ROWLANDS, Spr. HARRY, 13101253. 233 Field Coy., Royal Engineers. 6th June, 1944. Age 40.

SAMBROOK, Marine WILFRED DENNIS, PLY/X. 111491. Royal Marines. No. 47 R.M. Commando. 6th June, 1944. Age 19.

SAUNDERS, Cpl. JAMES BERNARD, 4617936. 5th Bn. The East Yorkshire Regt. 6th June, 1944. Age 24.

SCOTT, Marine FRANK LEONARD, PO/X. 105848. Royal Marines. No. 47 R.M. Commando. 6th June, 1944. Age 22.

SCRIVENS, Pte. ALFRED WILLIAM, 5728781. 1st Bn. The Dorsetshire Regt. 6th June, 1944. Age 27.

SHELBOURNE, Pte. HAROLD, 4986029. 1st Bn. The Hampshire Regt. 6th June, 1944. Age 20.

SIDEBOTTOM, Pte. BERNARD, 14672954. 7th Bn. The Green Howards (Yorkshire Regt.). 6th June, 1944.

SMITH. Lt. EDWARD CHARLES SIDNEY, 277665. The Hampshire Regt., attd. 2nd Bn. The Devonshire Regt. 6th June, 1944. Age 24.

SOUTHERN, Pte. HARRY, 3909649. 2nd Bn. The South Wales Borderers. 7th June, 1944. Age 25.

STEFFE, L/Cpl. ALFRED JOHN, 5626059. 2nd Bn. The Devonshire Regt. 6th June, 1944. Age 28.

STIFF, Cpl. HERBERT WALTER SYDNEY, 5501971. 2nd Bn. The Devonshire Regt. 6th June, 1944. Age 26.

STONEMAN, Pte. JOHN, 4626373. 7th Bn. The Green Howards (Yorkshire Regt.). 6th June, 1944. Age 24.

SUTTON, Pte. WILLIAM, 3658315. 7th Bn. The Green Howards (Yorkshire Regt.). 6th June, 1944. Age 28.

TATE, Pte. FRANK THOMAS, 4756501. 5th Bn. The East Yorkshire Regt. 6th June, 1944. Age 29.

ROE, Cpl. LESLIE JOHN WILLIAM, 5672102. 2nd Bn. The Devonshire Regt. 6th June, 1944. Age 24.

ROSE, Cpl. DENNIS EDWIN, 5505032. 1st Bn. The Hampshire Regt. 6th June, 1944. Age 27.

RYAN, Pte. ALFRED, 5961360. 6th Bn. The Green Howards (Yorkshire Regt.). 8th June, 1944. Age 21.

SATCHELL, Pte. HENRY CHARLES, 5724979. 1st Bn. The Dorsetshire Regt. 6th June, 1944. Age 27.

SAUSSEY, Cpl. WILLIAM THOMAS, 13037383. 1st Bn. The Hampshire Regt. 6th June, 1944. Age 34.

SCOTT, Pte. HEBER, 14229136. 6th Bn. The Green Howards (Yorkshire Regt.). 7th June, 1944. Age 20.

SELFE, Cpl. ALBERT EDWARD, 5623074. 2nd Bn. The Devonshire Regt. 6th June, 1944. Age 25.

SHERRIFF, Pte. HORACE, 5735086. 1st Bn. The Dorsetshire Regt. 6th June, 1944. Age 19.

SMITH, Marine BERNARD GEORGE, CH/X. 107029. Royal Marines. No. 47 R.M. Commando. 6th June, 1944. Age 20.

SOUTHAM, Pte. FREDERICK GEORGE, 14660997. 2nd Bn. The Devonshire Regt. 6th June, 1944. Age 19.

STAIN, Pte. JAMES WILLIAM, 4860585. 1st Bn. The Hampshire Regt. 6th June, 1944. Age 24.

STEPHENS, L/Cpl. JOHN, 3915542. 2nd Bn. The South Wales borderers. 7th June, 1944. Age 21.

STONE, Pte. BURNARD JOHN, 14625051. 2nd Bn. The Devonshire Regt. 6th June, 1944. Age 19.

STRINGER, Pte. ARTHUR EDWARD, 4755408. 6th Bn. The Green Howards (Yorkshire Regt.). 6th June, 1944. Age 24.

SWEENEY, Marine EDWARD JOHN, PO/X. 105867. Royal Marines. No. 47 R.M. Commando. 6th June, 1944. Age 22.

TAYLOR, Pte. CHARLES ARTHUR, 5512517. 1st Bn. The Hampshire Regt. 6th June, 1944. Age 20.

TAYLOR, Cpl. JOHN WILLIAM. 2000769. 280 Field Coy. Royal Engineers. 6th June, 1944. Age 26.

THEOBALD, L/Cpl. THOMAS HENRY, 5624472. 2nd Bn. The Devonshire Regt. 6th June, 1944. Age 24.

THOM, Spr. JOHN GRAY. 2102319. 280 Field Coy. Royal Engineers. 6th June, 1944. Age 20.

TOOZE, L/Cpl. IVOR, 2073460. 233 Field coy., Royal Engineers. 6th June, 1944. Age 23.

TULIP, Pte. THOMAS, 4392218. 6th Bn. The Green Howards (Yorkshire Regt.). 7th June, 1944. Age 25.

TURNER, Marine STANLEY HENRY RICHARD, CH/X. 103820. Royal Marines. No. 47 R.M. Commando. 6th June, 1944. Age 23.

VAUGHAN, Sgt. KENNETH ROBERT. 7882667. 4/7th Royal Dragoon Guards. RAC. 6th June, 1944.

WALKER, L/Cpl. HENRY NOEL, 4392431. 7th Bn. The Green Howards (Yorkshire Regt.). 8th June, 1944. Age 26.

WALKER, Marine RAYMOND, PLY/X. 103183. Royal Marines. No. 47 R.M. Commando. 7th June, 1944. Age 23.

WALTON, Pte. ARTHUR EDWARD, 3117458. 1st Bn. The Hampshire Regt. 6th June, 1944. Age 36.

WARBOYES, Tpr. JESSE ARTHUR. 5054355. The Nottinghamshire Yeomanry. RAC. Age 29.

WEST, Pte. CHARLES RICHARD, 5616858. 2nd Bn. The Devonshire Regt. 7th June, 1944. Age 28.

WHITE, Capt. JAMES HELIER, 130714. The South Lancashire Regt., attd. 5th Bn. The East Yorkshire Regt. 6th June, 1944. Age 35.

WHITE, Pte. OLIVER, 14275021. 1st Bn. The Hampshire Regt. 6th June, 1944. Age 20.

WILLIAMS, Pte. DAVID ARTHUR, 5507143. 1st Bn. The Hampshire Regt. 6th June, 1944. Age 29.

TAYLOR, Pte. PATRICK WILLIAM, 5728399. 1st Bn. The Dorsetshire Regt. 6th June, 1944. Age 26.

THORBURN, Pte. FRANK DOUGLAS, 4459828. 6th Bn. The Green Howards (Yorkshire Regt.). 6th June, 1944. Age 25.

TIDEY, Pte. ALBERT WILLIAM, 4618107. 5th Bn. The East Yorkshire Regt. 6th June, 1944. Age 25.

TOWLE, Marine WILLIAM HARRY, PLY/X. 103401. Royal Marines. No. 47 R.M. Commando. 7th June, 1944. Age 21.

TULL, Marine ARTHUR FREDERICK PERCIVAL CH/X. 104128. Royal Marines. No. 47 R.M. Commando. 7th June, 1944. Age 22.

VAN BOCHOVE, JAN CHARLES HENRY (served as VANE, Sigmn. J., 2385858). Royal Corps of Signals, 50th Div. Sigs. 6th June, 1944. Age 24.

WALKER. Tpr. ERIC NORMAN. 14344156. 4/7th Royal Dragoon Guards. RAC. 6th June, 1944. Age 20.

WALKER L/Cpl. NEVILLE. 2991388. 4/7th Royal Dragoon Gurards. 6th June, 1944. Age 21.

WALLIS, L/Cpl. LESLIE ARTHUR. 4858463. 280 Field Coy. Royal Engineers. 6th June, 1944. Age 24.

WALTON, Pte. THOMAS, 3661928. 2nd Bn. The Essex Regt. 6th/25th June, 1944. Age 31.

WAYGOOD, Marine LEONARD THOMAS, CH/X. 107580. Royal Marines. No. 47 R.M. Commando. 6th June, 1944.

WHEWALL, Pte. GILBERT ROLAND, 5616825. 2nd Bn. The Devonshire Regt. 6th June, 1944. Age 30.

WHITE, Pte JOE, 4343146. 5th Bn. The East Yorkshire Regt. 6th June, 1944. Age 28.

WILKINSON, Marine ROBERT MOORELVIN, PO/X. 119052. Royal Marines. No. 47 R.M. Commando. 6th June, 1944. Age 19.

WILLIAMS, Pte. DONALD FREDERICK, 14648182. 1st Bn. The Hampshire Regt. 6th June, 1944. Age 20.

WILLIAMSON, Lt. CHARLES-YOUNG, 253674, M.C. 1st Bn. The Hampshire Regt. 6th June, 1944. Age 30.

WILLS, Pte. FREDERICK ARTHUR, 5624777. 2nd Bn. The Devonshire Regt. 6th June, 1944. Age 27.

WOOD, Pte. THOMAS, 5724622. 1st Bn. The Dorsetshire Regt. 6th June, 1944. Age 33.

WORMALD, Pte. JOHN ERNEST, 14648607. 2nd Bn. The Devonshire Regt. 6th June, 1944. Age 27.

WYATT, Gnr. ALFRED, 955355. 90 Field Regt., Royal Artillery. 6th June, 1944. Age 24.

YOUNG, Pte. KENNETH FRANCIS, 14219467. 1st Bn. The Hampshire Regt. 6th June, 1944. Age 20.

WILLIAMSON, Pte. LEWIS, 13403925. 7th Bn. The Green Howards (Yorkshire Regt.). 8th June, 1944. Age 20.

WITHINGTON, Marine JOHN VERNON, PO/X. 120713. Royal Marines. No. 47 R.M. Commando. 7th June, 1944. Age 19.

WOOLRIDGE, Pte. LEONARD, 4924190. 7th Bn. The Green Howards (Yorkshire Regt.). 6th June, 1944. Age 34.

WORTON. Tpr. WILFRED. 3912764. 4/7th Royal Dragoon Guards. RAC. 6th June, 1944. Age 29.

YOUD, Pte. GILBERT GEOFFREY, 5727747. 1st Bn. The Dorsetshire Regt. 6th June, 1944. Age 25.

YOUNGS, Pte. GEORGE LESLIE, 6031616. 6th Bn. The Green Howards (Yorkshire Regt.). 6th June, 1944. Age 20.

BROUAY WAR CEMETERY

BOWL, Pte. WILLIAM JOHN, 14663589. 1st Bn. The Dorsetshire Regt. 8th June, 1944. Age 18.

JEFFERY, Pte. CUTHBERT, 5728832. 1st Bn. The Dorsetshire Regt. 8th June, 1944.

TUCKER, Capt. ROBERT WALLIS, 121129, MC. 1st Bn. The Dorsetshire Regt. 8th June, 1944. Age 24.

HANCOCK, Lt. ROBERT DAVID, 288001. 4th/7th Royal Dragoon Guards, R.A.C. 8th June, 1944. Age 21.

PEARCE, Cpl. GEORGE ALFRED, 5723656. 1st Bn. The Dorsetshire Regt. 8th June, 1944. Age 33.

RYES WAR CEMETERY

BECKWITH, Pte. DERRICK, 14612515. 6th Bn. The Green Howards (Yorkshire Regt.). 6th June, 1944. Age 19.

BLOSSE, Pte. DENNIS FREDERICK, 14650048. 1st Bn. The Dorsetshire Regt. 8th June, 1944. Age 19.

CHILTON, L/Cpl. GEORGE HENRY, 4451025. 7th Bn. The Green Howards (Yorkshire Regt.). 6th June, 1944.

BIRCH, Tpr. LESLIE CLAUDE, 7886809. 2nd County of London Yeomanry (Westminster Dragoons), R.A.C. 6th June, 1944.

CATTS, L/Cpl. JOHN HENRY, PLY/X. 3877. Royal Marines. No. 47 R.M. Commando. 7th June, 1944. Age 21.

DELANEY, Gnr. DANIAL, 1127335. 90 Field Regt., Royal Artillery. 8th June, 1944. Age 31.

HANN, Pte. LEONARD, 14671216. 1st Bn. The Dorsetshire Regt. 7th June, 1944. Age 18.

HORTON, L. Cpl. PETER JAMES, 2584043, MM. Royal Corps of Signals, 50 Div. Sigs. 6th June, 1944. Age 25.

MARTIN, Maj. ARTHUR CHARLES WOOLCOTT, 69156, D.S.O. The Dorsetshire Regt. 6th June, 1944. Age 27.

MAYES, Lt. ERNEST FREDERICK, 284965. 1st Bn. The Dorsetshire Regt. 7th June, 1944. Age 27.

WRIGHT, Sgt. SAMUEL L., 5045632. 7th Bn. The Green Howards (Yorkshire Regt.). 6th June, 1944. Age 36.

HOTTOT-LES-BAGUES WAR CEMETERY

BARLOW, Pte. WILLIAM HENRY, 4987501. The Durham Light Infantry. 8th June, 1944. Age 21.

BAYEUX MEMORIAL TO THE MISSING

ANDERSON, L/Sgt. WILLIAM, 409411. 4th/7th Royal Dragoon Guards, R.A.C. 6th June, 1944. Age 30.

BENNETT, Pte. ERNEST JAMES REGINALD, 1110263. 2nd Bn. The Devonshire Regt. 6th June, 1944. Age 38.

BURNS, Sgt. FRANK, 4923918. 6th Bn. The Green Howards (Yorkshire Regt.). 6th June, 1944. Age 33.

CLARK, Pte. HENRY THOMAS, 5501401. 1st Bn. The Hampshire Regt. 6th June, 1944. Age 40.

DYER, Pte. LEONARD, 5511661. 1st Bn. The Hampshire Regt. 6th June, 1944. Age 21.

ELSON, Pte. JACK, 5504956. 1st Bn. The Hampshire Regt. 6th June, 1944. Age 27.

GAZEY, Pte. LESLIE JACK, 6399434. 1st Bn. The Dorsetshire Regt. 6th June, 1944. Age 25.

GREEN, Cpl. LEONARD WILLIAM, 7684823. 50 Divisional Provost Coy., Corps of Military Police. 6th June, 1944. Age 27.

HIRD, Tpr. JOHN HENRY, 7963386. 4th/7th Royal Dragoon Gurards, R.A.C. 6th June, 1944. Age 21.

MATTHEWS, L/Cpl. KENNETH JOHN, 5337856. 1st Bn. The Hampshire Regt. 6th June, 1944. Age 24.

NEWALL, Pte. CYRIL, 14612006. 2nd Bn. The Devonshire Regt. 6th June, 1944.

PHILPOTT, Pte. GEORGE FREDERICK, 5500360. 1st Bn. The Hampshire Regt. 6th June, 1944. Age 23.

SANDERSON, Pte. ERIC, 4867606. 6th Bn. The Green Howards (Yorkshire Regt.). 6th/7th June, 1944. Age 21.

SMITH, Pte. CHARLES WILLIAM, 5500000. 1st Bn. The Hampshire Regt. 6th June, 1944. Age 26.

STEVENS, Pte. WALTER, 5724571. 1st Bn. The Dorsetshire Regt. 6th June, 1944. Age 33.

WALLIS, Spr. FREDERICK, 2073801. 233 Field Coy., Royal Engineers. 6th June, 1944. Age 24.

WALTERS, Tpr. WALTER JAMES, 1427600. 4th/ 7th Royal Dragoon Guards, R.A.C. 7th June, 1944. Age 20.

WILLIS, Pte. THOMAS JAMES, 4924889. 6th Bn. The Green Howards (Yorkshire Regt.). 6th June, 1944. Age 33.

WILSON, Spr. THOMAS HENDERSON. 1909030. 280 Field Coy. Royal Engineers. 6th June, 1944. Age 25.

WILLIAMS, Dvr. GEORGE ERNEST, 2119439. 295 Field Coy., Royal Engineers. 6th June, 1944. Age 28.

WRIGLEY, Sigmn. ERNEST, 2375217. Royal corps of Signals, 86 Field Regt., R.A., Sig. Sec. 6th June, 1944. Age 22.

PORTSMOUTH NAVAL MEMORIAL

SMITH, Marine. JOHN J. PO/X105847. 47 R.M. Commando. 6th June, 1944. Age 22.

FEWTRELL. Marine. CHARLES HENRY. PLY/ X112746. 47 R. M. Commando. 6th June, 1944. Age 35.

APPENDIX 'C'

ORDER OF BATTLE: MAY 1944

50TH NORTHUMBRIAN DIVISION
Divisional Commander:
Major General D. A. H. Graham, CBE, DSO, MC.

56TH INFANTRY BRIGADE
Commanding Officer: E. C. Pepper, OBE.

2ND BN. THE ESSEX REGIMENT
Commanding Officer: Lieutenant-Colonel J. F. Higson, MC.
Second in Command: Major C. G. Elliott.
Adjutant: Captain J. Townrow.

2ND BN. THE GLOUCESTERSHIRE REGIMENT
Commanding Officer: Lieutenant Colonel D. W. Biddle, DSO.
Second in Command: Major J. O. Hopper.
Adjutant: Captain R. C. Nash.

2ND BN. THE SOUTH WALES BORDERERS
Commanding Officer: Lieutenant Colonel R. W. Craddock, MBE.
Second in Command: Major F. F. S. Barlow.
Adjutant: Captain K. V. Coles.

69TH INFANTRY BRIGADE

Commanding Officer: Brigadier F. Y. C. Knox, DSO and BAR.
Brigade Major: Major C. P. N. Parker.
G.S.O.3: Captain C. W. Mallinson.
Staff Captain: Captain N. H. Nicholson.
Intelligence Officer: Captain J. M. B. Isaac.

5TH BN. THE EAST YORKSHIRE REGIMENT

Commanding Officer:
Lieutenant Colonel G. W. White, MBE.
Second in Command: Major J. H. F. Dixon.
Adjutant: Captain T. G. Fenwick.

6TH BN. THE GREEN HOWARDS

Commanding Officer:
Lieutenant Colonel R. H. W. S. Hastings, DSO., MC.
Second in Command: Major C. M. Hull.
Adjutant: Captain G. S. Piper.

7TH BN. THE GREEN HOWARDS

Commanding Officer: Lieutenant Colonel P. H. Richardson.
Second in Command: Major H. R. D. Oldman, MC.
Adjutant: Captain F. W. M. Underhay.

151ST INFANTRY BRIGADE

Commanding Officer: Brigadier R. H. Senior, DSO., TD.
Brigade Major: Major The Viscount Long.
G.S.O.3: Captain J. W. Thompson.
Staff Captain: Captain R. R. Coddin.
Intelligence Officer: Captain W. W. Teggin.

6TH BN. THE DURHAM LIGHT INFANTRY

Commanding Officer: Lieutenant Colonel A. E. Green.
Second in Command: Major G. L. Wood, DSO., MC and Bar.
Adjutant: Captain R. S. Loveridge, MC.

8TH BN THE DURHAM LIGHT INFANTRY

Commanding Officer: Lieutenant Colonel R. P. Lidwell, DSO.
Second in Command: Major A. H. Dunn.
Adjutant: Captain J. C. Walker.

9TH BN. THE DURHAM LIGHT INFANTRY

Commanding Officer: Lieutenant Colonel H. R. Woods, DSO., MC.
Second in Command: Major H. J. Mogg.
Adjutant: Captain R. C. Rickett.

231ST INFANTRY BRIGADE

Commanding Officer: Brigadier Sir A. B. G. Stanier, Bt., DSO., MC.
Brigade Major: Major I. A. Robertson.
G.S.O.3: Captain D. Montgomery.
Staff Captain: Captain H. M. Johnson.
Intelligence Officer: Captain K. S. Hollebone.

1ST BN. THE HAMPSHIRE REGIMENT

Commanding Officer: Lieutenant Colonel H. D. N. Smith, MC.
Second in Command: Major A. C. W. Martin, DSO.
Adjutant: Captain F. H. Waters.

1ST BN. THE DORSETSHIRE REGIMENT

Commanding Officer: Lieutenant Colonel E. H. M. Norie, OBE, DSO.
Second in Command: Major A. E. C. Bredin.
Adjutant: Captain L. Browne, MC.

2ND BN. THE DEVONSHIRE REGIMENT

Commanding Officer: Lieutenant Colonel C. A. R. Nevill, OBE.
Second in Command: Major G. B. Brown.
Adjutant: Captain T. A. Holdsworth.

61ST RECONNAISSANCE REGIMENT

Commanding Officer: Lieutenant Colonel Sir W. M. Mount, Bt., TD.
Second in Command: Major P. H. A. Brownrigg.
Adjutant: Captain E. E. Mocatta.

2ND BN. THE CHESHIRE REGIMENT

Commanding Officer: Lieutenant Colonel S. V. Keeling, DSO.
Second in Command: Major H. R. Moon.
Adjutant: Captain L. J. Cutler.

ROYAL ARTILLERY

Commanding Officer: Brigadier C. H. Norton, DSO., OBE.
Brigade Major: Major H. A. C. Dundas.
Staff Captain: Captain E. N. Briscomb.
Intelligence Officer: Captain N. S. Harrison.

74TH FIELD REGIMENT

Commanding Officer: Lieutenant Colonel H. W. W. Harris, DSO.
Second in Command: Major E. N. Dawson.
Adjutant: Captain R. B. Hutt.

86TH FIELD REGIMENT

Commanding Officer: Lieutenant Colonel G. D. Fanshawe, OBE.
Second in Command: Major J. B. M. Smith, DSO.
Adjutant: Captain R. R. Thornton.

90TH FIELD REGIMENT

Commanding Officer: Lieutenant Colonel I. G. S. Hardie.
Second in Command: Major J. F. Murphy.
Adjutant: Captain M. H. Shepheard.

124TH FIELD REGIMENT

Commanding Officer: Lieutenant Colonel P. H. Gough.
Second in Command: Major E. H. Colville.
Adjutant: Captain L. G. Heptinstall.

147TH FIELD REGIMENT

Commanding Officer: Lieutenant Colonel R. A. Phayre, DSO.
Second in Command: Major C. V. Broke.
Adjutant: Captain P. W. Gee.

102ND ANTI TANK REGIMENT

Commanding Officer: Lieutenant Colonel A. K. Matthews, DSO.
Second in Command: Major D. J. Cowen.
Adjutant: Captain G. S. Spence.

25TH LIGHT ANTI-AIRCRAFT REGIMENT

Commanding Officer: Lieutenant Colonel G. G. O. Lyons, MBE.
Second in Command: Major C. D. B. Campling.
Adjutant: Captain J. D. Johnson.

ROYAL ENGINEERS

C.R.E: Lieutenant Colonel R. L. Willott, DSO.
Adjutant: Captain R. G. Bishop.
Intelligence Officer: Lieutenant R. L. Rolt.

233RD FIELD COMPANY

Officer Commanding: Major J. R. Cave-Browne.
Second in Command: Captain A. D. Campbell.

295TH FIELD COMPANY

Officer Commanding: Major C. W. Wood.
Second in Command: Captain R. E. Sperling.

505TH FIELD COMPANY

Officer Commanding: Major C. A. O. B. Compton, MC.
Second in Command: Captain W. L. Kent.

235TH FIELD PARK COMPANY

Officer Commanding: Major I. L. Smith.
Second in Command: Captain E. G. Richards, MC.

280TH FIELD COMPANY

Officer Commanding: Major L. Clayton, MC.

73RD FIELD COMPANY

Officer Commanding: Major L. E. Wyatt.

82ND ASSAULT SQUADRON, RE.

Officer Commanding:
Major H. J. A. Elphinstone. (killed 6th June, 1944)

15TH BRIDGING PLATOON

Officer Commanding: Lieutenant G. Sumner.

ROYAL CORPS OF SIGNALS

Commanding Officer: Lieutenant Colonel G. B. Stevenson.
Second in Command: Major G. St. L. King.
Adjutant: Captain J. E. Sergeant.

ROYAL ARMY SERVICE CORPS

C.R.A.S.C: Lieutenant Colonel G. W. Fenton, MBE.
Second in Command: Major D. Dalton, MBE.
Adjutant: Captain L. Panton.

346 COMPANY

Officer Commanding: Major A. B. Belcher.
Second in Command: Captain J. B. Adams.

508 COMPANY

Officer Commanding: Major V. H. J. Carpenter.
Second in Command: Captain J. E. Osborne.

522 COMPANY

Officer Commanding: Major H.S. Butterworth, MC.

524 COMPANY

Officer Commanding: Major L. Carrick.
Second in Command: Captain J. V. Marlow.

ROYAL ARMY MEDICAL CORPS

149TH FIELD AMBULANCE

Commanding Officer: Lieuenant Colonel S. R. Trick.
Second in Command: Major O. G. Prosser.

186TH FIELD AMBULANCE

Commanding Officer: Lieutenant Colonel C. W. Arnot, OBE, MC.
Second in Command: Major W. S. Gale.

200TH FIELD AMBULANCE

Commanding Officer: Lieutenant Colonel W. A. Robinson, OBE.
Second in Command: Major M. N. S. Duncan.

22ND FIELD HYGIENE SECTION

Commanding Officer: Major R. W. Elliott.

47TH FIELD DRESSING STATION

Officer Commanding: Major H. S. H. Gilmer.

48TH FIELD DRESSING STATION

Officer Commanding: Major J. M. C. Almond.

ROYAL ARMY ORDNANCE CORPS

50TH DIVISION ORDNANCE FIELD PARK

Officer Commanding: Major D. C. H. Merrill.

69TH BRIGADE WORKSHOPS SECTION

Officer Commanding: Captain W. Kirkby.

151ST BRIGADE WORKSHOPS SECTION

Officer Commanding: Captain H. L. Smith.

231ST BRIGADE WORKSHOPS SECTION

Officer Commanding: Captain P. A. W. Turner.

ROYAL CORPS OF ELECTRICAL AND MECHANICAL ENGINEERS

C.R.E.M.E: Lieutenant Colonel E. H. Rundle.
Second in Command: Major R. E. Thornton.
Adjutant: Captain N. R. Earnshaw.

69TH BRIGADE WORKSHOPS COMPANY

Officer Commanding: Major S. F. Coaten.

151ST BRIGADE WORKSHOPS COMPANY

Officer Commanding: Major C. Whitehead.

231ST BRIGADE WORKSHOPS COMPANY

Officer Commanding: Major T. J. A. Hunter.

APPENDIX 'D'

716TH INFANTRY DIVISION

Commanding Officer:
LT. GENERAL WILHELM RICHTER.

726TH INFANTRY REGIMENT

736TH INFANTRY REGIMENT

716TH ARTILLERY BATTALION

716TH RECONNAISSANCE COMPANY

716TH ENGINEER BATTALION

716TH SIGNAL COMPANY

Formed in April 1941, the 716th Division consisted of older personnel. In May of that year it moved to the Caen area of Normandy where it remained until D-Day.

APPENDIX 'E'

BRITISH FORCES ASSAULTING 'GOLD BEACH'
0725 hrs - 6th June, 1944.

LEADING FORMATIONS:

69TH BRIGADE

6th BN. THE GREEN HOWARDS RGT.
5th BN. THE EAST YORKSHIRE RGT.
PLUS DD TANKS OF THE 8th ARMOURED BDE. AND
73rd FLD COY - RE: BEACH CLEARANCE PARTY.

231 BRIGADE

1st BN. THE DORSETSHIRE RGT.
1st BN. THE ROYAL HAMPSHIRE RGT.
PLUS DD TANKS OF THE 8th ARMOURED BDE.
280 FLD COY - RE: BEACH CLEARANCE PARTY AND
82ND ASSAULT SQUADRON - RE.
EQUIPPED WITH CHURCHILL AVRE'S

50th Division Commander: Major General D. A. H. Graham

Bombarding Force K: **Cruisers:** HMS Orion
HMS Ajax
HMS Argonaut
HMS Emerald
Gunboat: HNMS Flores (Dutch)
13 destroyers including
ORP Krakowiak (Polish)

APPENDIX 'F'

COMPANY SERGEANT MAJOR STANLEY ELTON HOLLIS. VC.

6TH BATTALION THE GREEN HOWARDS.

Stanley Elton Hollis was born in Archibald Street, Middlesbrough, Yorkshire, on 21st September 1912. He was the second son of a Fishmonger and grew up in the difficult time of the first 'Great War' and its aftermath. He attended school in Middlesbrough and Saltburn - leaving at the tender age of 13 years, for the next four years he worked in his father's shop only to leave at the age of 17 to become an apprentice in the Merchant Navy working on tramp steamers. His sea going career was cut short when he found he had an ulcerated stomach and was detained for a while in Hospital at Aarhus, Denmark. Stanley followed medical advice, took a shore job and became a lorry driver and mechanic, eventually he settled down and married Miss Alice Clixby.

In 1939 he joined the 4th Battalion Green Howards Territorial Army - and was mobilised with his unit at the outbreak of war and moved to the 6th Battalion. After the battle for France was lost his unit was evacuated from Dunkirk and he had to swim out to 'HMS Halcyon' before being picked up. The 50th Division then moved on to Iraq, Palestine, and Cyprus before being moved into the Western Desert - taking part in the Gazala Battles before falling back to El Alamein. The 50th Division fought Major actions in the North African Campaign at El Alamein, Mareth and the Wadi Akarit - after which Stanley Hollis was promoted to Company Sergeant Major. The Division then landed in Sicily during 1943, staying until the Axis Forces were defeated, returning home they trained as the assault troops that would land in Normandy on 'Gold Beach'.

C.S.M. Stanley Elton Hollis won the only Victoria Cross to be awarded for the 6th June 1944, his award appeared in the London Gazette on 17th August 1944 and read as follows:

VC Citation

In Normandy on June 6th, during the assault on the beaches and the Mont Fleury battery, C.S.M. Hollis's Company Commander noticed that two pill boxes had been by passed and went with C.S.M. Hollis to see that they were clear. When they were 20 yards from the pill box a machine gun opened fire from the slit and C.S.M. Hollis instantly rushed straight at the pill box, firing his Sten gun. He jumped on top of the pill box, recharged his magazine, threw a grenade in through the door and fired his Sten gun into it, killing two Germans and making the remainder prisoner. He then cleared several Germans from a neighbouring trench. He undoubtedly saved his company from being fired on from the rear and enabled them to open the main beach exit.

Later the same day, in the village of Crepon, the company encountered a field gun and crew armed with Spandaus at 100 yards range. C.S.M. Hollis was put in command of a party to cover an attack on the gun. But the movement was held up, seeing this C.S.M. Hollis pushed forward to engage the gun with a Piat from a house at 50 yards range. A sniper fired and grazed his right cheek and at the same moment the gun swung round and fired at point blank range into the house. To avoid the falling masonry C.S.M. Hollis moved his party to an alternative position. Two of the enemy gun crew had by this time been killed and the gun was destroyed shortly afterwards. He later found that two of his men had stayed behind in the house, and immediately volunteered to get them out. In full view of the enemy, who were continually firing at him, he went forward alone, using a Bren gun to distract their attention from the other men. Under cover of his diversion the two men were able to get back.

Wherever fighting was heaviest C.S.M. Hollis appeared, and in the course of a magnificent day's work he displayed the utmost gallantry, and on two separate occasions his courage and initiative prevented the enemy from holding up the advance at critical stages. It was largely through his heroism and resource that the company's objectives were gained and casualties were not heavier, and by his own bravery he saved the lives of many of his men.

C.S.M. Hollis was badly wounded in the leg during the inland battles of July 1944 and was sent home on leave at the age of 32 to his family at Park Avenue North, Old Ormesby. When notification of his award arrived he showed little interest - He was broken mentally and physically, his wife Alice commented in 1983:

> "When the Kings telegram came saying he'd got the VC he was still suffering from war wounds. He just glanced at it, screwed it into a ball and threw it at the fire. I daren't touch it or he'd have torn it up, when he wasn't looking I rescued it - ironed it out and it's a precious souvenir now."

Stanley Hollis was decorated with his award by His Majesty King George VI at Buckingham Palace on 10th October 1944. Once back in Civvy street he went back driving and then tried his hand at running a business without success. Eventually he took over the management of a Public House in the Market Square, North Ormesby and re-named it the Green Howards. This venture was to prove a great success and Stanley Hollis was a very popular landlord, most of his customers were hardy steel workers from the area but Mr Hollis enforced a strict no swearing rule and commented:

> "My customers know I won't stand for any nonsense."

In 1970 he transferred to the Holywell View Public House, Liverton Mines, but his health deteriorated quickly and he died in North Ormesby Hospital on 8th February 1972 at the age of 59.

Stanley Hollis was buried in Acklam Cemetery, Middlesbrough, on 12th February 1972, his old regiment turned out in force to pay their respects to a brave man, six pall bearers from the Green Howards carried the coffin and a bugler played The Last Post. Two other VCs were also present, Sergeant Bill McNally and Major Edward Cooper, the latter representing the Victoria Cross and George Cross associations. Other officers in attendance were Colonel John Forbes from the Green Howards Head-Quarters and Brigadier Cook-Collis who commanded the Green Howards in 69 Brigade, 50th Northumbrian Division.

In 1982 Mrs Alice Hollis, at the age of 71, sent her husbands group of eight medals for auction at Sotheby's where they fetched a record £32,000. Alice received abusive letters when it became known the VC her husband had won was up for sale - but it was his dying wish the money raised should be used for the benefit of the family. Alice commented:

"He was a wonderful man, so much fun to be with, but he wouldn't have approved of my holding on to his medal, he used to keep it in the button box with the milk tokens. It was not that he wasn't proud of it - that was just him. I wish I'd sold the medal ten years ago, he always said it should be sold for the grand children, it was doing no good lying in a drawer getting scratched among the bottle tops and I couldn't afford to insure it.

He had terrible nightmares for five years after the war, reliving the battles, screaming out. When he first came home , he said: 'I'm a cripple, lamed for life, and then he shut himself in the bedroom for a week, pushing letters under the door, telling me to push off and leave him.'

The next time he came home he'd had a plate put in his head, and the pain had subsided. He began to take an interest in his son.

'Brian grew up to be a Scotland Yard Detective. He didn't want me to sell the medal, but it was what his dad wanted. It's all for the grandchildren. All I've bought for myself is a car my daughter drives. I just use the interest on the money to pay household bills.

Everyone thought Stan was a hero except for the Government. He died with bullets in his feet, yet they said he wasn't entitled to a disability pension.

I don't think we treat our heroes right. One man stopped me in the street and said it was thanks to Stan that his boy came back alive. Stan would be down sometimes and talk about sending his medal back. But he soon bounced up again. He was that kind of man. Stan was a wonderful man, and when he died everything collapsed, but he never really left me."

OFFICIAL FUNCTIONS ATTENDED BY
STANLEY HOLLIS BETWEEN 1946 AND 1968:

8th June, 1946   The Victory Parade, Whitehall, and the Dinner at the Dorchester Hotel, London.

26th June, 1956   On parade at the VC Centenary Review held by HM Queen Elizabeth II in Hyde Park.

17th July, 1962   The Garden Party given to the VC & GC Association by HM Queen Elizabeth II at Buckingham Palace, London.

17th July, 1962   The Banquet given by The Rt. Hon. The Lord Mayor of London to the VC & GC Association, at The Mansion House, London.

18th July, 1962   The 3rd Dinner of the VC & GC Association at the Café Royal, Regent Street, London.

18th July, 1962   The Reception of the V.C & GC Association by the Queen at Buckingham Palace.

19th July, 1962   The 3rd Memorial Service at St. Martin's in the Fields, London.

19th July, 1962   The 6th Reunion Dinner of the VC & GC Association at the Café Royal, Regent Street, London.

APPENDIX 'G'

CASUALTIES, REINFORCEMENTS AND PRISONERS OF WAR OF 50TH (NORTHUMBRIAN) DIVISION IN B.L.A.

6TH JUNE TO 1ST DECEMBER, 1944

	KILLED		WOUNDED		MISSING		MISSING Rejoined		TOTAL CASUALTIES		REINFORCEMENTS	
	Officers	O.Rs.	Officers	O.Rs.	Officers	O.Rs.	Officers	O.Rs.	Officers	O.Rs.	Officers	O.Rs.
June	52	436	157	2,012	28	1,104	4	439	223	3,113	173	3,102
July	17	168	54	849	2	102	—	62	73	1,057	29	924
August	16	159	46	940	2	190	—	127	64	1,162	56	1,360
September	15	150	44	470	6	233	3	112	62	741	35	712
October	12	111	30	611	7	107	3	89	46	740	38	1,204
November	1	21	8	85	1	16	—	3	10	119	27	717
Total	113	1,045	339	4,967	46 ·	1,752	10	832	488	6,932	358	8,019

Total POW taken – 17,202   Total POW at June 9 – 2,300   POW taken on September 5 – 4,865

    August 30 – 4,838
    September 4 – 8,901
    September 5 – 13,766
    October 22 – 16,998
    December 1 – 17,202

4

NOTE:- Figures for total casualties exclude normal wastage, e.g., cases of sickness, etc.

APPENDIX 'H'

JUNE, 1944

SPECIAL D-DAY MESSAGE FROM THE DIVISIONAL COMMANDER TO ALL RANKS OF THE 50TH (NORTHUMBRIAN) DIVISION

The time is at hand to strike - to break through the Western Wall and into the Continent of Europe.

To you, officers and men of the 50th (Northumbrian) Division, has been given the great honour of being in the vanguard of this mighty blow for freedom.

It is my unshakeable belief that we, together with Force "G" of the Royal Navy, the special regiments of the Royal Armoured Corps, the Royal Artillery and the Royal Engineers attached to us and with the help of the R.A.F. and American Air Force, will deliver such an overpowering punch that the enemy will be unable to recover. Thus shall we be well set to carry through to a glorious and successful end to all that is now entrusted to us.

Much has been asked of you in the past and great have been your achievements, but this will be the greatest adventure of all. It will add yet another fine chapter to your already long and distinguished record - the grandest chapter of all.

Very best of luck to every one of you.

D. A. H. GRAHAM, Major-General
Commander, 50th (Northumbrian) Division.

APPENDIX 'I'

POINT 103 - TIGER HILL
12TH JUNE, 1944

MESSAGE SENT TO THE 50TH DIVISIONAL COMMANDER FROM BRIGADIER CRACROFT:-

"1st Dorset, who have been under command for three days, left me today to return to their own brigade.

"I am very anxious to draw attention to the excellent work that this unit has carried out. At the time the unit joined me it had done considerable fighting after a very wet landing. In spite of this, no one showed signs of distress or fatigue. This speaks highly of their state of training.

"To the best of my knowledge this unit had never before been part of an armoured formation. In spite of this, they immediately undertook the difficult task and the arduous task of assisting in a break through and occupation of a position with completely exposed flanks some miles into enemy occupied territory.

"Throughout the time the unit was with me, both officers and other ranks worked with the greatest of energy and showed the greatest dash, determination and steadiness in battle. In fact, the whole behaviour of the unit was exceptional.

(Signed) H. J. B. CRACROFT, Brigadier
Commanding 8th Armoured Brigade."

APPENDIX 'J'

SUBJECT:- CONGRATULATORY MESSAGES

List 'A'   **14 June 1944**

The following copy of congratulatory message is forwarded for information.

Captain.
Adjutant.
5 E York R.

Field.
IC

SECRET

Rear HQ.
50th (N) Div.

I have received the following letter from the Army Commander:-
"Now that the first phase of the operations are over, I want to congratulate you on 50 Division's magnificent work and to tell you how much I admire and appreciate all that they have done.

You have a very difficult task, the result shows how splendidly you carried it out.

Yours ever,
(sgd) M.C. DEMPSEY.

This is most gratifying and I am indeed proud to command such a grand Division. Please ensure that the appreciation of the Army Commander is brought to the knowledge of all ranks under your command. At the same time let them all know how much I realise all they have done during and since the assault and how deeply grateful I am.

(sgd) D.W.H. GRAHAM.

Major-Gen.
Commander.

50th (Northumbrian Division).